MICHAEL SHERMIS
ARTHUR E. ZANNONI, editors

Introduction to Jewish-Christian Relations

PAULIST PRESS
New York/Mahwah, N.J.

Library of Congress Cataloging-in-Publication Data

Introduction to Jewish-Christian relations/[edited by] Michael Shermis, Arthur E. Zannoni.
    p. cm.
    Includes bibliographical references and indexes.
    ISBN 0-8091-3261-3 (pbk.)
    1. Judaism—Relations—Christianity.   2. Christianity and other religions—Judaism. 3. Chrisitianity and antisemitism. I. Shermis, Michael, 1959– . II. Zannoni, Arthur E., 1942–
BM535.I495   1991
296.3'872—dc20   91-23524
                                                     CIP

Published by Paulist Press
997 Macarthur Boulevard
Mahwah, New Jersey 07430

Printed and bound in the
United States of America

Table of Contents

In memory of our dear friend, mentor, and colleague
Larry E. Axel, Ph.D.
(1946–1991)

THE EDITORS

Introduction

This volume of essays is an example of something new and exciting which is going on in North America, especially between Jews and Christians. For the first time in almost two thousand years Jews and Christians can sit down as equals around the table, to reflect upon their profound sameness and their deep differences. Dialogue groups are springing up all over the world. Christians are eager to claim their Jewish faith roots while Jews want to learn how to live as an ethnic and religious minority in a world that is a Christian majority. Jews want to understand some Christian theological concepts that seem to make no sense to them and Christians want to learn how to treat minorities with more dignity and respect. This book represents another step Christians and Jews have taken together on the road to deeper understanding.

Although numerous works continue to be published on Jewish-Christian relations, we have found none that would serve well as a college textbook or for use in adult education groups. This volume was written with those express audiences in mind. Each of the contributors was asked to write specifically for college age students and adults who had a general knowledge of their own religion, but who were unaware of what was happening in the emerging field of Jewish-Christian relations. The result is a text that can serve as a springboard to more study and dialogue on each of the ten topics we have chosen to present in this volume.

The reader will discover that the book is organized into ten chapters. The first four on Hebrew scriptures, New Testament, the holocaust, and Israel have been organized chronologically. These are followed by an essay on anti-Semitism

1

and anti-Judaism which spans the whole of the Jewish-Christian relationship. The next two chapters look at theology in general and christology in particular. The two following essays are on issues that are beginning to receive more attention in the Jewish-Christian dialogue: intermarriage and feminism. Although the book concludes with some educational strategies, students and other newcomers to the dialogue could usefully read the final essay first. In order to provide readers with more information a short explanation of each chapter follows.

In the first chapter, *The Challenge of Hebrew Scriptures in Jewish-Christian Relations,* Arthur Zannoni discusses the scriptural heritage Jews and Christians share in common as well as their different interpretations of this heritage. Over the centuries Christians dominated Jews, not only socially and economically, but also religiously. Christians belittled Jewish traditions and misinterpreted their sacred scriptures. Zannoni contends that the Christian grasp of the Hebrew scriptures has been continuously weakened and distorted by the relationship of hostility between Christianity and Judaism. He examines the spiritual and dialectical interpretations of the Hebrew scriptures, suggests a constructive alternative interpretation, and proposes a need for willingness by Christians and Jews to recognize and respect a wider range of possibilities inherent in any religious text.

In the probing chapter, *The New Testament: Confronting Its Impact on Jewish-Christian Relations,* Michael Cook thoroughly examines the disparaging references to Jews in the New Testament. He discusses misleading stereotypes that the New Testament presents. Explaining how the New Testament became an obstacle for Jews and how it poses a quandary for Christians even today, he then suggests ways to cope with the problems of the anti-Jewishness of the New Testament.

The holocaust is a part of both Jewish *and* Christian history. In his moving chapter, *The Holocaust: Tragedy of Christian History,* Michael McGarry asserts that it is necessary to understand ourselves by making the memory of the holocaust part of our common memory. He assesses the history of the holocaust and then examines the people involved: the perpetrators, the victims, and the bystanders. Finally, he discusses the aftermath, including Jewish survival, Christian survival, and shared feelings.

As we enter the twenty-first century, one of the most entangled issues facing not merely Christians and Jews but the whole world is the state of Israel, the Palestinians, and the Arab nations. In *The Land: Israel and the Middle East in Jewish-Christian Dialogue* Robert Everett explores Christian and Jewish views of the land tradition, modern Zionism and the state of Israel, and the debate about power and powerlessness in the Jewish community.

In the fifth chapter, Mary Christine Athans defines and distinguishes the differences between antisemitism and anti-Judaism. She traces the historical roots of Christian anti-Jewish attitudes in the New Testament, those negative attitudes which evolved in the writings of the fathers of the church, in the medieval canons of church councils against the Jews, and then in Martin Luther's tracts on the Jews. She questions the relationship between antisemitism and the holocaust, examines antisemitism in the United States, and then cogently asks if there is reason to hope for a better relationship between Christians and Jews.

In *The Seventy Faces of the One God: The Theology of Religious Pluralism* Philip Culbertson examines many theories of the theology of covenant, including the multi-covenant, dual-covenant, and single-covenant theories. He traces some of the early church fathers' contributions to Christian theology in relationship to truth, salvation, and revelation and he then proceeds to assess the views of some Jewish and Christian theologians in the twentieth century. Finally, he summarizes some denominations' official church policy on God's truth and salvation outside of Christianity and on the relationship of Christianity to Judaism.

In the chapter on christology, *Jesus—A Pharisee and the Christ*, John Pawlikowski discusses the distinguishing characteristics of the Pharisaic movement, the central conviction shared by Jesus and the Pharisees, and the unique dimension of Jesus' message. Pawlikowski shows why today's scholars, not only Jewish but also Christian, see the Pharisees of Jesus' day as heroes—and not as the villains many Christians interpreted them to be. He elaborates upon two ways of categorizing the complexity of the ongoing

Jewish-Christian relationship, the single and double theories of covenant. Finally, he emphasizes that Christianity is incomplete without the incorporation of the themes of human goodness, creation, and community which still characterize the Jewish people.

In *Interdating and Intermarriage: Jews and Christians* Sanford Seltzer talks about interdating and intermarriage in the context of conversion, children and divorce. He also suggests issues that couples planning to intermarry should consider.

Susannah Heschel, in her essay *Feminism and Jewish-Christian Dialogue,* shows that the feminist critique of religion parallels, in numerous respects, issues addressed by Jewish-Christian dialogue. Heschel traces the development of feminist theology and then poses the problem of anti-Judaism in Christian feminist theology. She suggests that a shift is required, from Christian feminists criticizing Judaism's sexism in order to elevate Christianity, to a recognition that feminism is a challenge shared by both Jewish and Christian feminists.

Readers who are first-time participants in the Jewish-Christian dialogue will appreciate the essay by S. Samuel Shermis entitled *Educational Dimensions of the Jewish-Christian Dialogue.* Shermis discusses the status of the dialogue in the United States, the world, and the classroom. He then examines the goals, language, and terminology of the Jewish-Christian dialogue. Finally, he suggests what strategies to use to make the dialogue a fruitful one.

Wherever possible we eliminated as much jargon as we could. In places where this was not possible, we have asked each contributor to explain complex terms. The authors have done this in their own style. So as not to impede the flow of the text, notes are located at the end of each chapter, as well as questions to stimulate discussion. The short lists of suggestions for further reading are not meant to be inclusive, but to list some of the many good works that might be consulted for a fuller understanding of the topic in the field of Jewish-Christian relations.

The editors wish to acknowledge a generous grant from the Center for Jewish-Christian Learning of the University of St. Thomas in St. Paul, Minnesota to defray some of the costs involved in editing the book. We are grateful for the constant support and encouragement of Christine Athans, Larry E. Axel, Max A. Shapiro, S. Samuel Shermis, Richard Sparks, and Kathleen Flannery Zannoni. Particular thanks for word processing and layout of the entire text are expressed to Gerald J. Milske, to Sue Moro for her help with computer translation, and to Karen Schierman for proofreading.

It is hoped that what the reader will learn from this book will contribute to better relations between Jews and Christians and further the ongoing dialogue.

I.

ARTHUR E. ZANNONI

The Challenge of Hebrew Scriptures in Jewish-Christian Relations

I. Common Scriptural Heritage

One of the common heritages shared by both Jews and Christians is their love of stories.

> God decided to select a nation to be God's chosen people. First God interviewed the Greeks. "If I were to be your God and you were to be my people, what could you do for me?" God asked.

> "O God," the Greek people replied, "if you were to be our God and we would be your people we would honor you with the finest art and the loftiest systems of thought. Our great thinkers would extol you in their great writings."

> "Thank you for your offer," God said.

> Next God visited the Romans. "If I were to be your God and you were to be my people, what could you do for me?"

> "Great ruler of the universe," the Romans said, "we are a nation of builders. If you were to be our God and we were to be your people we would erect great buildings in your name and wonderful road systems so that your people could travel to worship in these great buildings."

> God seemed pleased with the offer, and thanked the Romans.

From Rome God went all over the world interviewing one nation after another. Finally, God interviewed a mideastern group, the Jews, who had a reputation for being astute traders.

Once again God asked the question. "If I were to be your God and you were to be my people, what could you do for me?"

"God," the Jewish people said, "we are not known for our power or our art or our buildings. However, we are a nation of storytellers. If you were to be our God and we were to be your children we could tell your story throughout the whole world."

God, who also had a reputation for being a wise trader, said, "It's a deal!"[1]

The sacred book that records the many faith stories of the Jewish people is known by Jews as the Hebrew scriptures and by Christians as the Old Testament. Both Jews and Christians consider themselves "people of the book." This not only means that over the centuries they have preserved a relatively stable collection of religious writings, but also that each generation of believers has held that the teachings found in "the book" are inspired by God, or, for Orthodox Jews, the word of God. For this reason they have looked to these writings for their religious identity and inspiration. Since these two religious communities hold some of the same religious traditions in common, one might wonder why they do not always agree on their interpretation. The reason for this difference, as will be discovered later, is found in the way various traditions work within the respective communities.

As stated above, the sacred scriptures function as religious literature. This does not mean that they contain merely religious themes, but, more importantly, that they work as an agent informing a religious consciousness. A formative influence in the development of this consciousness is the actual experience of the individual group. Because this reality can be significantly different for religious groups, the same literature can be understood in quite diverse ways. An explanation of this might serve to clarify this point.

The Jewish community of the first century of the common era continued to perceive itself, as it had for centuries before, as the chosen people of God. (The term "common era" should be understood as the era Jews and Christians share in common. It is an inclusive term replacing the terms B.C. and A.D. where calendric dating was based entirely on the Christ event.)

The earliest Christians came from the same community and shared that self-perception. When this Jewish community split over the identity of Jesus, both factions continued to claim that *they* were the people of God and thus interpreted their religious traditions (the Hebrew scriptures) in such a way as to support their own claims. Hence, the same scriptures came to be understood in quite different ways by these two believing communities.

One of the major challenges that Christianity faced during the second century concerned the relevance of the Old Testament (Hebrew scriptures). Marcion, one of Christianity's staunchest critics—eventually condemned as a heretic —did not believe that this first Testament (Hebrew scriptures) had any religious value for Christians. His rejection of the Hebrew traditions went to such an extreme that he accepted as scripture only those Christian writings that he could interpret as repudiating the first Testament (Hebrew scriptures). Marcion's denigration of the Old Testament has remained a serious option within Christianity, or at least on its borders. Although the church denounced this position, Christian interpreters continued to struggle to understand the relationship between the Testaments.

Today, no one can deny that the entire Bible—both the Old and the New Testaments—has had a profound impact on world civilization. Its epic stories, sensitive prayers, and powerful language and images have left their imprint on human society and history, especially in cultures touched by Judaism and Christianity. In a sense, the Bible is a common heritage of both of these religious traditions.

Although the Bible is bound together under one cover and bears a single title, the Bible is *not* a single, unified book. It is a library of books composed by different authors, using very different styles and perspectives, compiled over several centuries. The gathering of these diverse writings into a single library collection or "book" (which is the literal meaning of the word "Bible") was itself a long-term, complicated, and laborious process. The technical term used to designate which books belong to the Bible is the "canon" (which means "a measurement").[2] Both Judaism and Christianity had to make choices about which books to include and which books to exclude from their respective "Bible." Judaism would not make any official decision about which books belonged to its "Bible" until the end of the first century of the common era. Jews and Christians have a different table of contents for their respective "Bibles." Christians include in their "Bible" the twenty-seven books of the New Testament. Jews do not. The actual naming of the major divisions of the books of the Hebrew scriptures, which Christians call the "Old Testament," differ.

However, before we look at this difference, it is important to speak about a problem that arises with the use of the expression "Old Testament."[3] It is the usual or normal way for Christians to refer to the first and largest section of their Bible. Yet for Jesus of Nazareth it was by no means an "Old Testament"; for him it was the *only* Bible, the living word of God. Recently the suggestion has been made by scholars that the terms "Old" and "New" Testaments be replaced with either the terms "first Testament" and "second Testament" or "Hebrew scriptures" and "Christian scriptures" or "Hebrew scriptures" and "apostolic writings." If this suggestion is not accepted, then the term "Old" when applied to one section of the Christian "Bible" cannot mean "displaced" or "antiquated," but rather should be seen to mean "prior" or "earlier" or "basic." The challenge is to be both respectful of and sensitive to both Judaism's and Christianity's vocabulary.

Recently, a church leader commented on the importance of accepting the Hebrew scriptures on their original level of meaning.

> There has been a gradual but persistent shift in emphasis away from the viewpoint that regarded the Hebrew Scriptures simply as background material for understanding the New Testament. In its place has come an emerging sense that the books of the Hebrew Bible are worth studying in their own right, apart from whatever legitimate insight they may offer us into the meaning of Jesus' life and mission.

These documents are no longer seen as mere "preludes" or "foil" for the teachings of Jesus in the New Testament. Rather, we are recognizing, however slowly, that without deep immersion into the spirit and texts of the Hebrew Scriptures, Christians experience an emaciated version of Christian spirituality and know but a very truncated version of Jesus' full religious vision.[4]

Jews call their Bible either "the holy scriptures" or *Tanak*. The consonants in *Tanak* come from the first letters of three Hebrew words: *Torah* (or law and instruction), *Neviim* (or prophets), and *Kethubim* (or writings). These three words are the titles for the three major parts of the Hebrew Bible. Or put more simply, *Tanak* is an acronym like, for example, AMA which stands for the American Medical Association.

The Jewish sacred scriptures are divided as follows:

Torah or The Five Books of Moses

Genesis, Exodus, Leviticus, Numbers and Deuteronomy;

Neviim or Prophets

Former Prophets: Joshua, Judges, 1 and 2 Samuel, 1 and 2 Kings.
Latter Prophets: Isaiah, Jeremiah, Ezekiel and the Book of the "Twelve"

(Hosea, Joel, Amos, Obadiah, Jonah, Micah, Nahum, Habakkuk, Zephaniah, Haggai, Zechariah, Malachi)

Kethubim or Writings

Psalms, Proverbs, Job
Megilloth or "Scrolls" for special feasts:

Song of Songs, for the feast of Passover
Ruth, for the feast of weeks or Pentecost
Lamentations, for the feast mourning the destruction of the temple
Ecclesiastes, for the feast of Tabernacles

Esther, for the feast of Purim
Daniel, Ezra and Nehemiah, 1 and 2 Chronicles.

You will note that there is no special section called "historical books." Jews have the greatest respect and reverence for tradition and history. Nonetheless, they do not look upon their holy scriptures as primarily a history book. Rather it is considered a book of instruction and prayer whose meaning is inexhaustible.

For Christians the books of the Old Testament are subdivided (a) the Pentateuch and historical books, (b) the wisdom books, and (c) the prophetical books. The following list indicates what Jews, Roman Catholics, and Protestants hold in common:

Pentateuch (Law):   Genesis, Exodus, Leviticus, Numbers, Deuteronomy

Historical Books: Joshua, Judges, Ruth, 1 and 2 Samuel, 1 and 2 Kings, 1 and 2 Chronicles, Ezra, Nehemiah, Esther

Wisdom Books: Job, Psalms, Proverbs, Ecclesiastes, Song of Solomon (Song of Songs)

Prophetical Books:

Major Prophets: Isaiah, Jeremiah, Lamentations, Ezekiel, Daniel,

Minor Prophets: Hosea, Joel, Amos, Obadiah, Jonah, Micah, Nahum, Habakkuk, Zephaniah, Haggai, Zechariah, Malachi

The above arrangement of the Christian canon is an adaptation of the Jewish Bible that was produced in Alexandria in Egypt, before the common era. In the second and third centuries before the common era the Jewish *Torah* was translated into Greek by Jews in Alexandria. The reason for this translation was that, following the conquest of Alexander the Great a century earlier, Jews living in Alexandria had become thoroughly influenced by the Ptolemy kings and the Greek culture that existed in Alexandria. The Alexandrian Jews consequently needed to read their sacred scriptures in their own language, Greek. And so the *Torah,* the prophets, and the writings (*Tanak*) were translated into Greek from the original Hebrew. The name of this translation is the Septuagint. (The Roman numeral LXX is used to symbolize the Septuagint because according to the tradition there were seventy Jewish scribes who came from Jerusalem to Alexandria in order to engage in that particular translation process.) You will note that the books in both lists are arranged differently but they are the same books for Jews and Christians—a common scriptual heritage.

If we compare the official list of the Hebrew scriptures or Old Testament in Roman Catholic editions of the Bible with that of Jewish and Protestant editions we will notice seven more books in the Roman Catholic list: Tobit and Judith, 1 and 2 Maccabees among the historical books; Wisdom and Sirach among the wisdom books; Baruch among the prophetical books. Parts of the books of Esther and Daniel are also not shared by Protestant and Jewish editions of the canon. Roman Catholics call these sections that are not found in Jewish and Protestant editions the "deuterocanonical" books; Protestants use the word "apocrypha" for the same books. The term "deuterocanonical" means the "second" or "wider" canon; "apocrypha" means "concealed" or "hidden." These books were either unknown or later under dispute by some sectors of Jews and/or Christians. What is important to know, however, is that they were Jewish books.

If you have a Bible of your own that includes a separate section on what Protestants call the "apocrypha" you will note that it includes much more than the seven books mentioned above. According to widespread usage in scholarship today, "apocrypha" is a designation applied to a collection of fourteen or fifteen books, or portions of books, written during the last two centuries before the common era and the first century of the common era. The following are the titles of these books as given in the Revised Standard Version of the Bible: (1) First Book of Esdras, (2) Second Book of Esdras, (3) Tobit, (4) Judith, (5) the editions of the book of Esther, (6) the Wisdom of Solomon, (7) Ecclesiasticus, or the Wisdom of Jesus son of Sirach, (8) Baruch, (9) the Letter of Jeremiah,

(10) the Prayer of Azariah and the Song of the Three Young Men, (11) Susanna, (12) Bel and the Dragon, (13) the Prayer of Menasseh, (14) the First Book of Maccabees, and (15) the Second Book of Maccabees.[5]

The books of the apocrypha represent several different literary forms and were written at different historical times. However, they were seen to have their origin within the Jewish religion. Even though these extra books do not appear in the *Tanak* (the Hebrew Bible) they are nonetheless Jewish writings that Christians have chosen to use as Christian scripture. They are not used as Jewish scripture.

There are other writings that were produced around the same time as the biblical writings and the apocryphal writings, a whole collection of what we call the pseudepigrapha. Pseudepigrapha means "false writings." They are so called because these writings are falsely ascribed to Jewish leaders of the past, to the heroes of the past, for example, the Apocalypse of Daniel, the Testament of Adam, the Testament of Abraham, the Book of Enoch, the Apocalypse of Zephaniah, the Book of Jubilees, and many others.[6] So the ancient world that produced our sacred scriptures that we share in common as Jews and Christians was a world that was teeming with literary products, cultural artifacts that the ancient Jews had produced. And many of these cultural artifacts became a part of the sacred canonical tradition of the Jews and also of the Christians. We share much in common.

II. Different Interpretations

Christians have a tendency to look at the Hebrew scriptures through the eyes of the New Testament. The New Testament becomes for Christians the principal collection of sacred scripture. Christians make the claim that the word of God is revealed in both Testaments, but in practice the New Testament has taken a position of priority over the Old Testament, and so Christian practice is to interpret the Old Testament in light of the New Testament.

Within Judaism, sacred writings did not cease when they had produced the *Tanak*. They continued to produce other writings such as the apocryphal books and the pseudoepigraphical books mentioned above. That tradition of writing sacred literature continued until eventually they produced works that were given the status of canonical literature alongside of the *Tanak.* This literature is called the *Mishnah,*[7] a massive collection of Jewish law based upon the *Torah.* The *Mishnah* developed the legal traditions from the *Torah* to new levels of understanding and observance. The *Mishnah* was assembled and published around 200 C.E. The production of Jewish literature continued; there were commentaries on the *Mishnah,* and eventually all the commentary and discussions about the *Mishnah* produced what is known as the *Talmud.* There were two different editions of the *Talmud,* one produced in Jerusalem, completed around 400–500 C.E. and another *Talmud* produced in Babylonia where there was a very significant Jewish community around 500 or 600 C.E.

Jews interpret *Tanak* with the aid of the *Mishnah* and the *Talmud.* Christians interpret the Old Testament through the eyes of the New Testament. Hence we frequently arrive at different interpretations for the same passages of sacred scripture that we share in common.

On the Christian side the tendency has been to give the prophets a place of prominence in the Hebrew scriptures (Old Testament). The prophets are looked upon as being the most important part of the Old Testament by many Christians. Christians have found in the prophets passages they believe are prophecies of the coming of the messiah. The reason Christians consider the prophets the most important part of the Old Testament is because they see Jesus as the messiah and maintain that the prophets predicted his messiahship. A good example of this is the gospel of Matthew which often quotes from the prophetic books to substantiate its interpretations about Jesus (see Mt 1:23; 2:6, 18; 3:3).

To be a Christian, to make a confession of Jesus Christ as the messiah, is the principal basis of interpretation. That causes Christians to approach the Old Testament (Hebrew scriptures) section of the prophets in a different way than Jews approach them. To be Jewish, one is called to be observant. And in Jewish tradition, *Tanak,* especially the *Torah,* as interpreted by the sages (rabbis), forms a commentary on everyday life and may be used as a guide to doing God's will and attaining salvation.

On the Jewish side the practice has been to give the pre-eminent position to the *Torah*, first part of the *Tanak*, because it is in the *Torah* that Jews find the basis of their worldview and the way of life they have developed over the centuries. This view came to a more complete expression in the *Mishnah* and the *Talmud*. Jews begin with the *Mishnah* and the *Talmud* to find the foundation of their worldview and way of life which has become so important to them. To be a Jew means primarily to be observant of that way of life. This has been the emphasis over the centuries. To embrace that way and to live that way is what it is to be called a Jew. To do that, Jews must necessarily turn to the *Torah* in order to be observant and to the interpretation of *Torah* in *Midrash*, *Mishnah*, and *Talmud*. Through the careful reading of the holy scriptures, the rabbis located eternal truths. They had a name for the process, *midrash*, derived from the root *darash*, "to seek," "to investigate."

> Holy Scripture posed to the Rabbis a more perplexing problem than just uncovering the plain meaning of the sacred words. Their problem, which still troubles book- or text-centered religions, was how to discover in ancient writings continuing truths and meaning for a very different time. Their answer to this problem . . . is in Midrash, the exposition of revealed Scripture.[8]

The tendency to be selective of which part of the Old Testament that we use in our appropriation of tradition for our respective Christian and Jewish lives can be illustrated by showing how we have developed differing views of redemption. The temptation story of the garden of Eden in Genesis 3 in the Old Testament (Hebrew scriptures) illuminates our Jewish and Christian differences on the point of redemption.

In the Christian view this is a story of the fall. Here is the beginning of sin in human life. There has been much discussion about original sin beginning with Adam and Eve and then transmitted through generations so that all of humankind is infected with the condition of sinfulness. If human beings are innately sinful, they cannot redeem themselves because they do not have that which is necessary for their own redemption. They must necessarily rely upon the act of

God to deliver them from the bondage of sin and death. The messiah is the one who has been sent, in the Christian tradition, in order to break those bonds of sin and death and to effect the work of redemption—something human beings could not accomplish by themselves. Christians look upon the garden of Eden story as a story of a fall, and many texts in the New Testament reflect upon Adam and Eve as great sinners. This is where sin came into the world according to the Christian view. Sin is therefore a universal phenomenon and all humankind participates in it.

When we turn to the Jewish view of the garden of Eden story, Christians are astounded that Jews don't see in that story evidence of a fall as such. They don't see there the basis for the view that all humankind is innately sinful. But rather Jews see in that particular story two things. The rabbis from antiquity had a creative way of interpreting how those texts should be understood and they wrote down their understanding in the *Mishnah* and *Talmud*. They looked at the garden of Eden story because the Christians were claiming it was a story of innate sinfulness and the rabbis noticed that the Hebrew telling of that story was different.

The rabbis discovered that where it says God "formed" Adam from the clay of the earth, God shaped Adam and breathed into him the breath of life, he became animated. The word in Hebrew that was used for "formed" is a word that can be transliterated normally *yatzar* with one "y." Wherever that word *yatzar* appears in the Old Testament (Hebrew scriptures), it is written with one "y." In this particular case (Gen 2:7), for some reason, it was written with two "y's," and the rabbis said that it was surely significant that *Tanak* has two "y's" here. And the rabbis asked why are there two "y's" when the text is talking about the forming of humankind. Their interpretation was that it is to tell us that every human being has two *yetzers*. *Yetzer* is the Hebrew word for "inclination" or "tendency." According to rabbinic interpretation every human being has within himself or herself two tendencies. One is the tendency for good and the other is the tendency for evil. And so this story is designed to teach us about the tendency for either good or evil. It does not say that humankind is innately evil. Human beings can go either way. God has so endowed each and every individual with the innate capacities that a person needs in order to be good. God has created everyone in the image of God, and that is good; and that possibility of being good is open to every human being even after the garden of Eden. So the garden of Eden is a constant reminder that the possibility of being good is real. Hence, the rabbis see this story in a considerably different way.

If there is no general or universal condition of human sinfulness of an innate nature, then there is no particular need for a messiah to come and rescue these people from the bondage of sin and death. If human beings have within themselves the capacity to live the good life, to be ethical, and to be moral, then they can uphold the *Torah;* they can live according to the law; they can be observant doing what God wants them to do. So beginning with this particular story we can see differing views of human nature unfold: one, the Christian notion of the "fall"; the other, the Jewish notion of the two tendencies. And there are other views about, God, creation, the messiah, to mention but a few, that Jews and Christians look at somewhat differently.

III. Reflections on the Christian Church's Interpretations of the Hebrew Scriptures

Writing from a Berlin prison cell in 1943, awaiting an uncertain fate at the hands of the Nazi regime whose downfall he had sought, German Lutheran theologian and pastor Dietrich Bonhoeffer expressed to his friend and fellow pastor Eberhard Bethge that he was experiencing a breakthrough to the Old Testament in his reading of scripture. "My thoughts and feelings seem to be getting more and more like those of the Old Testament and in recent months I have been reading the Old Testament much more than the New . . . . In my opinion it is not Christian to want to take our thoughts and feelings too quickly and too directly from the New Testament."[9] Bonhoeffer's concern about "the Christian significance of the Old Testament" is a timely one, because it was Bonhoeffer who at the end of his road of resistance to the most furious attempt to eliminate the Jewish people—the holocaust—was able to break through to a new and profound grasp of the revelation of Israel's God in the Bible.

The position of this essay is that the Christian grasp of

the Hebrew scriptures has been continuously weakened and distorted by the relationship of hostility between Christianity and Judaism, for whom these writings are authoritative revelation. The prevailing Christian anxiety to develop a view of the Old Testament which would *exclude* its use as sacred scripture by Judaism has blinded the church in a variety of ways to the real message of the Old Testament (Hebrew scriptures).

It is at this point that we encounter the perennial problem of the shared canon of scripture. The Hebrew scriptures, *Tanak* for Jews, Old Testament for Christians—serves as a "root metaphor"[10] for both faiths. By "root metaphor" I mean the controlling story of a religious tradition: in the case of Judaism the exodus story, in the case of Christianity the Jesus story. Hence, each religious tradition must regard its rights to that document as inalienable. A denial of these rights would mean disinheritance and consequently disillusionment. Therefore, defense of its "root metaphor" seems essential to the continuing existence of each believing community. Judaism and Christianity, however, interpret their "root metaphor" in contrasting ways. For Jews, *Tanak,* is a covenantal document, establishing a relationship between God and the people with two foci, law and the land. For Christians, on the other hand, the Old Testament is read as a history of human sin and divine redemption that culminates in the coming of Jesus as the messiah. Since the Christian gospel, especially as interpreted by Paul, appears to leave concern with the law and the land behind, Christianity seems bound to insist that these themes cannot be truly central in the Hebrew scriptures, and for precisely that reason, Judaism insists on their centrality. The two interpretative communities, then, have developed mutually exclusive interpretations of their common "root metaphor." If one is right, must the other be wrong? And if that is so, then the community that offers the "false" interpretation is a usurper, a standing danger to the true community.

Social theorists have coined the term "nihilation" to describe the conflict that results from such a situation.[11] The intellectual leaders of Christianity, who were responsible for interpreting the scriptures and defending the faith, were compelled by this competitive relationship not only to find Christ and the church in the Old Testament, but also to eliminate any basis Jews might have for finding the law and the land as the central focus. To reduce the Jewish interpretation to nothing—to "nihilate" it—required either a thoroughgoing reinterpretation of the Old Testament in exclusively Christian terms, or else a change in the status of the Old Testament in the Christian canon, which would neutralize the potentially Jewish elements. Throughout the history of Christianity, various strategies and different degrees of nihilation were often a major shaping force in Christian analysis of the Old Testament. As a result the church's understanding of the Olc Testament has been diminished.

IV. Spiritual Interpretation of the Old Testament (Hebrew Scriptures)

From the beginnings of Christianity there was another understanding that would be the dominant one for an entire millennium. In this interpretation, the Old Testament was accepted fully as part of the Christian Bible, but only as interpreted spiritually, that is, in a way that demonstrated its immediate relevance to the gospel. The Christian movement arose within Judaism and needed to justify itself to the Jews by means of the Hebrew scriptures. Therefore, a way of understanding the scriptures that would warrant the conviction that Jesus Christ was the goal and fulfillment of God's revelation was needed. There are indications that the earliest Christian apologetic writings, which may underlie portions of the New Testament, consisted of collections of Old Testament *testimonia,* which gave witness to Jesus as the messiah.[12] Sometimes these passages were taken in a simple prophetic sense (e.g. Is 7:14); but increasingly the events and characters of the Old Testament were seen as types or shadows of Christ, the church, and redemption. (Paul's use of Sarah and Haggar as types of two communities in the history of redemption—see Gal 4:21–31—is an example of such typological interpretation, as is the symbolic use of Melchizedek and the tabernacle in the epistle to the Hebrews—see chapters 7–9.)

Eventually this method of analysis was extended from specific passages to the Old Testament (Hebrew scriptures) in general. Borrowing from the surrounding Greco-Roman culture the technique of allegory—by which a passage of ancient sacred literature could be read as speaking in a hidden way about current concerns of philosophy or morality— Christian analysts fashioned a unique and powerful tool for discerning a witness to Christ throughout the Old Testament. Allegory continued to be an important weapon in the Christian arsenal against the Jews. For nearly all the Christian analysts before the reformation, allegory in some form was the dominant mode of interpreting scripture. The reformers, while they abandoned some elements of medieval allegorizers, were far from rejecting the general intent of finding Christ foreshadowed throughout the Old Testament. Although eclipsed by the rise of historical consciousness during the enlightenment, the tradition of spiritual interpretation has found new proponents among scholars and theologians, both Catholic and Protestant, in the twentieth century.

Over this long period of development the origins of spiritual interpretation in the controversy with the Jews remained evident even when its use had become less directly polemical. An interpretation that did not lead to Christ, which was merely literal or historical, was held to be "Jewish," and hence decrepit, outmoded, transcended. Jewish analysis of the Hebrew scriptures, apart from Christ, could produce only superstition and legal ceremonial excess. Henri de Lubac summarizes the prevailing view in the middle ages: ". . . those Jews who, by refusing to recognize Jesus Christ, refused to recognize the New Covenant, lost their understanding of Scripture itself."[13]

Once again, the strategy of nihilation is evident. The Christian interpretation of scripture must exclude and destroy the Jewish interpretation. As a consequence, elements in the text of the Hebrew scriptures that cannot be interpreted christologically are problematic. There is a strong temptation either to force such passages into a christological framework, through fair means or foul, or to ignore them altogether. Both solutions serve to weaken Christian analysis: first by making the entire method of spiritual interpretation implausible, and second by placing certain portions of scripture out-of-bounds for Christianity. The Song of Solomon (Song of Songs) with its lavish and earthy erotic imagery can serve as a case in point. If it is allegorized to make it less erotic for Christians, the result can be a reduction to meaninglessness of the entire poem. By doing so the Christian church has lost the healthy sensuality and sexuality presented in the Song of Songs.

V. Dialectical Interpretation of the Old Testament (Hebrew Scriptures)

Despite their considerable diversity in detail, the two views just considered (nihilation and spiritual interpretation) have in common one major feature: they take the Old Testament (Hebrew scriptures) in its entirety, viewing it as a single, non-reflective, non-historically conditioned entity in relation to a New Testament conceived in a similarly static and uniform fashion. In reality, however, the two parts of the Christian canon are each collections containing considerable variety. The New Testament contains the epistle of James as well as those of Paul, John's gospel as well as Matthew's. Likewise, the Hebrew scriptures (Old Testament) from an historical point of view consist of documents representing more than a millenium of Israelite religious and secular history. As a collection it presents tensions on fundamental issues: the relative importance of temple-cult and morality, the function and significance of a monarchy, the centrality of Jerusalem, the criteria for recognizing true prophecy, and so on. Hence, the possibility arises that a Christian appropriation of the Hebrew scriptures (Old Testament) might need to take into account this dynamic process: all biblical texts are culturally and historically conditioned, forging a link between the Testaments through historical developments. This process is more accurate than the pre-conceived teachings of Christianity, which are known as dogmas, namely a body of doctrines concerning faith or morals formally stated and authoritatively proclaimed by a church.

These doctrinal interpretations of the Hebrew scriptures (Old Testament) were less prominent before the rise of historical consciousness during the enlightenment, although they were not wholly absent. Yet the breakthrough in the historical understanding of the Hebrew scriptures which occurred during the eighteenth and nineteenth centuries of the common era forced many Christian theologians to consider seriously whether a static, dogmatic understanding of the Old Testament would be an appropriate interpretation. Within this context, Julius Wellhausen's[14] presentation of the "Documentary Hypothesis"—the view that the first five books of the Old Testament are the product of an evolutionary process in Israelite religion and thus contain material representing different ages of that evolution—held enormous appeal and soon came to dominate the work of "critical" Old Testament scholars, much as the views of Charles Darwin were becoming dominant in the natural sciences. Wellhausen viewed the evolution of Israel's religion as an ongoing process. But this evolution developed in a series of stages from the primitive to the more advanced. Even in the latter phases of development, it was possible for ancient Israel to lapse into superstitious or legalistic forms of religion. Other forms of Old Testament religion, more primitive than the prophets, led, if anywhere, to rabbinic Judaism, which Wellhausen regarded as a dead-end.

Wellhausen's hypothesis continued to be accepted in broad outline by succeeding generations of scholars. Among the most important syntheses of Old Testament theology, which took the dialectical approach as a basic point of departure, was Walther Eichrodt's *Theology of the Old Testament*.[15] Eichrodt employed the concept of "covenant" as an organizing concept for the ideas of the Old Testament. Ancient Israel's faith, in his view, centered around the covenant of God with the nation, and its spiritual journey became manifest in the evolution of the covenant-concept through its history. The covenant in Eichrodt's hands becomes a tool for tracing the dialectical movement within the history of ancient Israel, through which ancient Israel's understanding of God was continually challenged, corrected, and enriched by the pattern of God's activity in relation to the nation. It was in "the manifestation of Christ" that this dialectical movement reached its climax and fulfillment.[16]

Once again, it is just at this point that the nihilating element in the approach becomes visible. It is one thing to say, with Eichrodt, that in Christ "the noblest powers of the Old Testament find their fulfillment," but quite a different note is sounded when he continues: "negative evidence in support of this statement is provided by the torso-like appearance of Judaism in separation from Christianity."[17] The latter statement implies that Christianity's claim to the Old Testament must be established by the exclusion of Judaism's right of

inheritance. Yet, since Judaism is obviously rooted in the Hebrew scriptures, it must be the case that Judaism draws its
sustenance from the "less noble" elements to be found there.
For Eichrodt, these are overcome and left behind by
Christianity.

The selectivity inherent in this approach, by which some
elements of the Hebrew scriptures are declared enduring and
others transitory, is employed by Eichrodt and other similar
interpreters who argue that the "Jewish" interpretation is
mistaken from the outset, and hence religiously irrelevant.[18]
All that classical rabbinic Judaism has to offer—the legal
traditions which led to the *Mishnah* and the *Talmud*, and the
collections of the *Midrashim*—are declared null and void for
Christian interpreters. It is worth asking whether such
Christian analysis in its zeal to hear the witness of the Old
Testament through the filter of the New Testament, and not
also through the insights of the other believing community
that has endeavored to remain faithful to the Hebrew scriptures, has not stifled some crucial understandings of
revelation.

VI. Toward a Constructive Alternative

All the strategies of Old Testament interpretation which
we have considered here have in common a fundamental
starting point: the conviction that there is in the Old Testament a "surplus" of meaning which cannot be immediately
reduced to or assimilated by a theology based exclusively on
the New Testament. Whatever label is given to this concept
—legalism, primitivity, or national particularism—it is regarded as an alien element whose presence within the biblical canon must be accounted for or counteracted. Marcion
and his theological disciples demoted the Hebrew scriptures
to an inferior status within the Christian canon, or excluded
them altogether. The allegorical interpreters contrived an
analysis that would transpose the alien elements into a more
familiar christological interpretation. Dialectical interpreters
saw certain elements of the Hebrew scriptures as dead-ends,
bypassed by the dynamic moment of Israel's history, and
hence not of direct or positive significance for Christian analysis. Whether the problematic elements are excluded, trans-

posed, or bypassed, the outcome is eventually the same: the witness of the Old Testament (Hebrew scriptures) to the saving power of God is in some respect muted, distorted, or impoverished.

This impoverishment is perhaps most clearly visible in a loss of a sense of concrete engagement with the world for Christian preaching and instruction. When the New Testament message of salvation is not understood in continuity with Israel's traditions, there is a danger that the church will forget some part of God's claim on the whole world, and the will of God is reduced to the sphere of individual piety. This means that the salvation of the individual takes on overwhelming importance, and the realization of God's will in the world is pushed into the background or forgotten.

The continued presence of the Hebrew scriptures in the Christian canon is an implicit recognition by the church that it cannot finally cut itself off from the "worldly" roots of its own gospel. The Hebrew scriptures are the Jewish roots of the Christian faith. Yet sacred scripture must be interpreted and applied in order to be meaningful. The development of a hermeneutic (method of interpretation) that does justice to the Old Testament within the context of the whole canon is a task of the church with no less urgency today than two millennia ago. The following challenges are offered as a possible alternative method of interpretation.

The God of Abraham, Isaac, Sarah, Rachel, and Jesus Christ must be at the center of any Christian interpretation of the Hebrew scriptures to be significant for Christian preaching and instruction. The analysis of the Hebrew scriptures by Christians must interpret the proclamation of salvation through the God of Jesus Christ. The status of the Hebrew scriptures in the canon of the Christian church is predicated on this assumption. The church needs to be theocentric (God-centered) in its interpretation of the Hebrew scriptures.

Further, the Hebrew scriptures are not to be subjected to the New Testament as a criterion of interpretation, for Christ is *not* identical with the New Testament. The notion that the New Testament as a document stands in a more immediate relationship to Christ than the Hebrew scriptures, and must therefore serve as the key to the interpretation and the authority of the Hebrew scriptures, has no basis in scripture and must be resisted.

We should not deal with any passage of the Old Testament in order to show that in it we find only the type or shadow of what later becomes reality or light in the New Testament . . . we should not treat the Hebrew Scriptures in any way that suggests Christianity has superseded or displaced Jews and Judaism in the covenant with God, in God's love or favor. 'Supersede' is derived from two Latin words *super* ("on" or "upon") and *sedere* ("to sit"). It refers to the act in which one person takes a seat that has been vacated by another, thus preventing that person from sitting there again. All the ways in which we should not deal with the Old Testament are ways of claiming that Christianity has superseded, taken the place of, Judaism and the Jewish people in God's grace.[19]

For the Christian the Old Testament is the necessary presupposition for understanding the revelation of Jesus of Nazareth as the Christ. God's work in Christ is fully comprehensible only within the context created by the Old Testament (Hebrew scriptures), with its understanding of the condition of humanity before God, regardless of whether it be the notion of the "fall" or the two tendencies. The Old Testament (Hebrew scriptures) shows us humankind in the midst of the concrete realities of life: yearning for God and yet rebellious in self-assertion, delighting in the world's blessing and yet conscious of its tragedy. It is for this concept of humankind—that Christians need to understand—that Christ assumed. Therefore, the line of interpretation runs not from Christ to the Old Testament, nor from the New Testament to the Old Testament, but *rather* from the Old Testament to Christ.

The New Testament, which portrays explicitly the fact of Christ and the consequences of his appearance and work, must inevitably sharpen our Christian perspective on the Old Testament. Yet, since the world which God loves and Christ redeems is the world of the penultimate, the "things before the last," the Old Testament is *not* to be superseded by the New Testament. Any view of the Old Testament that regards its "this-worldliness" as a "barrier" that must be overcome if we are to strive toward the New Testament has stripped away from the center the context which gives it meaning.

Rather, "the Old Testament's love for life and the earth forms the context within which the Christian resurrection hope can alone be properly interpreted and lived."[20]

All of the foregoing challenges imply that a Christian interpretation of the Hebrew scriptures need not—must not—exclude the Jewish understanding from consideration. The significance of the law (*Torah*) and the land as focal points of Hebrew scriptures for Judaism, as well as the interpretations found in the *Mishnah* and *Talmud,* may constitute an ultimate difference between Jewish and Christian analysis. But within the context of the penultimate, this-worldly boundaries of the Hebrew scriptures, the scene of the sanctification of the world before God, through the law (*Torah*) and within the land, as well as the *Mishnah* and *Talmud,* is an irreducible given that must be more deeply understood, respected, and celebrated by Christians if they are to fully grasp the meaning of the Christ event. Neither believing community can absolutize its interpretation of the sacred scriptures, for the God who is revealed through these inspired texts is both *greater* than, and not *limited* by, *either* Judaism or Christianity's interpretation. For the freedom of God's activity is greater than any human interpretation.

The appropriate stance of the Christian toward Jewish analysis is one of respectful dialogue rather than nihilation. The dialogue which has been initiated with courtesy and vigor amidst the tragedies of our century by Jewish thinkers, such as Leo Baeck, Martin Buber, Abraham Joshua Heschel, and Elie Wiesel,[21] is not merely a luxury of the pluralistic age; rather it is, or should become, an essential element in the self-understanding of Christianity and its grasp of the Old Testament (Hebrew scriptures).

Since the task of teaching and instruction is carried out in the church not first of all by theologians but by pastors and lay people, a sympathetic knowledge of Judaism and an ability to encounter and benefit from the Jewish reading of sacred scripture should become a component of minimal literacy in the church. Admittedly, the barriers to realizing this ideal are serious. But for the sake of its own mission and for the sake of the truth, Christianity can no longer afford to make Judaism into a marginal element, alienated or trivialized, within its own consciousness.

Whenever the Hebrew scriptures have been used as a

barrier between the church and synagogue, Christians have discovered their own grasp of the Bible made alien or trivial (i.e. the unwarranted notion that the God of the Old Testament is the God of wrath and judgment that robs Christians of the beauty of God's compassion in the Hebrew scriptures). "Then let us no more pass judgment on one another, but rather decide never to put a stumbling block or hindrance in the way of a brother" (Rom 14:13 NAB). "Behold how good it is and how pleasant, where brethren dwell at one" (Ps 133:1). Making the Hebrew scriptures into a bridge between church and synagogue is a vital step in recovering their meaning for Christians, Jews, and the world whose redemption we await in common.

In sum, dialogue between Christians and Jews on the Bible, most especially the Hebrew scriptures, means a conscious willingness to recognize and respect the other possibilities inherent in any religious text. Honestly admitting one's own bias and prejudice is a vital preparation for, and an integral part of, dialogue; allowing the viewpoint of one's partner in the dialogue the same validity one gives to oneself is an essential aspect of any interreligious dialogue. The true challenge in Jewish-Christian relations is not to make the Bible divisive but rather revelatory of the God whom Jews and Christians all worship.

NOTES

[1] Paraphrased from William R. White. *Stories for the Journey* (Minneapolis: Augsburg, 1988), p. 32.

[2] "Canon" is a transliteration of a Hebrew word (*kaneh*) for "reed" or "stalk" which grows in swampy areas and when cut and trimmed was used at times as a yardstick or ruler; from this came the transfer to what was a "norm" or "rule" of faith and prayer. For an extensive treatment of the issue of canonicity see "Canonicity" in *The New Jerome Biblical Commentary*, edited by Raymond E. Brown, Joseph A. Fitzmyer, and Roland E. Murphy (Englewood Cliffs: Prentice-Hall, 1990), pp. 1034–54. For a brief explanation of the Jewish understanding of the process of canonization see S. Daniel Breslauer, "Bible: Jewish View" in Leon Klenicki and Geoffrey Wigoder, eds., *A Dictionary of Jewish-Christian Dialogue* (New York: Paulist Press, 1984), pp. 16–19.

[3] Commenting on the use of the term "Old Testament" John T. Pawlikowski states:

> The time has come to eliminate the term 'Old Testament' from the Christian vocabulary about the Bible. Though admittedly the word 'old' can connote 'reverence' or 'long-standing experience,' used in reference to the first part of the Bible it tends to create an attitude that these pre-Christian books are inferior and outdated in their religious outlook when compared with passages of the New Testament. In such a context the Hebrew Scriptures at best appear as a foreword to the fullness of faith found in the Gospels and Epistles and at worst as works motivated by legalism and spiritual shallowness which Christians can ignore without in any way impoverishing their spirituality. Continued use of the term 'Old Testament' tends to keep Christians from the realization that the Hebrew Scriptures contain rich spiritual insights vital in their own right. It likewise continues to give credence to the discredited contrast between Christianity as a religion of love with Judaism as a faith perspective marked by cold legalism.

John T. Pawlikowski, "Jews and Christians: The Contemporary Dialogue," in *Quarterly Review,* 4 (Winter 1984), pp. 26–27. Paul M. van Buren suggests that instead of the terms "Old" and "New" Testament we speak of Hebrew scriptures and the apostolic writings. The merit of van Buren's suggestions is that the terms "Old" and "New" Testament do not themselves occur anywhere in the scriptures. Van Buren's suggestion, therefore, has the merit of appropriateness. See Paul M. van Buren, *A Theology of the Jewish-Christian Reality, Part I: Discerning the Way* (San Francisco: Harper & Row, 1980), pp. 122ff. For discussion and use of the term "Prime Testament" for "Old Testament", see André Lacocque, "The Old Testament in the Protestant Tradition" in Lawrence Boadt, Helga Croner, and Leon Klenicki, eds., *Biblical Studies: Meeting Ground of Jews and Christians* (New York: Paulist, 1980), pp. 120–43.

[4] Joseph Cardinal Bernardin, "A Cardinal Looks at 25

Years of Jewish-Catholic Relations," *Proceedings of the Center for Jewish-Christian Learning* 4 (1989), pp. 35–37.

[5] For an extensive treatment of each of the books of the apocrypha, see "Apocrypha; Dead Sea Scrolls; Other Jewish Literature" in *The New Jerome Biblical Commentary*, edited by Raymond E. Brown, Joseph A. Fitzmyer, and Roland E. Murphy (Englewood Cliffs: Prentice-Hall, 1990), pp. 1055–82.

[6] For a complete treatment of the pseudepigrapha, see James A. Charlesworth, ed., *The Old Testament Pseudepigrapha*, 2 vols. (Garden City: Doubleday and Co., Inc., 1983).

[7] Commenting on the meaning of *Mishnah* and *Talmud*, Jacob Neusner, in *Between Time and Eternity: The Essentials of Judaism* (Encino: Dickenson Publishing Co., 1975), pp. 53, 63, states:

> The *Mishnah* is the first and most important document of Rabbinic Judaism. It reached its present form at about the beginning of the third century, C.E. and is based upon traditions at least two hundred years older than that. . . . The *Mishnah* is essentially a law code. It is divided into six major parts, called *Sedera* or *Orders*, encompassing the vast themes of "reality" covered by the Oral *Torah*. These are, first, agricultural law; second, Sabbath and festival laws; third, family laws; fourth, civil and criminal laws; fifth, laws concerning sacrifices in the cult; and finally, laws concerning purities.
>
> To use more general language, *Mishnah* deals with the *Torah*'s governance of the economy and means of production, the material basis of life (agriculture); the organization and differentiation of time into the holy and profane (Sabbath and festivals); the structure and definition of the family, in particular the rights of women; the regulation of society and human interactions and transactions outside of the family; the mode of service to the divinity through sacrifice and cult; and the regulation of the unseen world of purity and impurity as these affect the cult, society, the economy, and the home. The "theory" of the *Mishnah*, therefore, is that all of reality is to be

suitably organized and rationally governed through the law of *Mishnah*.

. . . the great and authoritative commentary to the *Mishnah* is the *Gemara*, which also is simply called the *Talmud*. This is a compilation of materials relevant to a given paragraph of *Mishnah*, developed from the third through the fifth centuries C.E. In point of fact, two *Talmuds* exist for the same *Mishnah*, one edited in Palestine, called the Palestinian or Jerusalem *Talmud*, the other edited in Babylonia, and called the Babylonian *Talmud*. It is the latter that is widely studied to this day and which supplies the authoritative interpretation of *Mishnah*.

[8] Ibid., 48. Also see Jacob Neusner, *Christian Faith and the Bible of Judaism: The Judaic Encounter with Scripture* (Grand Rapids: Wm. B. Eerdmans, 1987).

[9] Dietrich Bonhoeffer, letter to Eberhard Bethge, 5 December 1943. See Eberhard Bethge, *Dietrich Bonhoeffer* (New York: Harper and Row, 1970), p. 360.

[10] For a treatment of the stories that serve as root metaphors for both Judaism and Christianity see Michael Goldberg, *Jews and Christians, Getting Our Stories Straight: The Exodus and Passion-Resurrection* (Nashville: Abingdon Press, 1985).

[11] See Peter Berger and Thomas Luckman, *The Social Construction of Reality* (Garden City: Doubleday, 1966), pp. 114ff for a lucid discussion of this concept.

[12] See C.H. Dodd, *According to the Scriptures* (London: Nisbet, 1952) for an exposition of this view.

[13] Henri de Lubac, *The Sources of Revelation* (New York: Herder and Herder, 1968), pp. 90f.

[14] Julius Wellhausen, *Prolegomena to the History of Israel* (New York: Meridian, 1957).

[15] Walther Eichrodt, *Theology of the Old Testament*, 2 vols. (Philadelphia: Westminster Press, 1961.)

[16] Eichrodt, *Theology of the Old Testament*, I, p. 26.

[17] Ibid., 26.

[18] Ibid., 63, 133, 168ff.

[19] Clark M. Williamson, *When Jews and Christians Meet: A Guide for Christian Preaching and Teaching* (St. Louis: CBP Press, 1989), pp. 15–17. Also see Rolf Rendtorff, "The

Jewish Bible and Its Anti-Jewish Interpretation," *Christian-Jewish Relations* 16 (1983), 3–20, and Joseph Blenkinsopp, "Tanakh and the New Testament: A Christian Perspective" in Lawrence Boadt, Helga Croner, and Leon Klenicki, eds., *Biblical Studies: Meeting Ground of Jews and Christians* (New York: Paulist, 1980), pp. 96–119.

[20] Martin Kuske, *The Old Testament as the Book of Christ: An Appraisal of Bonhoeffer's Interpretation* (Philadelphia: Westminster, 1976), p. 106.

[21] For an exploration of contemporary Jewish exegesis (analysis) see Elie Wiesel, *Five Biblical Portraits* (Notre Dame: University of Notre Dame Press, 1981); Abraham Joshua Heschel, *The Prophets* (New York: Harper and Row, 1969); Martin Buber, *On the Bible: Eighteen Studies,* edited by N. Glatzer (New York: Schocken Books, 1982).

Discussion Questions

1. How do Jews and Christians understand the term "Bible"? Explain.

2. Do you feel the Bible has been abused by both Jews and Christians? Explain why or why not.

3. Explain why the term "Old Testament" might be offensive to Jews.

4. If the Hebrew scriptures were to be removed from the Bible, would the New Testament make sense by itself?

5. What do you see as the challenge Christians face when interpreting the Old Testament (Hebrew scriptures)? What do you see as the challenge Jews face when interpreting the New Testament (Christian scriptures)?

For Further Study

Boadt, Lawrence, Helga Croner, and Leon Klenicki, eds. *Biblical Studies: Meeting Ground of Jews and Christians.* New York: Paulist Press, 1980.

Fisher, Eugene, James Rudin, and Marc H. Tanenbaum, eds. *Twenty Years of Jewish-Catholic Relations.* Mahwah:

Paulist, 1986. See "The Role of Scripture in Catholic-Jewish Relations" by Lawrence Boadt, pp. 89–109.

Fornberg, Tod. *Jewish-Christian Dialogue and Biblical Exegesis.* Uppsala: University Press, 1988.

Greenspan, Frederick E., ed. *Scripture in the Jewish and Christian Traditions: Authority, Interpretation, Relevance.* Nashville: Abingdon, 1982.

Harrelson, Walter. "Christian Misreading of Basic Themes in the Hebrew Scriptures." *Quarterly Review* 2 (1982) 58–66.

Neusner, Jacob. *Christian Faith and the Bible of Judaism: The Judaic Encounter with Scripture.* Grand Rapids: W.B. Eerdmans, 1987.

Nickelsburg, George. "Reading the Hebrew Scriptures in the First Century: Christian Interpretations in Their Jewish Context." *Word and World: Theology for Christian Ministry* 3 (1983) 238–50.

Rendtorff, Rolf. "The Jewish Bible and Its Anti-Jewish Interpretation." *Christian-Jewish Relations* 16 (1983) 3–20.

Thoma, Clemens, and Michael Wyschogrod, eds. *Understanding Scripture: Exploration of Jewish and Christian Tradition of Interpretation.* Mahwah: Paulist Press, 1987.

Wilson, Marvin. *Our Father Abraham: Jewish Roots of the Christian Faith.* Grand Rapids: William B. Eerdmans, 1989.

II.

MICHAEL COOK

The New Testament: Confronting Its Impact on Jewish-Christian Relations

I. Introduction

Jews receive frequent mention in the Christian scriptures, commonly called the New Testament. But the tenor of these references is usually disparaging, and many of the criticisms lodged against Jews or their religious practice are, regrettably, ascribed to Jesus personally. Aside from rare reports of camaraderie between Jesus and the Jews' leaders, the gospels generally show him chiding, sometimes even maligning, the scribes and Pharisees, priests and Sadducees. And these authorities, in turn, are regularly depicted as bent on embarrassing or tricking Jesus and, particularly toward the end of his ministry, even on destroying him. Nor is such malevolence limited to the leaders; sometimes the Jews as a people are also thus portrayed, especially once they too seem to join in clamoring for Jesus' execution.

Negative depictions of Jews punctuate not only the four gospels but also the book of Acts, and appear occasionally in Paul's epistles as well. It is hardly difficult, therefore, to surmise the likely impact of these texts on the history of Jewish-Christian relations: over the centuries, not only have many Jews come to consider the New Testament a virtual catalogue of anti-Judaism, but many Christian readers have been unable to ignore how consistently the Jews come across as villainous. Moreover, since the figure of Jesus serves as a role model for Christians, they may naturally assimilate as their own those same disapproving attitudes toward Jews apparently advanced by Jesus himself.

II. Sample Passages and Stereotypes

Most scholars view the "scribes" and "Pharisees" as having been forerunners of the rabbis, who, a generation after Jesus' death, began laying the foundations of Judaism as it has evolved even to the present day. It becomes especialiy instructive, therefore, to observe how the New Testament depicts Jesus in relation to these two groups in particular, for his assessments of them were undoubtedly determinative of how many later Christians, readily appropriating his sentiments, came to relate both to the Jews and the Judaism of their own day.

The gospels show us Jesus addressing these scribes and Pharisees with hostility, often accusing them of "hypocrisy." One well-known chapter, Matthew 23,[1] features Jesus relentlessly berating or belittling these groups with a repetitive refrain, "Scribes and Pharisees, hypocrites!" Further condemnations are also included: "you blind fools" (v. 17); "you blind guides, straining out a gnat and swallowing a camel!" (v. 24); "you . . . whitewashed tombs . . . outwardly . . . beautiful, but within . . . full of dead men's bones and all uncleanness . . . full of hypocrisy and iniquity" (vv. 27–28); "you . . . sons of those who murdered the prophets" (v. 31); "you serpents, you brood of vipers, how are you to escape being sentenced to hell?" (v. 33).

In the synoptic gospels (Mark, Matthew, and Luke), only the Jews' chief priests and other leaders are cast as orchestrating Jesus' arrest and trial, and plotting his execution; ultimately, however, the Jews as a people are themselves enlisted in urging Pontius Pilate, the Roman governor, to "crucify him! . . . crucify him!" (Mk 15:13–14). And Matthew, for good measure, adds the infamous "blood curse," wherein the Jews, already collectively to blame for Jesus' death, now also eagerly foist responsibility on their offspring as well: "Let his blood be on us and on our children!" (27:25). In Mark and Matthew, the Jewish masses need to be "stirred up" (Mk 15:11) or "persuaded" (Mt 27:20) by their priests to demand Jesus' death, but in Luke they require no encouragement whatsoever.

While in the synoptic gospels it is only near the conclusion of Jesus' ministry that the Jews as a people emerge actively as his adversaries, in the gospel of John they surface in this capacity far earlier. John's frequent use of the collective term "the Jews"—seventy-one times compared to but five or six times in each synoptic gospel—suggests his desire not only to cast "the Jews" as Jesus' enemies, but to do so *throughout* Jesus' ministry, not merely at its end.

Thus, John informs us (italics added) that "*the Jews* persecuted Jesus" (5:16), and that "*the Jews* sought all the more to kill him" (5:18; also 7:1). Some who accepted Jesus as the Christ dared not admit it publicly "because they feared *the Jews*" (9:22; also 7:13). Joseph of Arimathea had to ask for Jesus' body secretly "for fear of *the Jews*" (19:38). The disciples' doors were kept shut "for fear of *the Jews*" (20:19). Strangely, John even has Jesus denounce Jews *accepting* of him: they are of their "father the devil . . . a murderer from the beginning . . . a liar and the father of lies" (8:44), with the reason why they do not hear the word of God being that they "are not of God" (8:47).

This antagonism, so intense in John, may even obscure from readers Jesus' Jewish identity and that of his inner circle. John 10:34, for example, presents Jesus as saying to Jews (italics added): "Is it not written in *your* law?" (why not "*our* law"?); John 13:33 has Jesus address his disciples (italics added): "as I said to *the Jews* so now I say to you" (why not "as I said to *our fellow* Jews"?). Such texts may only reinforce an already erroneous impression that Jesus somehow perceived himself as *outside* the Jewish people.

When viewed most broadly, the New Testament appears to have spawned negative stereotypes persisting for centuries—in some circles, even to the present day: that the Jews are responsible for crucifying Jesus and, as such, guilty of deicide; that their tribulations throughout history constitute God's punishment of them for killing Jesus; that Jesus originally came to preach only to Jews but, when they rejected him, he urged their abandonment in favor of Gentiles (non-Jews) instead; that Christianity (typified by Jesus and his teachings) emphasizes love, while Judaism (typified by the Pharisees and the "Old" Testament) stands for an oppressive legalism, stern justice, and a God of wrath; that, by Jesus' day, Judaism had entirely ceased to be a living faith; and, above all, that while the children of Israel were God's original chosen people by virtue of an ancient covenant, in rejecting Jesus they forfeited that chosenness—and now, through a new covenant, Christians (the "new" Israel) have replaced the Jews as God's chosen people, with the church now becoming the people of God.

III. The Modern Legacy

The legacy of these themes and developments remains influential today because the New Testament continues to serve as such a vibrant stimulus of Christian teaching: aside from regular scripture readings in church (wherein the selections frequently happen to include anti-Jewish verses), and textual sermons (many based on passages targeting the Pharisees as models of what *not* to be[2]), the New Testament is also the central focus of thousands of books as well as university courses, not to mention adult education and sectarian training in churches and religious schools. Added to these is the seemingly endless citation of New Testament texts heard on an ever-growing number of radio and "televangelism" programs on national broadcasting networks.

Jews today frequently encounter expressions of the New Testament's anti-Jewish bias. Naturally they sometimes expect that Christians, in addition to looking askance, unjustifiedly, at the Jews of *Jesus'* day, will also carry this over when viewing *modern* Jews as well. This suggests that the ways in which the New Testament refers to Jews and Judaism may continue to set much of the tenor of Jewish-Christian relations in the future even as they have in the past—that these texts still constitute an imposing *obstacle for Jews* and a serious *quandary for Christians* interested in improving Jewish-Christian relations today.

IV. The New Testament: How It Became an Obstacle for Jews

When most Jews think of Jesus, the image they readily conjure up is not that of the actual historical figure but rather of the gospel portraits of him completed long after his ministry. The difference is notable, for there is no reason to believe that the historical Jesus was himself anti-Jewish, even though his later gospel image indisputably *is*.

It was this latter depiction that first induced Jews to dismiss Jesus as an apostate, i.e. as someone who had turned against his own religion, Judaism. And because missionaries sought to draw Jews into Christianity in Jesus' name, the rabbis condemned Jesus himself for attempting to deceive the Jewish people and lead them astray. It is probable that the proliferation of Christian writings toward the end of the first century catalyzed the rabbis into "closing" the Jewish Bible so as to prevent any such "external books" from gaining acceptance among the Jewish populace at large.

Of course, religious opinions of one age are not always consequential for subsequent eras. But the rabbis' disaffection with the New Testament did, in point of fact, set the trend for centuries of later Jews who, identifying the historical Jesus by the New Testament's depiction of him, came to relate to Christianity accordingly.

The New Testament's anti-Jewish Jesus also determined the attitudes of many Christians. During the middle ages, by which time the church had established a virtual monopoly on European learning, gospel teachings in particular conditioned the mindset of the masses against Jews. And since the laity was generally illiterate, church art became employed to teach that the Jews were accursed, with the "synagogue" depicted as either blindfolded or literally blind (cf. 2 Cor 3:14ff).[3]

Since, moreover, the gospels held the Jews as a people responsible for Jesus' execution, they gave rise to the epithet that Jews were "Christ-killers." This identification often inflamed popular passions against Jews in Christian Europe, who lived with perpetual anxiety that the gospels' accusations would become pretexts for pogroms (massacres of Jews). Nor was their fear without good reason: during the various crusades (beginning in 1096), Christian armies, trekking through Europe to recapture Jerusalem from the Muslim "infidel," routinely ransacked Jewish communities en route and murdered the inhabitants—justifying these actions by appeals to the gospels' own assessments of Jews as murderers of Jesus and infidels themselves. Other pogroms were triggered by outrageous "blood libels," to the effect that Jews were regularly reenacting their execution of Jesus by kidnaping Christian children to secure blood Jews supposedly needed to bake Passover *matzah* (unleavened bread).[4]

Etched even deeper into the modern Jewish psyche, after centuries of such continual prejudice, was Nazism's malicious exploitation of the New Testament's supersessionist theology. This conviction—that Gentile Christians had superseded the Jews, displacing and replacing them as God's chosen people—was now manipulated by Hitler's ideologues to suggest that the persistence of Jews into the twentieth century was an anomaly, a quirk or mistake of history, that they were a fossil meant to have disappeared far earlier. Such a ploy lessened potential resistance to Hitler's "final solution," the plan to exterminate the entire Jewish people.

Since Christian anti-Judaism has thus been such a source of anxiety for Jews over the centuries, it should come as no surprise how many Jews today continue to bristle or flinch, even to cringe, upon hearing the name of Jesus, and to view the New Testament with varying degrees of dismay and distrust, if not dread. This explains why these Christian texts loom up for Jews as such a fundamental and imposing obstacle in interfaith relations today.

V. The New Testament: How It Poses a Quandary for Christians

It should be obvious now that these texts likewise pose a serious dilemma for Christians committed to interfaith relations. Their quandary is inescapable: what to do when their scriptures, sacred repository of their cherished teachings, also seem to generate such intensely anti-Jewish sentiment?

Their responses have usually resolved themselves into at least three different avenues of approach: (1) a *denial* that the New Testament itself is anti-Jewish; or (2) an acknowledgment of anti-Jewishness in the New Testament, but mainly in terms that tend to *minimize* its importance or otherwise explain it away; or (3) an open recognition that the New Testament is profoundly anti-Jewish and that this is a serious problem requiring full *confrontation.* It is important to recognize that these three categories of response are largely incompatible with each other: that is to say, either the New Testament is not anti-Jewish (#1) or it *is,* and if it *is,* either this problem is not especially serious (#2) or it is definitely so (#3). Agreement in these regards may be a necessary precondition for achieving any significant progress in Jewish-Christian relations in the future.

Avenue #1—Denial That the New Testament Is Itself Anti-Jewish

Christians espousing this approach believe interfaith relations will improve once Jews and Christians come to view the New Testament itself as neither a source nor a cause of Christian anti-Judaism. In the service of this viewpoint, at least a fourfold argument has been advanced:

(a) Inspired by God, the New Testament reflects the ultimate revelation of divine love and could in no way have been intended to encourage the contempt of any people. Jesus himself spoke this language of love: he preached the turning of the other cheek, even the love of one's enemies. Therefore, those recording his spiritual teachings, and deeply committed to him themselves, could hardly have written works that are anti-Jewish.

(b) The New Testament's apparently harsh language against the Jews is not anti-Judaism at all but simply prophetic rebuke out of love. Just as the Hebrew prophets of old, reprimanding the Israelites in their day, are surely not to be judged anti-Jewish, neither then should Jesus' criticisms of Jews be so construed. Diatribes against the Jews —whether by Jesus or Paul—were only a kind of oratorical style or a literary device intended not to be final but merely to shock people into repentance before it was too late.

(c) The gospels and the book of Acts show us, approvingly, thousands of Jews accepting Jesus' message, or at least eager to hear what he had to say. How then, when the New Testament so *approvingly* presents so many Jews so positively disposed, can modern Jews consider it anti-Jewish?

(d) Though, in subsequent eras, Christian theology did evolve along anti-Jewish lines, this later orientation toward Jews should not be confused with that in the New Testament itself, where such bias is not evident, even latent. Denunciations of Jews by church fathers, especially in the third century and following, were a function of a time long after the New Testament was completed, when Christian preachers were forging new weapons for the church in the church's ongoing conflict with Judaism. Interpreting the sacred gospel, the church fathers added their own errors and prejudices against Jews to the holy, eternal, and infallible truths of the New Testament itself. Thus, it is misunderstandings by *later* Christian interpreters which must be confronted, not sentiments of the New Testament writers themselves.

Assessing Avenue #1

This first category of approach—*denying* as it does that the New Testament is anti-Jewish—strikes me as serving no constructive purpose; well-intentioned as it may be, it nevertheless depends on arguments which, from a Jewish point of view, are simply not compelling:

(a) Respecting the first argument advanced—that the New Testament reflects the ultimate revelation of divine love —I do not wish to respond insensitively. But since Jews do not include the New Testament among their sacred texts, any argument proceeding, as if self-evidently, from the New Testament's divine inspiration is not seen as persuasive. Moreover, that Jesus himself spoke this language of love hardly guarantees that all those committed to him (including the later gospel authors) did so as well.

(b) I welcome the second argument, that the admittedly harsh language against the Jews in the gospels, Acts, and Paul's epistles is only prophetic rebuke out of love. But I also experience a nagging sense that these reprimands far exceed any rebuke I know of by the Hebrew prophets of old. After all, were not the prophets acting out of love for and loyalty to the Jewish people, with their message designed to *solidify* the covenantal bonds between God and the Jewish people? Yet many censures of Jews in the New Testament predict that God will choose *others* to replace them! While Jesus himself may well have scolded some fellow Jews out of love, the particular intensity and animosity characterizing rebukes attributed to him by the gospels most likely reflect interjections by the gospel authors themselves, not the sentiments of the historical Jesus personally. And given the prominence of this editorial element, the New Testament, while sacred to Christianity, is nonetheless unavoidably to be construed as *it-self* anti-Jewish.

(c) How should we address the argument that, since it represents approvingly so many Jews as having accepted or at least having been open to Jesus, the New Testament cannot itself, therefore, be considered anti-Jewish? While the gospels, Acts and Pauline epistles are not biased against *all* Jews, they are biased against Jews not accepting Jesus. Not biased against Christian Jews (those accepting Jesus as the "messiah," or "Christ"), they *are* biased against *non*-Christian Jews. Since, in terms of Jewish theology, a Jew who professes belief in Jesus as the messiah has thereby, by definition, become a Christian—and is no longer a Jew[5]—in effect the only persons mentioned in the gospels with whom modern Jews can readily identify is with those not accepting Jesus, and the New Testament *is* hostile toward these Jews. It *is* therefore anti-Jewish.

(d) In terms of the fourth argument cited—that anti-Jewish stereotypes originated in later Christian theology but not in or with the New Testament itself—my own reading of New Testament texts leaves me unpersuaded by the argument for this defense. I still feel that the four evangelists themselves have conveyed anti-Jewish sentiment in the very process of describing Jesus' ministry in their gospels.

Avenue #2—The New Testament's Anti-Jewishness Is Acknowledged, But Mainly in Terms That Tend To Minimize Its Importance or Otherwise Explain It Away

Christians espousing this general approach, while acknowledging the New Testament's anti-Judaism, hope nonetheless to reduce its impact. They offer a variety of mitigating interpretations, or suggest a number of extenuating circumstances, which make that bias appear to be of only minor consequence. Their intent is to induce Jews to feel less offended by New Testament texts, and to move Christians themselves to take these texts less seriously. Arguments reflecting this position are quite varied, and not necessarily consistent with one another:

(a) The Christian scriptures were hardly unique in attacking opponents; other religious or philosophical literatures of that age partook of this same tendency, and New Testament polemics even turn out to be relatively *mild* by comparison. This realization may help blunt any current-day effects of the New Testament's rhetoric by robbing it of "its capacity for mischief"[6]—since now Jews as well as Christians, identifying these diatribes as but the convention of a bygone era, will be able to dismiss them as inconsequential for the modern day.

(b) It would be beneficial if Jews apprised themselves of the polemical nature of their *own* ancient literature! The Hebrew Bible itself, for example, abounds in condemnation of Israel's enemies. The first century Jewish historian Josephus, meanwhile, considers hostile Gentiles "frivolous and utterly senseless specimens of humanity,"[7] and caricatures his opponent, Apion, for having "the mind of an ass and the impudence of a dog, which his countrymen are wont to worship."[8] The first century Jewish philosopher Philo terms his Gentile opponents in Egypt "a seed bed of evil in whose souls both the venom and the temper of the native crocodiles and wasps are reproduced."[9] Moreover, rabbinic literature as well engages in considerable invective, directed even—it should be noted—against Christians and Christianity! In fact, if Jews themselves had ever become a majority presence, would not anti-Christian sentiment, imbedded within their own tradition, have occasioned the same kind of predicament for *them* vis-à-vis Christians as is now faced by Christians vis-à-vis Jews?

(c) Also constructive would be the realization that authors of New Testament writings were not consciously contributing to a new corpus of scripture. In their day, their only Bible, recognized or envisioned, was the *Jewish* Bible. Had they imagined the importance their writings might someday assume, or surmised the detrimental effect of a "New" Testament on the Jewish people, such authors— themselves good Christians—may well have been more judicious in their presentations of Jews.

(d) Anti-Judaism, moreover, hardly began with the New Testament since Jews had already become negatively perceived by many pagans well before these writings even emerged. This suggests that influxes of pagans into Christianity may have played a significant role in the introduction of anti-Jewish bias into Christian traditions. Thus, while the New Testament's anti-Judaism may now be admitted, its substantial origin *outside* Christianity should also now be more widely acknowledged—in the hope both of lessening resentment toward the New Testament among modern Jews and of weakening the attachment of modern Christians to prejudices so at variance with truly Christian ethics.

(e) Conceivably, Jews whom the New Testament attacked were not all "the Jews" but only a *segment* of them, or perhaps even a group *outside* them altogether! When Jesus denounced the Pharisees, for example, he may have been targeting only a minority of "hypocrites" amongst them—or only the disciples of Shammai.[10] Alternatively, what appear to be anti-Judaic diatribes could actually have been rebukes only of particular Christians called "Judaizers."[11] Whichever the case, *modern* Jews, themselves akin neither to disreputable Pharisees nor to partisans of Shammai, and still less to Christian Judaizers, need in no way feel attacked by New Testament censures which only inadvertently became misapplied to them. And all the more so, therefore, should modern Christians understand that Jesus' and Paul's criticisms were in no sense applicable to all Jews of the first century, still less to those of later times.

(f) The most formidable argument falling within this general approach offers an alternative way of viewing matters. The apparent anti-Jewish polemic in the New Testament was actually only *intra*-Jewish: admittedly intense, it was nevertheless only "in-house squabbling" between one segment of Jews (who had accepted Christianity) over against another (who had not). If what appears to be anti-Jewish rhetoric is thus merely recorded argument against those within the *same* family, then those scolding the Jews turn out still to be Jews *themselves*—with their condemnations therefore ceasing to be *anti*-Jewish in any meaningful sense.

Assessing Avenue #2

The sentiments of this second approach also are well-intentioned. But do they effectively address our problem? Several arguments strike me as not genuinely relevant; and some, possibly relevant, may be unfounded.

(a) Yes, the New Testament's invective was hardly unique; perhaps it was even relatively mild. But how many Christians today are sufficiently conversant with the conventions of ancient polemic to bring them to bear in an evaluation of the New Testament's anti-Judaism? Moreover, for Christians the New Testament, in sharp distinction from most other ancient writings, is *sacred* literature; as such, its polemics, whether comparatively tame or not, command authority as the inspired word of God. This sanctified status of their scripture accords its censures of Jews a compelling quality, and thus more than compensates for what is supposedly the *comparative* mildness of its anti-Judaism.

(b) Yes, Jews too were certainly polemical in their own literature and should at the least consider whether, had they themselves become dominant in history, a Christian minority might not have suffered accordingly. But conjecture must pale before reality: Christianity, not Judaism, has been dominant, and Jews the victims of persecution fueled and justified by recourse to New Testament texts.

(c) Yes, New Testament writers may have been unaware that their criticisms of Jews would become enshrined in a new corpus of scripture. To suggest, however, that such an awareness would have induced them to abstain from abusive language, or at least to tone it down, is again conjectural, and not relevant to realities at hand.

(d) Yes, Jews were disliked by other peoples even prior to the rise of Christianity. Yet, for most Christian readers, would not such an awareness tend to *universalize* the New Testament's polemic rather than neutralize it? Arguing that other peoples (prior to and independent of Christians) also disapproved of Jews may have the unintentional effect of reinforcing if not validating the New

Testament's prejudice by seeming to suggest that it was somehow justified or warranted.

(e) Were the New Testament's rebukes against Jews actually directed only against a minority among them, or even persons outside them altogether? I am unconvinced. Even if correct, however, such speculation would render us little assistance in coping with the modern-day effects of these censures which especially after centuries of Christian preaching are still often *heard* today as attacks on *all* Jews of the first century (if not now as well).

(f) Finally, I must take issue with the "in-house squabbling" argument which is sufficiently crucial to this discussion to require, at this juncture, an extended treatment.

Scholars holding to this theory usually accept the testimony of the book of Acts, which would have us believe that *early* Christianity had been swelled by "myriads" (literally, "tens of thousands"[12]) of Jews. This huge number of Jewish entrants feeds—or renders more plausible—the idea that, even in the post-70 era when the gospels were being composed, anti-Jewish polemics could have been essentially only "in-house" rebukes by one segment of Jews (accepting Christianity) against others (rejecting it). Gospel writers, assigned by this theory to the former category, would thus turn out to be polemicizing only against *fellow* Jews.

In responding, I feel that we must first dispense with one preliminary: at the least, let us not be misled by the *titles* of the gospels. While persons named Mark, Matthew, and John may indeed have been among Jesus' *Jewish*[13] contemporaries back around 30 C.E.,[14] these (together with Luke[15]) were not the actual authors of gospels written and ascribed to them so many years later. The four gospels apparently circulated initially as *anonymous* writings. Only belatedly, probably in the second century, did they come to be incorrectly attributed to contemporaries of Jesus.[16] Since we do not know the identity of the actual authors, certainly any names of *Jews* assigned to the gospel titles should not be enlisted in support of the "in-house squabbling" argument alleging that the gospels were written *by* Jews against *other* Jews. For some, possibly even all, of the actual authors could have been

Gentiles themselves (i.e. of no Jewish extraction or affilia-
tion)—and anti-Jewish ones at that.[17]

As for the "myriads" of Jews claimed originally to have
joined Christianity's ranks, this is myth, not history. Paul's
own epistles, dating from the 40s into the 60s, are not only
far earlier than Acts (ca. the late 80s), but emanate from the
very time frame when Acts insists "myriads" of Jews had
already flocked to Christianity. Yet Paul advances a radically
different assessment of Christian demography, expressing
disappointment that so *few* Jews (only "a remnant" [Rom
11:5]) had become Christian. Most "were hardened" (2 Cor
3:14), resisting Christ and not attaining righteousness (Rom
9:31–33); "not enlightened" (10:2); a "contrary people"
(10:21) who, in a "stupor," neither "see" nor "hear . . .
down to this very day" (11:8; italics added), branches "broken off because of their unbelief" (11:20). Hence, Christianity's successful inroads, as early as Paul's own day, were already predominantly among *Gentiles,* hardly Jews.

Paul's statements should caution readers to be wary of
Acts' alternative statistics and should prompt the question:
Where is the huge critical mass of *Jewish*-Christians necessary to sustain the theory that the anti-Judaism of the post-
70 gospels was only "*in*-house squabbling"? After 70 C.E.,
Christianity was no longer "in" the Jewish house at all—the
"church" had severed itself from the "synagogue," with the
Jewish revolt of 66–70 C.E. playing a crucial role in culminating this process (see below). Since the reality is that only
relatively few Jews had become Christian at *any* time, surely
the truth to be stressed is "not that some [Jews] accepted [the
gospel], but that many rejected it," and that to "overempha-
sise the references to the conversion of the Jews . . . [is to get]
hold of the wrong end of the stick."[18] The "in-house squabbling" argument, therefore, convenient and even comforting
as it may be, is in my view simply not soundly-based.[19]

Avenue #3—The New Testament's Anti-Jewishness Is Recognized as a Serious Problem Requiring Full Confrontation

I personally not only espouse this third, remaining avenue of approach, but also believe the other approaches have
now, regrettably, become part of our dilemma—for their ori-

entation actually impedes our understanding of *why* the New Testament came to be anti-Jewish and our determination of how best to *cope* with this problem today. The remainder of this chapter is devoted to these two questions.

VI. Why the New Testament Came To Be Anti-Jewish

A General Dynamic

The New Testament may have *had* to be anti-Jewish. A new religion (Christianity), developing from its mother (Judaism) and wishing to establish a viable separateness, needed to justify its existence, and such self-justification actually necessitated expressions of negativity toward the parent. Especially since Christianity drew so heavily upon Judaism in terms of its ethics, scripture, and liturgy, as well as some of its theological teachings, would not the question naturally have surfaced: given Judaism, why Christianity?

One response by early Christians was a claim that *they* had supplanted the Jews in God's favor, that they had become the "new" Israel. Accordingly, for Christianity now to justify its worth, Judaism somehow had to be shown as possessing *less* value, and whatever value it was granted had to be explained as only a function of God's plan in preparing the world for *Christianity.* Since such a natural dynamic actually *required* Christian writers to express anti-Jewish sentiments, we should interpret many New Testament passages as precisely what they *appear* to be: namely, anti-Jewish. To deny the problem (Avenue #1) or even mitigate it (Avenue #2) thus becomes misleading, or at the least counter-productive.

Some Specific Dynamics

We may surmise, as well, three more specific reasons why the New Testament came to be anti-Jewish:

(a) By insisting not only that Jesus was the messiah or "Christ," but also that others should agree, Christians inevitably became embroiled in acrimonious debate with *Jewish* adversaries, especially Pharisees, whose objections to the Christian message were sufficiently disconcerting to necessitate point-by-point refutations. As a vehicle for conveying and preserving these Christian rebuttals, stories arose of alleged controversies between Jesus and various Jewish leaders ("Pharisees," "scribes," "Sadducees," etc.), traditions which eventually achieved incorporation into the gospels themselves.

What is striking to realize, however, is that the early Christians mistakenly came to assume that their own immediate problems with Jewish opponents, for the most part *first* arising only in the decades *subsequent* to Jesus' death, had instead actually originated *during* his ministry itself, and that the answers to these problems were therefore discoverable in *his* words. That is to say, Christians naturally imagined that their omniscient Christ had anticipated all possible objections potentially confronting his followers after his death, and had therefore bequeathed to these followers the very responses they should emulate in disarming their critics. This explains why, later on in the gospels themselves, we find that harsh words silencing Jewish opponents—first surfacing only with the developing Christian tradition—are instead now attributed to *Jesus personally,* even though the issues being argued arose only after he died, and concerning them, in my view, the historical Jesus had no advance awareness.

By thus gaining inclusion in the gospels themselves, such depictions of Jesus vanquishing Jewish opponents generated the ineradicable image of his aversion to fellow Jews, and in this fashion markedly contributed to the New Testament's anti-Judaism. For centuries of later Christians, having no reason to question the authenticity of these gospel confrontations, naturally accepted what were heavily fictionalized[20] exchanges at face value instead. Thereby, they grew to dislike not only those Jews who had allegedly harassed Jesus himself, but also those who continued to vex generations of his later followers down to their own day.

What were these objections that Jews lodged against Christianity? In the main, they were attempts to refute claims of Jesus' messianic identity, and included the following: that Jesus had in no way resembled the *triumphant* messiah expected to overthrow Rome—his crucifixion therefore only *dis*confirmed his credentials (cf. Mk 15:29ff);[21] that Elijah, the herald of the Christ's coming, had yet to appear (cf. Mk 9:11);[22] that the messiah was not expected to come from *Galilee* (cf. Jn 7:41, 52), as did Jesus, who was neither born in

Bethlehem of Judea, King David's birthplace,[23] nor was himself a Davidic descendant (cf. Jn 7:41–43; Mk 12:35–37); and that Jesus himself[24] had broken with the law of Moses, thereby abandoning the very essence of Judaism (cf. Mk 7:19; Jn 9:16; Acts 6:13ff). As for Jesus' resurrection, crucial to Christianity, Jews denied its occurrence, and dismissed the claim of the empty tomb as a hoax (cf. Mt 28:13–15).[25]

Naturally, given the Christian authorship, each gospel debate was resolved in favor of the Christian viewpoint (just as, in the writings of the pro-Pharisee and pro-Hillel rabbis, Pharisees out-debated Sadducees and the school of Hillel that of Shammai). But the net effect of the controversy traditions, as far as centuries of later Christian readers and churchgoers were concerned, was an overwhelming impression of a relentless anti-Judaism on the part of Jesus himself.

(b) A second factor productive of the New Testament's anti-Judaism was the emergence of severe tension between Christianity and *Rome,* a problem which the church found it most expedient to address by assuming an *anti-Jewish* stance. In 64 C.E., Emperor Nero had initiated a brutal persecution of Christians, whom he made scapegoats for a fire in Rome. Shortly thereafter, in 66 C.E., Jews in Judea launched a major revolt. This extraordinary act of sedition raised the ominous specter of Roman vengeance not only against Jews but against *Christians* as well. For in the eyes of Rome, the two were often confused since Christianity, arising from Judaism, perpetuated so many of its beliefs, teachings and practices. When the Jews revolted, therefore, it became imperative for Christians to distinguish themselves from Jews in such a way that Christians would also appear to be the allies of *Rome,* and in this fashion be able to deter any further persecution of Christians at Roman hands.

The major hurdle, however, was that Jesus had been *crucified,* a Roman punishment meted out notably to subversives. A crucified Jesus inevitably invited speculation that not only had Christianity's founder and Lord been himself a seditionist,[26] but that this same stigma adhered to his later followers as well.

Faced, then, with the urgency of establishing Jesus' loyalty, Christian tradition could hardly depict *Rome* as culpable in Jesus' execution. Responsibility had to be shifted, assigned to some other party. In view of the later antipathy being directed at Christianity by the Jewish community, it is not surprising that Jewish leaders (and, ultimately, "the Jews") became saddled with the blame in *substitution* for Rome—especially since Jewish opposition to later Christians was easily assumed to have originated as opposition to Jesus himself. This replacement of Rome by "the Jews" was accomplished through a literary device—a fictional trial of Jesus before the Roman governor—wherein the normally ruthless Pontius Pilate (symbolizing Roman officialdom) was now presented as actually desiring Jesus' exoneration but forced instead to yield to pressure *by the Jews* to crucify him.[27] Complementing this picture was the introduction of various other traditions suggesting harmony, or at least compatibility, between Jesus and Rome,[28] along with the story of another fictional, but earlier, trial in which Jesus had been condemned by judges of a specifically *Jewish* sanhedrin.[29] When viewed against the backdrop of the great Jewish revolt (66–70 C.E.), the sum effect of all these factors was to ally Christians with Rome, and to present the Jews as the enemies of *both*. Thus, paradoxically, did a Jew put to death by Romans become, instead, a Christian put to death by Jews.

(c) As previously mentioned in another connection, prejudice against Jews had already existed in *pagan* circles even prior to Christianity's emergence; accordingly, Gentiles entering Christian ranks may naturally have brought this antecedent bias into Christianity along with them. The reasons for such prejudice were varied: Jews in the Diaspora (lands outside Palestine) understandably tended to settle together, set apart from, rather than interspersed among, Gentiles; this apparent unsociability intensified xenophobia, fear or dislike of foreigners (both of Jews, by Gentiles; and of Gentiles, by Jews). Not to go unmentioned, of course, was the Jews' refusal to worship the gods of the Greco-Roman pantheon, even though the God of Israel had received hospitable welcome. In addition, Jews observed what struck others as bizarre customs: circumcision, for example, and seemingly curious dietary laws; these only alienated them further in the eyes of some outsiders. One can well imagine, moreover, that whatever preferential treatment Jews received from Rome[30] only aggravated Gentile resentment.

The Jewish revolt of 66–70 C.E. must itself have played a profound role in intensifying this antipathy and thereby in stimulating anti-Judaism in gospel traditions. The auxiliary forces Rome drafted to crush the revolt in Judea were drawn from neighboring regions, particularly Syria. Many Gentile recruits died in putting down what their families probably considered only a needless disturbance by a fanatic upstart people. The casualties sustained fanned hatred of Jews especially by natives of Antioch, Syria's major city, which had a large Jewish population.[31] Josephus informs us that Jews in Antioch were harassed, even murdered, by Gentiles, who libeled them, spread rumors of Jewish plots, and asked the Roman general Titus to expel Jews, or at least revoke their privileges.[32]

With Gentile passions in Antioch now so inflamed against anyone Jewish, whether Jews per se or Christians of Jewish extraction, the latter must have realized how precarious it was to be viewed by others as still having *Jewish* ties. They may therefore have sensed it expedient to shed Jewish associations and instead to submerge their identity within Antioch's *Gentile*-Christian Church—whose members no doubt harbored some of the same anti-Jewish biases then typifying Antioch's wider Gentile community. These considerations may largely explain the extreme anti-Jewish bitterness permeating the gospel of Matthew, produced, I believe, in Antioch's Gentile-Christian community in the 80s.[33]

VII. Coping with This Problem Today

It was Nazi exploitation of Christian anti-Judaism which first drove home to many modern Christians the critical need to confront their scripture, stimulating in turn not only a large number of church declarations disavowing anti-Semitism, but also hundreds of books and essays on the problem. Several noteworthy contributions deserve special mention, even within the confines of this brief chapter.

The Second Vatican Council's *Declaration on Non-Christian Religions* in 1965 delineated specific dimensions of biblical and theological study requiring revision, with the particular end in view of enhancing of Catholic-Jewish relations. Roman Catholics (and, by extension, all Christians) were now urged to recognize the Jewish ancestry of Jesus, his mother, and closest followers; to understand Christian faith in terms of its continuity with Judaism rather than its displacement of it; to realize that Jesus' death, as recorded in the gospels, should not be blamed upon all Jews then living, without distinction, nor upon Jews of today;[34] to view Jewish scripture in such a way that it not seem to espouse only legalism, fear, and justice devoid of love of God and humanity; and generally to achieve familiarity with how Jews themselves understand their own Bible and religion.

Rosemary Ruether's seminal volume, *Faith and Fratricide*,[35] published in 1974, is still considered by many the most important impetus in bringing Christians and Jews to their current state of progress in Christian-Jewish dialogue. Ruether argued that the presence of anti-Jewish bias in the New Testament is blatant and undeniable, and asked us to believe, moreover, that this bitter dialectic of christology and anti-Judaism is rooted not simply in the period of the gospels' composition (after 70 C.E.), but rather far earlier, in the days of Christianity's very emergence. (Also controversial was her conjecture that Jesus' disciples, mortified by their abandonment of him, had compensated for their sense of guilt by projecting blame upon the Jewish authorities instead.)

Another important and highly innovative work, published in 1985, has been Norman Beck's *Mature Christianity*.[36] Viewing religions as passing through developmental phases, Beck believed that a willingness to initiate self-criticism signals the dawning of a religion's maturity. Hence, Christianity could best demonstrate its own maturity by self-critically reevaluating the New Testament's traditions of antipathy toward Jews and Judaism. He challenged Christians to "stand in significant judgment over our scriptural traditions just as [these traditions] stand in significant judgment over us," and incisively added that "subscription to them as infallible . . . is idolatrous." He also listed quite sobering illustrations of how Christianity has adapted scripture throughout its history by reinterpreting some sections and progressively ignoring others. Among sections Beck wanted to see Christians today ignore are the New Testament's anti-Jewish passages, this to be best accomplished by a process of retranslation. He insisted that gospels thus purged of their apparent hate could thereby be brought into closer conformity with the actual demeanor of the historical Jesus himself.[37] Beck's contributions to Avenue #3 encourage me to raise additional considerations.

Christians view the New Testament as sacred, but does this sanctity inhere in the texts themselves or rather with the *interpreters* thereof? Some religious outlooks profess to root their sole authority in what their scriptures say; yet in practice they rely additionally on a tradition of interpretation that clarifies how these texts are to be understood, and prioritizes them in terms of importance. What has often resulted in the history of religions is that sacred written texts do not actually command in practice the degree of authority laid claim to by the texts themselves. As applied to the topic at hand, the *influence* of New Testament passages biased against Jews could well be more a function of what modern Christian interpreters will *allow* than of the scriptural texts in and of themselves.

Many Christians recognize that the Bible ("Old" and New Testament together) expresses some attitudes that, in the modern day, seem quite objectionable—e.g. passages endorsing animal sacrifices, condoning slavery, maligning homosexuals, or demeaning women. Yet despite their genuine presence in the Bible itself, such views are usually routinely ignored by many Christians who, not feeling constrained by *these* attitudes, could likewise be induced to dispense with the New Testament's anti-Judaism as well.

Posing the matter differently, what should be done when we encounter a conflict between sacred literature and religious *values*? Many interpreters of Matthew, for example, have asserted that included among the sacred values of Christianity are the mandates to turn the other cheek and to love one's enemies (5:39, 44). What, then, do we do with the text, found in the same gospel, which presents Jesus assailing the Pharisees as children of hell (cf. Mt 23:15)? A sacred image in Christianity is often said to be a "God of *love*"; how is this to maintain itself alongside a prophecy that a wrathful God will destroy Jerusalem to avenge the Jews' rejection of Jesus (Mt 22:7)? Does there not devolve upon interpreters of Christian values a responsibility to declare anti-Jewish passages *devalued*?

Undoubtedly, the most formidable obstacle we face is unawareness on the part of the Christian laity of the role of *historical conditioning* in the formation of the New Testament's anti-Jewish passages. I have consistently argued that developments reflecting decades well after Jesus' death were

mitment, from now on, for joint endeavor in hastening the day when "the Lord shall be one and the Lord's name one" (Zec 14:9).

NOTES

[1] Scriptural citations follow *The Oxford Annotated Bible with the Apocrypha: Revised Standard Version* (New York: Oxford University Press, 1965).

[2] Even though Jesus may well have been a Pharisee himself; cf. my essay, "Jesus and the Pharisees: The Problem As It Stands Today," *Journal of Ecumenical Studies* 15 (1978): 441–60.

[3] Cf. Wolfgang Seiferth, *Synagogue and Church in the Middle Ages*, trans. by Lee Chadeayne and Paul Gottwald (New York: Frederick Ungar, 1970).

[4] Cf. R. Po-chia Hsia, *The Myth of Ritual Murder* (New Haven: Yale University Press, 1988).

[5] Cf. Dennis Prager, "Is There Such a Thing as a 'Jew for Jesus'?" *Ultimate Issues* 5 (1989): 6–7; also my article, "Anti-Judaism in the New Testament," *Union Seminary Quarterly Review* 38 (1983): 135, n.2.

[6] Quoted from Luke Johnson's insightful essay, "The New Testament's Anti-Jewish Slander and the Conventions of Ancient Polemic," *Journal of Biblical Literature* 108 (1989): 441. He suggests (pp. 434–35) the examples cited below, nn. 7–9.

[7] *Against Apion* 1.25 §225–6; trans. by Henry St. John Thackeray, *Josephus* (Cambridge: Harvard University Press, 1926).

[8] Ibid. 2.7 §86.

[9] *Embassy to Gaius* 26.166.

[10] An apparently arrogant teacher whose views were criticized later in the literature of rabbinic Judaism itself, where he is often contrasted with his contemporary, Hillel, reputed to have personified patience and loving-kindness.

[11] These elicited the scorn of some fellow Christians for insisting that Gentiles accepting Christianity should nonetheless "live like Jews," as, e.g., by accepting the Mosaic law as binding and incorporating Jewish observances into the practice of their Christian faith.

[12] "Myriads" literally means "tens of thousands," but

some scholars understand the term as "thousands" only. Cf. Acts 2:41; 4:4; 5:14; 6:7; 21:20.

[13] Church tradition considers Mark to have been Peter's (Jewish) interpreter and associate in Rome, and locates Matthew within Jesus' inner circle of twelve Jewish followers. John is also often identified as among the twelve.

[14] "C.E." ("common era") is a more inclusive formulation than "A.D." (*anno Domini*, "in the year of our Lord"), a Christian theological term.

[15] Luke is usually identified as Paul's (Gentile) physician.

[16] Cf. Norman Perrin, *The Resurrection According to Matthew, Mark, and Luke* (Philadelphia: Fortress, 1977), p.x: "All the [gospels] were written and circulated anonymously. Names were attributed to them only in later ecclesiastical tradition."

[17] This could have been the case even with the author of Matthew, the gospel most frequently cited as "Jewish"; cf. my article, "Interpreting 'Pro-Jewish' Passages in Matthew," *Hebrew Union College Annual* 54 (1983): 135–47.

[18] Stephen Wilson, *The Gentiles and the Gentile Mission in Luke-Acts* (Cambridge: At the University Press, 1973), pp. 232–33.

[19] Why then does Acts exaggerate the number of Jews joining early Christianity? The author was disturbed by the anomaly that, while Jesus' preaching naturally extended the essence of *Judaism,* Jews affirming Christianity in the author's day (ca. the late 80s) were embarrassingly few. How explain that Christianity's intuitively obvious truths had been rejected by those most expected to have intuited them? His explanation: while Christianity's truths were not perceived by Jews in his own late day, by no means had they been lost on Jews of a bygone age; for when Christianity had first emerged, Jewish entrants had numbered even in the (tens of) thousands! Only subsequently, upon beginning to experience rebuffs by Jews, did Christian missionaries turn to Gentiles instead; and it was their phenomenal success among Gentiles that accounted for the disconcertingly high percentage of Gentile-Christians in the church of the author's own day. Cf. my chapter, "The Mission to the Jews in Acts: Unraveling Luke's 'Myth of the "Myriads," ' " in *Luke-*

Acts and the Jewish People: Eight Critical Perspectives, edited by Joseph Tyson (Minneapolis: Augsburg, 1988), pp. 102–03, 152–58.

[20] I am not denying that Jesus engaged in controversies with religious opponents, only that the gospels can be confidently used to confirm *specific* disputations during his ministry, reconstruct their *exact* substance, or even identify *precise* disputants. See my volume, *Mark's Treatment of the Jewish Leaders* (Leiden: Brill, 1978), pp. 15–28.

[21] Rejoinders by the church, attesting that Jews lodged this objection, include: Jesus *expected* execution (Mk 10:33f); he could have prevented it but *chose* not to (Mt 26:53); he died to *fulfill* scripture (Mt 26:54). Stated in more modern terms, the objection would be that Jesus died without bringing the messianic age, typified by an end to war, oppression, and ill-will.

[22] The church's attempted solution: cf. 9:13; Mt 17:13.

[23] His birth was later assigned to Bethlehem to neutralize this Jewish objection. Cf. Raymond Brown, *The Birth of the Messiah* (Garden City: Doubleday, 1979), pp. 412ff., and Appendices 3 and 7; Howard Teeple, "The Historical Beginnings of the Resurrection Faith," *Studies in New Testament and Early Christian Literature: Essays in Honor of Allen P. Wikgren,* edited by David Aune (Leiden: Brill, 1972), p. 109.

[24] Jews did not realize that it was developing Christianity (not Jesus) which broke with the law and then attributed the break to Jesus. The oft-cited, "Think not that I have come to abolish the law . . ." (Mt 5:17ff), is not relevant here; this reflects not words of Jesus but rather of *Matthew,* who casts Jesus as a lawgiver modeled on Moses.

[25] They alleged that the disciples had stolen the body and proclaimed it resurrected. Matthew's reaction was to insist that a stone had been sealed and a guard set (27:66; cf. 28:11ff.), so an undetected theft was impossible. John responded by having the resurrected Jesus standing near the tomb (20:14ff). The empty tomb tradition is unmentioned and, I submit, unknown by Paul. Since the author of Mark (unlike that of Matthew) seems unaware of Jewish rebuttals, the story must have *first* surfaced either with Mark himself (ca. 70), or only shortly before him. This means that, while early Christians believed in Jesus' resurrection, they did not

do so initially on the basis of any empty tomb tradition, which only originated as a Christian response to Jews and possibly others denying Jesus' bodily resurrection.

[26] The gospels themselves may inadvertently preserve telltale clues of Jesus' possible subversive image: his "cleansing" of the temple (which must have involved *some* militancy); his followers' possession of weapons (on a holiday, no less; cf. Lk 22:36ff); his crucifixion between seditionists (the Greek, *lestes,* meaning, in this context, "seditionist," not "thief"); the title atop the cross: "king of the Jews" (worded from Rome's perspective and indicating that sedition, not "blasphemy" [Mk 14:64], was the actual reason for Jesus' arrest).

[27] That this trial is fictional is accepted by many scholars today, especially after their recourse to Tacitus, Josephus, and Philo, ancient sources attesting to Pilate's ruthlessness and to his execution of opponents without trials.

[28] E.g. Jesus' dicta, "render to Caesar the things that are Caesar's" (Mk 12:17) and "all who take the sword will perish by the sword" (Mt 26:52)—whether originating with Jesus or not—became useful in persuading Rome of Jesus' harmlessness and in downplaying any suggestion of his incompatibility with Roman interests.

[29] Such sanhedrins could be legally convened by Jewish leaders only with the Roman governor's express consent (Josephus, *Antiq.* 20:197–203). The gospels present us with a fiction that the Jewish leaders, here in the case of Jesus, acted *independently.* The intent of this tradition was at least threefold: to show that the Jews arrested and tried Jesus without Rome's direction; to demonstrate that Jesus was formally condemned only by a specifically *Jewish* body; and to substitute "blasphemy," a non-significant offense in Roman eyes, for "sedition," the actual reason for Jesus' crucifixion (by Rome).

[30] Jews were excused from participation in the cult of the emperor and could both administer their own funds (including export of dues to the Jerusalem temple) and settle their own legal affairs in civil suits involving one Jew against another. Some correctional authority may also have been conceded their communal leaders. Additionally, Jews were exempted from military service and court appearances on the sabbath. Cf. my article, "Judaism, Hellenistic," *The Inter-*

preter's Dictionary of the Bible Suppl. Vol. (Nashville: Abingdon, 1976), pp. 505–06.

[31] Conjectured today at having been anywhere between 22,000 and 45,000.

[32] *The Jewish War* 2 & 7.

[33] Cf. "Interpreting 'Pro-Jewish' Passages."

[34] Even this much-heralded statement, however, leaves gospel depictions essentially unchallenged since Roman involvement still goes unmentioned and Jesus' death remains solely the responsibility of Jews (only *fewer* of them).

[35] Rosemary Ruether, *Faith and Fratricide: The Theological Roots of Anti-Semitism* (New York: Seabury, 1974).

[36] Norman Beck, *Mature Christianity: The Recognition and Repudiation of the Anti-Jewish Polemic of the New Testament* (Selinsgrove: Susquehanna University Press, 1985).

[37] Ibid., 33–34.

[38] I myself would urge the following: scriptural selections read in church should not contain anti-Jewish verses, and sermons vilifying Pharisees should no longer be preached; publishers of Christian textbooks should: (1) strip their texts of anti-Jewish material; (2) introduce positive treatments about aspects of Judaism mentioned in the gospels (e.g. Jewish holidays such as Passover, institutions such as the synagogue, and teachings such as the *Shema* [Mk 12:29]); (3) introduce positive statements about Judaism of no particular relevance to Christianity (treating, e.g., Judaism's ongoing vitality in the modern world); and (4) indicate the role Christian teachings have played in unsavory periods of Jewish history (e.g. the crusades, pogroms, the Spanish inquisition, expulsions of Jews, the holocaust, etc.).

Discussion Questions

1. How do you react to the negative depictions of the Jews in the New Testament? How has the New Testament spawned negative stereotypes of Jews that have lasted for centuries?

2. In your opinion, was Jesus anti-Jewish or the gospel writers? Explain.

3. How do you react to the interpretation of the New Testa-

ment that gave rise to the claim that Jews were "Christ-killers"?

4. How can the New Testament be seen as an obstacle to interfaith relations today by Jews? Explain.

5. Even if all Jews living in Jerusalem were in fact guilty of killing Jesus, what is the responsibility of succeeding generations of Jews? What are the implications of your conclusion?

For Further Study

Baum, Gregory. *Is the New Testament Anti-Semitic? A Re-Examination of the New Testament.* Rev. ed. New York: Paulist, 1965.

Beck, Norman A. *Mature Christianity: The Recognition and Repudiation of the Anti-Jewish Polemic of the New Testament.* Cranbury: Susquehanna University Press, 1985.

Cook, Michael J. "Anti-Judaism in the New Testament." *Union Seminary Quarterly Review* 38 (1983): 125–38.

———. "The New Testament and Judaism: An Historical Perspective on the Theme." *Review and Expositor* 84:2 (1987).

Guignebert, Charles. *The Jewish World in the Time of Jesus.* New York: University Press, 1979.

Koenig, John. *Jews and Christians in Dialogue: New Testament Foundations.* Philadelphia: Westminster, 1979.

Perelmuter, Hayim Goren. *Siblings: Rabbinic Judaism and Early Christianity at Their Beginnings.* New York: Paulist, 1989.

Sandmel, Samuel. *A Jewish Understanding of the New Testament.* New York: Ktav, 1974.

———. *Anti-Semitism in the New Testament?* Philadelphia: Fortress, 1978.

———. *The First Christian Century in Judaism and Christianity: Certainties and Uncertainties.* New York: Oxford University Press, 1969.

III.

MICHAEL B. McGARRY

The Holocaust:
Tragedy of Christian History

I. Introduction

> "This is still the century of the *Shoah*, the inhuman
> and ruthless attempt to exterminate European
> Jewry."
>
> —Pope John Paul II[1]

Take away your birth certificate, your medical and school
records, your family photo album. In other words, take away
your memory. What are you? Who are you? How do you relate
to everyone in your neighborhood? For those who have had a
traumatic head injury, months of therapy may be required to
restore their memory so that they can know who they are.
Those of us who are living in the last decade of the twentieth
century resemble the person who needs to learn what we either forgot or denied so that we can know who we are.

As we study the many dimensions of the contemporary
Jewish-Christian encounter, we need to explore a part of our
memory—or, just as likely, to learn something of our collective North American memory so that we can know who we
are. What do I mean by this? I relate two short stories to respond to this question.

In 1988, I attended a conference about the holocaust, entitled "Remembering for the Future." Most of those attending
were older than I (who was born in 1948). They felt a strong
desire, indeed urgency, to remember those tragic years in
central Europe in the middle of this century. But for me who
was born after the event, grasping the holocaust meant *learn-*

ing about it from those who had experienced it and from those who had studied it. But the title of the conference gave us the reason for our presence: for the future. We did not want a future where the holocaust would be forgotten. For what reason? one might ask.

The second story: At a recent meeting among seminary and graduate theological professors, the question arose about sponsoring a holocaust remembrance service among the theological schools in the Washington, D.C. area. The academicians squirmed in their seats. The first professor questioned the timing: "It comes at a bad time: the end of April." Another asked what such a memorial might look like. Still another asked who had suggested such a thing. Finally someone expressed what was on the minds of more than a few: "Why do we have to go through this at all? Is it *psychologically* a good idea to go back to the holocaust? It's more important to look to the future."

And *that is* precisely the issue: If we do not claim our past by studying history, we will not know who we are and we will be less able to fashion the kind of future we want for ourselves and our children. Furthermore, we Jews and Christians will never know one another beyond a superficial level unless we seek to understand this extraordinarily tragic moment in both our histories. For the holocaust is not solely a part of Jewish history; it took place squarely in the middle of Christian Europe. The perpetrators were mostly baptized—even though in many cases non-practicing—Christians. It is part of Christian history. We study the holocaust so that we will know who we are and so that we can forge a common, mutually life-giving future.

So, in this chapter, we attempt to understand ourselves through making the memory of the holocaust part of our common memory. In too brief a space, we will seek to answer what happened during those awful years, who were the actors in that tragic moment, what is the aftermath, and how do we remember *for the sake of the future.*

II. What Happened?

The missionaries of Christianity had said in effect: You have no right to live among us as Jews. The secular rulers who followed had complained: You have no right to live among us. The German Nazis at last decreed: You have no right to live.

—Raul Hilberg[2]

The holocaust is the event wherein, from 1933 to 1945, German Nazis and their collaborators killed more than six million European Jews simply because they were Jewish, or, more accurately, simply because at least one of their grandparents was Jewish. This single-minded effort to eliminate the Jewish people from the earth also included the persecutions of many others for certain political, economic, or social reasons: Gypsies, Slavs, the mentally ill, the young incompetents, the Poles, homosexuals, and so forth. More than five million of these were barbarically killed. This, in a very limited sense, is "what happened" during the years of destruction and what we mean by the term "holocaust."

However, when we speak of "what happened" during the holocaust, we can also speak more generally: the holocaust was the culminating event of Jewish persecution witnessed through the centuries. In this more contextual view, the "what" of "what happened?" is seen as qualitatively but historically continuous with the victimhood of Jews throughout history. From the years of Constantinian rule (early fourth century), through the ghettoizing legislation of the middle ages, the expulsions from many parts of Europe, the pogroms (that is, vicious and regular attacks on Jews) of eastern Europe, to the "emancipation" of the late eighteenth and nineteenth centuries: all this can be seen as simply signposts along the way toward the destruction of the Jews.

But in a more proximate way, to understand "what happened" in the holocaust, we must look at the events before, and earlier in, the twentieth century. With the revolutions of the eighteenth century and the enlightenment, Europe was gradually becoming more secular. Jews were beginning to feel that they had finally "arrived." Their confidence was ill-founded, for they underestimated the antisemitism (Jew-hatred) which was hidden just under the German skin. In addition, the Germans had experienced tremendous devastation during and after World War I. Heaped upon this were the social and economic hardships of the 1920s and 1930s. The combination of these factors made Germany ripe for the rise of economic, social, and racial scapegoating. They were more than ready for someone to blame for their woes and someone to cast a new promise of German domination in Europe and in the world-at-large. The former they found in the Jews; the latter they found in the cunning and shrewd Adolph Hitler.

It was Hitler's calculated ability to galvanize cultural antisemitism, the resentments following World War I, and economic deprivation, with the dream of Germany once again triumphant and the world's master. The glorious future for the Germans found expression in the Germanic "Aryan," the northern European sterilized of the impure Jewish people. In his effort for global domination, Hitler took advantage of an array of economic, social, and religious stereotypes of the Jewish people that Christian and European history had given to him. He portrayed the Jews as demonic to the core, even subhuman "vermin"; the only antidote for "vermin," he reasoned, was annihilation. So he conceived the "final solution": the extermination of European Jewry. In the early 1930s, Hitler and his political party, the National Socialists ("Nazis"), began a gradually accelerating persecution of Jews. First, they enacted laws restricting Jewish employment, ownership of property, mobility, and other rights. This campaign reached a climax on November 9, 1938, *Kristallnacht,* the "Night of Shattered Glass." It was on that night that Nazis rounded up thousands of Jews and sent them to concentration camps. In many ways, *Kristallnacht* initiated the final stage of the war against the Jews. Up to that point, the Nazis had simply inconvenienced Jewish lives; now they were doing away with Jewish lives.

In 1939, after capturing Austria and Czechoslovakia, Hitler's Third Reich moved to a new phase by invading even more countries. Each new incursion was accompanied by the arrest, incarceration, and slaughter of Jews. In Poland, for instance, the Germans met a large Jewish community of three million which had lived there since the twelfth century. At the beginning they sequestered the Jews in increasingly cramped and crowded ghettos. Many Jews, taken in by the relatively innocent promise of "work camps," cooperated with this move. Word started to leak out, however, that something more awful was happening. Soon the Nazis began killing them. In 1942 the Germans stepped up their war against the Jews by fashioning concentration camps which quickly and efficiently disposed of large numbers of Jews. Methods of executing the Jews used at the outset wearied and depressed even the most hardened Nazis. "Cleaner and quicker" methods were soon found, with the concentration of killing centers located at Sobibor, Treblinka, and Auschwitz/Birkenau. By the end of the Second World War, more than ninety percent of Poland's Jews were dead.

As the German intent became clear, Jewish resistance in the ghettos became organized, systematic, and, for a time, successful. Despite this resistance the Nazi stranglehold slowly but surely tightened, not only on Poland, but on the Baltic states, Belgium, Denmark, Greece, Italy, the Netherlands, Norway, France, Hungary, Bulgaria, Romania, Czechoslovakia, and Yugoslavia. Amazingly swift deployment of entrance and processing plants moved thousands of Jews through the kingdom of death. Railroads and other methods of transportation were dedicated to transporting them to the camps. An entire national infrastructure was contrived to bring about the "final solution." The story is long, gruesome, and barely comprehensible. In the end, close to six million of Europe's nine million Jews had been murdered with swift, even amazing, efficiency.

Members of the Nazi party, however, were not the only cooperators in murdering the Jews. Amazingly, they enlisted not only the "rank and file" German people, but also some of the great minds of the university, eager physicians of the fatherland, and technicians and engineers who fashioned the complex but very efficient death machines. Sad to say, vigorous church resistance and courageous outcry were difficult to find. There were, however, some fascinating stories of courageous resistance which merit closer attention and study.[3]

Word about this unbelievable effort slowly reached the western sources and finally the press. Many at first refused to believe; it was too fantastic. Others gave credence to some of what they heard, but responded by concentrating more on the war effort. They reasoned that, after all, defeating Hitler would stop the slaughter of Jews. Others found the Jews expendable or not important enough to focus on. A small number urged Allied raids on the camps or at least on the railroads. Their pleading found deaf ears.

When all is said and done, the question we began with—

"What happened?"—remains pressing but too small. Merely to chronicle the rise of Hitler and the Nazis and their swift success in plundering eastern Europe seems all too inadequate to the immensity of what they sought to accomplish. The "what" is enormous, incomprehensible, indeed unique. That a modern European, "enlightened" country dreamt of empire and conquest, while not admirable, is certainly imaginable. What stands as incomprehensible is what came to light during the war—namely, even at the last hour as they saw defeat on the horizon and supplies and equipment were desperately needed for the war effort, Hitler and his henchmen enlarged their attempt at annihilating the Jews by diverting men and railroad equipment to the death camps.

The full story is obviously more complex than we have outlined here. So many other parts of the story—military, economic, social, scientific, and political—need to be told for the full depth of this history to be grasped. Quite interestingly, for instance, the Jewish fate in different countries varied as some Christian majorities resisted or hid Jews more eagerly than others; Italy and Denmark come to mind. Also, many peoples in addition to the Jews suffered during the Nazi madness. Still this much must be said: in a few short years, more than sixty percent of all European Jewry were slaughtered. At no other time in the history of western civilization (with the qualified exception of the Armenians by the Turks in the early part of this century) has there been the wholesale destruction of a people simply because they were that people.

In a book which introduces us into the world of Jewish-Christian relations, the significance of the holocaust has to be a major focus. The sometimes dispassionate recital of holocaust facts, punctuated by either gruesome anecdotes of torture or edifying stories of rescue, has to, in the end, lead to the question: Who were the people of the holocaust?

III. The People of the Holocaust

A. *The Perpetrators: The Nazis and their Collaborators*

> An Auschwitz survivor . . . asked, "Were they beasts or human beings?" I answered that they were human beings and that was the problem. . . .
> —Robert J. Lifton[4]

Adolph Hitler, a baptized Catholic, a native of Austria, had a most unremarkable upbringing. Many of his biographers have commented how unappealing he was. Nonetheless, Hitler possessed the practical brilliance to assess a number of factors that he forged into the Nazi project. He felt in himself, and recognized in his fellow Germans, the simmering nationalism that had been so humiliated by World War I. In Hitler, the German people found a voice promising a new age of glory and rescue from their international disgrace. Also, the extreme economic conditions of the 1920s made him desperate for a scapegoat. This he found in the Jews. Although antisemitism, expressed in his diabolic book *Mein Kampf,*[5] was at the center of his ideology, many of Hitler's opponents found its rashness and its extreme expressions too fantastic to take seriously. His followers absorbed his Jew-hatred in varying doses and with differing seriousness. Some historians have credited Ernst Moritz Arndt's German nationalism and Johann Gottlieb Fichte's antisemitism as the ideological grain that Hitler brought together and made into a deadly brew for his National Socialist policies.[6] Another potent, but sad, resource which the Nazi propaganda tapped was generations of what French historian Jules Isaac called the Christian "teaching of contempt" about Jews and Judaism.[7] The Nazis' rabid hatred of Christianity did not prevent them from occasionally using the Christian teaching of contempt to bolster their anti-Jewish policies. So with the help of many within the inner circle and unwitting outer circle, Adolph Hitler fashioned the dream of a Third Reich which would restore Germany to the global scene and inaugurate the first western genocide that was an official act of a democratically elected government.

The executive arm of the National Socialists were the *Reichsführer SS* (*Schützstaffel* = Defense Corps) headed by Heinrich Himmler. The SS were an elite corps of men who were bound together by their racial and elitist self-understanding. They organized the concentration camps and directed the "final solution," as the Nazi effort to exterminate the Jews came to be called. In the early years of the Third Reich, the SS found that the slow and crude killing by shooting and hanging had a depressing effect on the executioners. It fell to the SS to relieve their feelings by seeking less personal, more efficient, methods of execution. They came up with the idea of gassing people through ingeniously constructed death camps. With the plan of the concentration camps intact, this elite corps enlisted the participation of thousands of others who drove the trains, kept the records, ordered the gas for the camps, and managed the many other menial tasks of this kingdom of death.

Among these other perpetrators, one has to mention the physicians who conducted experiments on human beings and began to choose the children whose lives they deemed "unworthy of life"; these included the handicapped, the retarded, the deformed, and other such "undesirables." To accomplish this, the doctors disregarded their Hippocratic oath and left their moral conscience at the gate of the camps. They sought rather to explore some of the frontiers of science by macabre experiments on human subjects. They devised, for the sake of their homeland, how people might be most quickly and efficiently killed. As one Nazi doctor put it, "Ethical . . . the word does not exist [in Auschwitz]."[8]

In a civilized society, one often looks to the educational institutions to alert the general populace to a sickness that may be engulfing it. Sad to say, many university professors, hoping that Germany would rule Europe, subscribed to the poisonous doctrines of Hitler. Far from slowing the contagion down, these educators added to its momentum. To test the survival of the fittest, engineers found challenge in solving the intriguing problem of how to kill in large numbers very quickly. The emotionally detached, conscience-neutered person became the servant of the Reich. In short, the usual watchdogs of society became part of the very project about which they should have warned the people.

B. The Victims

We have already noted that there were many victims of the Nazi onslaught: the Poles (destined for eventual extermination), Slavs, Gypsies, mentally ill, Catholic priests, and others. But as Auschwitz survivor Elie Wiesel has noted, "although all Jews were victims, not all victims were Jews."[9] In the context of Jewish-Christian relations, we must focus on the plight of the Jews, all the time seeking not to minimize the utter pain of the other five million who died at the hands of the Nazis.

To be a victim of Hitler's exterminationist policies, one need have only one Jewish grandparent. No exceptions were made—no matter how old or young, infirm or strong, "vermin" were fit only to be killed. For some, however, the death sentence was mercifully swift; for others, death was delayed because some work could still be squeezed out of youthful and muscular bodies. But when those bodies were no longer useful, they were gassed and cremated quickly. Some went to death in silence, other screaming wildly in protest. Some in the camps bartered their family member's life for a ration of bread; others had babies in defiance and for the future. In other words, Jewish victims were human in their struggle, even if Hitler and his henchmen sought to deny them their very humanity. Indeed one dehumanizes the Jews every bit as much as Hitler if one generalizes too much about their reaction to the destruction. The voice of one does not represent the voice of all—but it is one. Etty Hillesum, a Dutch victim, wrote in her diary only days before the trip to Auschwitz:

> It is all so ugly. . . . I would much rather join those who prefer to float on their backs for a while, drifting on the ocean with their eyes turned towards heaven and who then go down with a prayer. I cannot help myself. My battles are fought out inside, with my own demons; it is not in my nature to tilt against the savage, cold-blooded fanatics who clamor for our destruction. I am not afraid of them either, I don't know why; I am so calm it is sometimes as if I were standing on the parapets of the palace of history looking down over far-distant lands. This bit of history we are experiencing right now is something I know I can stand up to. I know what is happening and yet my head is clear. But sometimes I feel as if a layer of ashes were being sprinkled over my heart, as if my face were withering and decaying before my very eyes, and as if everything were falling apart in front of me and my heart were letting everything go. But these are brief moments; then everything falls back into place, my head is clear again and I can once more bear and stand up to this piece of history which is ours. For once you have begun to walk with God, you need only

keep on walking with Him [God] and all of life becomes one long stroll—such a marvelous feeling.[10]

It is most important to remember, however, that the Jewish story of the holocaust is not simply one of victimhood.
Many Jews courageously resisted Hitler and the Third Reich.
Armed and fearless resistance was organized within the large
urban ghettos where, by 1942, almost all East European
Jews were gathered. Most famous of these were Lodz, Vilna,
and Warsaw. Resistance, too, was mounted in armed upris-
ings in the camps of Sobibor, Treblinka, and Auschwitz. Of
course, they were, in the end, unsuccessful, but they must be
remembered as extraordinary witnesses to Jewish bravery in
the face of overwhelmingly brutal force.

C. *The Others: Churches, Rescuers, and Bystanders*

First they came for the Communists
and I did not speak out—
because I was not a Communist.

Then they came for the Socialists
and I did not speak out—
because I was not a Socialist.

Then they came for the trade unionists
and I did not speak out—
because I was not a trade unionist.

Then they came for the Jews
and I did not speak out—
because I was not a Jew.

Then they came for me
and there was no one left
to speak out for me.
                    —Martin Niemoeller[11]

We have reviewed the perpetrators and the victims of the
holocaust. We have focused, in the former category, on the
leaders, their executive arm, and some of their collaborators;
in the latter category, on the Jews. What of the others? There
were so many involved in Germany during the war, some of
whom had no *direct* role to play in the holocaust—soldiers on

the battle front, factory laborers, civil servants, and the thousands of workers needed just to run the cities and work the farms. Here it is appropriate to itemize three: the church, the bystanders, and the rescuers.

The holocaust is part not only of Jewish history, but also of Christian history. This monstrous effort to wipe out European Jewry began in a country primarily made up of Lutherans and Catholics. It is true that more than twenty-five hundred Catholic priests were killed at Dachau, and hundreds of the Confessing Church of Germany were put to death. In light of these deaths, we ask: Where were the *Christian leaders*? Where were the pope, the priests, the pastors, the bishops? Where—we desperately search—were they when the atheistic movement of Nazism began to take its lethal hold? Sadly and honestly one must admit that clear, persistent voices from the churches were not to be heard. Yes, there were the heroes like Dietrich Bonhoeffer and Bernhard Lichtenberg, but these were few and far between.[12] Pope Pius XII spoke out in 1942 (which prompted stronger repression of Dutch Jews, including converts),[13] but his role looks, at this point, to be confused, even dubious.[14] What the church did publicly appears, on the surface, to be inadequate and sparse; what it did secretly to save individual Jews provides numerous stories of sacrificial heroism. Further historical research needs to be done in this delicate area, but it can at least be said that few church leaders distinguished themselves in speaking out against the Nazi onslaught.[15]

As pressing as it is to answer the question "Where was the church during the holocaust?" another more frightening question about "the others" in the holocaust precedes it: Was there something in Christian teaching itself which might have provided a seedbed, the groundwork for National Socialism? We already have noted that western Europe displayed an almost unbroken record of marginalizing and restricting Jewish life. Behind and parallel to that social history stands a theological lineage of teachings about Jews which questioned the very right of Jews to exist as Jews (it must be stressed, however, that despite scurrilous polemics, the church never endorsed a program of annihilation). These teachings, sometimes gathered under the term "supersessionism" (the notion that the church has replaced—superseded—the Jewish people in God's plan of salvation), included the following: (1) with the coming of Christ, the chosen people of old had lost their chosenness; this had been passed over to the Christian church; (2) because they killed their own messiah ("His blood be upon us and our children"—Mt 27:25), they were "Christ-killers," guilty of "deicide"; (3) with the destruction of the temple in 70 C.E. (common era, the present era shared by Christians and Jews), God left the Jews to wander the earth until the end of time; (4) with the coming of the messiah in Jesus, the Jews' old, legalistic law was replaced by a new law of love; (5) Jesus was the absolute fulfillment of all Old Testament prophecies and thereby the Jews' purpose in history had come to a close—they had become relics, obsolete.

But if these teachings appear to us as rather pitiful, there were some who were better than these Christian teachings. There were the *rescuers:*

> By saving the Jewish girl I simply did my duty. What I did was everybody's duty. Saving the one whose life is in jeopardy is a simple human duty. One has to help another regardless of who this human being is as long as he is in need, that is all that counts.
> —Ada Celka, Polish rescuer[16]

What turned anyone into a rescuer, in so many cases, we do not know. If anything is worth exploring after the holocaust and amid the Jewish-Christian encounter, it may well be this very issue. This question each of us—the readers—must ask: What would turn *us* into a resister or a rescuer? Nechama Tec has studied this phenomenon and her research has yielded quite surprising results.[17] Among Polish rescuers of Jews, she found that having the "right theology" was almost irrelevant: some who were very religious with the "teaching of contempt," who were even antisemitic, went out of their way to harbor Jews. As much as they disliked Jews, they would never participate in killing them. Others who were atheistic, or marginal, or just came from good families with no particular religious persuasion turned into rescuers. Some took money, others refused payment. In her research, however, Nechama Tec found that some common traits marked the rescuer: individuality, independence of convictions, a general commitment to help the helpless, a spontaneous decision to help Jews when the opportunity came to them, and a perception that Jews were totally dependent on the protection of others. With few exceptions, rescuers did not think that they had done anything more extraordinary than what any good human being would do; they certainly did not consider themselves courageous. And yet, in retrospect, the rescuers' story may be the most precious of the entire holocaust, for it may provide the hope for any credible uttering of "never again," the rallying cry of those who have confronted the world of the holocaust.

Finally, I believe it was Elie Wiesel who observed (although I cannot remember where), "In the end, we will understand the holocaust not in terms of the perpetrator nor in terms of the victim, but in terms of the bystander." The question of the Christian *bystander* comprises many factors: how much they knew, what their options were, what the reasonable chances were of successful resistance, and so forth. At the very least, however, one has to ask the question of what went through their minds as they heard about the early Nuremburg laws[18] which further and further ghettoized the Jews and confiscated their property. What went through their hearts as they saw some of their neighbors rounded up one day and gone the next? What torment—or numbing— touched their hearts as they plowed their fields and breathed the wind carrying the smoke from the crematoria? How could those who knew the truth live from day to day without completely disintegrating as human beings? In the end, can one conclude that the Nazi enterprise succeeded more at dehumanizing the bystander than the Jew?

IV. The Aftermath

A. Jewish Survival

According to Jewish philosopher Emil Fackenheim, a commanding voice was heard from Auschwitz, giving the Jewish people a new, 614th commandment.[19]

> We [Jews] are, first, commanded to survive as Jews, lest the Jewish people perish. We are commanded, second, to remember in our very guts and bones the martyrs of the holocaust, lest their memory perish.

We are forbidden, thirdly, to deny or despair of God, however much we may have to contend with Him or with belief in Him, lest Judaism perish. We are forbidden, finally to despair of the world as the place which is to become the kingdom of God lest we help make it a meaningless place in which God is dead or irrelevant and everything is permitted. To abandon any of these imperatives, in response to Hitler's victory at Auschwitz, would be to hand him yet other posthumous victories.[20]

At the very least, Fackenheim has articulated the most significant, even universally agreed upon, Jewish resolve following from the holocaust: the Jewish people must survive. While this is a common agreement, for many Jews the meaning of survival is elusive. It is around two major poles, however, that the meaning of survival seems to revolve: the question of God's existence and the significance of the state of Israel for the Jewish people.

If it throws into disarray every glib affirmation of human goodness and perfectibility, even more does the holocaust baffle the traditional notion of God. How could the God of Abraham and Sarah, of Jacob and Rebecca, of Moses and Miriam allow this catastrophe to befall God's people? Jewish voices stridently argue this question in their communities. There are some who claim that the experience of the holocaust has shown that God does not exist. Others suggest that belief in God be held in suspension, or even that God be held responsible for what happened to the chosen people. Others —a very small minority—view the holocaust as the punishment for the progressive secularization of European Jews. Some say that the holocaust has entirely bracketed the question of God; they simply cannot deal with it. There are even those who say that the holocaust does not affect whatsoever the question of God—the holocaust was of human cause and consequence; it has nothing to do with the existence of God. Responses to these arguments are not presented in this chapter. But for the sensitive believer, Jew or Christian, the holocaust must raise the fundamental question: What kind of God can we believe in after the holocaust?

The second pole of meaning around Jewish survival in a post-holocaust world is the significance of the state of Israel (see also the chapter on Israel). Too quickly some non-Jews may see the establishment of the state as the world's concession to the horror of the Nazi enterprise. History shows that the modern movement for a Jewish homeland had its roots in the European Zionist movement of the late nineteenth century. Theodor Herzl and others understood that the Jewish people could not live in complete freedom even in post-enlightenment Europe, and they sought a refuge where Jews could be Jews without seeking permission from a Christian majority. And so, through the early part of this century, thousands of European Jews joined their Sephardic (Middle Eastern Jews) brothers and sisters in the Ottoman empire of Palestine. Nonetheless, the United Nations 1948 vote to recognize Israel as the Jewish state carried great poignancy in the wake of the liberation of the concentration camps. Many saw the establishment of the state of Israel as the "resurrection" of the Jewish people. For many Jews and others, the establishment of the Jewish homeland not only answered the yearning of centuries to return to the land of Zion, but also the beginning of healing from the holocaust's trauma. However one interprets its meaning, the state of Israel, in the lived experience of the Jewish people—even those from non-European lands—stands as both the clearest symbol that the Jewish people have returned to world history and the repudiation of themselves as a wandering people.

In the larger post-holocaust Jewish experience, one reaction echoes regardless of how one understands God, the Jewish faith, or the meaning of the state of Israel—namely, "never again." The Jewish people, discriminated against for centuries in both Christian and Muslim lands, and victims of pogroms for centuries in eastern Europe, conclude that "never again" will they allow the conspirators of antisemitism to become powerful enough to ignite and cause another conflagration. For Jews in Israel and around the world keep constant watch so that even the hint of another holocaust will not occur.

B. Christian Survival

Was not the holocaust a terrible test—which the Church failed? It may be . . . that the question whether Christianity is to remember the Holocaust

or dismiss it is a question of the ability and the right
of Christianity to survive in any way conformable to
the Scriptures.

—Elwyn Smith[21]

That Christians survived the holocaust is clear; they
were not its primary victims. Indeed, too often they were
among its perpetrators or bystanders. But after the holocaust, how are Christians with integrity to survive as a blessing for the nations and for the nation Israel? In other words,
how is the holocaust relevant to a fully mature, divinely-
willed *surviving Christianity* moving into the twenty-first
century? We suggest that the holocaust's world-shaking dimensions move Christian self-understanding in four critical
directions.

First, the holocaust is not only a part of Jewish history,
but more importantly a part of Christian history. The holocaust is "an orienting event" in their own self-understanding
of what it means to be faithful to God today. From now on, in
the post-Auschwitz age, Christian history must include as a
significant chapter the experience of the holocaust.

Second, Christians are beginning to recognize that, every
bit as much as the holocaust raises theological concerns for
Jews, so does it for them. These concerns include the haunt-
ing, indeed terror-filled question: What kind of God can we
believe in after Auschwitz? From that fundamental question,
others come tumbling after: What can prayer mean when
children are tossed into burning ovens?[22] Can any post-
Auschwitz spirituality be credible that does not take history
seriously? What does the Christian gathering around the table of worship mean when it could be—and was—celebrated
in the midst of Nazi Germany?[23] And since the Jews have
survived, what is the Christian to make of this revelation that
God wants the Jews to survive as Jews? And if the Jews are to
survive as Jews, what implications has this for the age-old
Christian efforts to convert them to Christianity? Here one
can see the surface is only being scratched by the *theological*
relevance of the holocaust for Christian survival.

Third, Christian survival with integrity means to take
with some seriousness the *ethical* implications of the holocaust. That is, what is one to make of the behavior that so few
Christians saved their Jewish brothers and sisters in their

time of need? What is one to say about courage, about stepping out from the crowd to stop the evil onslaught of Nazism?
Somehow Christian survival requires that we carefully look
at the experience of the rescuers so that Christians might
know how to live with more integrity in the future.

Finally, the holocaust raises for the church its very
meaning, the very *definition* of the church in God's plan of
salvation. No longer can Christians simply mouth triumphal
clichés about God's preferential choice of Christians to the
exclusion of the Jews (or of other religious traditions for that
matter). Many Christians are asking, in this post-holocaust
world, "Can we ever be the same, can we ever understand
ourselves in the same way with the same theological, ethical,
and historical constructs? Who are we really, after the holocaust?" With some humility, Christians are concluding that
their survival with integrity requires that a self-definition
reached only in dialogue with their Jewish brothers and sisters can meet the requirements of a post-Auschwitz church.

If the meaning and purpose of Christian survival after the
holocaust raises the relevance of the holocaust in historical,
ethical, theological, and definitional terms for the Christian,
it also leaves the survival of the Christian people with a mandate strikingly similar to that of Jewish survival: that is,
"never again!" As they come to recognize that their own definition must be worked out in dialogue with their Jewish
brothers and sisters, Christians also recognize that their ultimate fate is tied inextricably to the fate of their Jewish
brothers and sisters. That is, post-holocaust Christian survival entails a divine mandate. That is, God has declared,
through the catastrophe, that Jews are to survive *as Jews*. It
falls to the Christians, therefore, to help carry out God's will
by protecting the original people of God, especially where
Jews may be threatened by prejudice, marginalization, and
oppression. Most assuredly, Christians under the commanding voice of "never again!" cannot allow their becoming op-
pressors again, but also in the post-Auschwitz world they
cannot tolerate being bystanders when others may threaten
the existence and well-being of the original people of God.[24]

C. Shared Feelings

The holocaust's aftermath raises serious questions of survival—different but related—for the Jews and Christians; it

also leaves feelings that each community shares, again different yet related. We note only four of these shared feelings and recognize that their roots are deep in the horror of the holocaust, and are often present just below the surface when Jews and Christians gather.

Jews and Christians often experience feelings of guilt. For many Jews, particularly those who survived in the safety of the United States, guilt may hover around the fate of surviving. Questions swirl through their psyche: Why did I survive? Why did my cousins, my uncles, my aunts, die in the hell of Auschwitz? Christian guilt, for those who take the time and can bear the honesty, revolves around the impotence of Christian leaders during the years of the holocaust or the almost total inadequacy of the Christian faithful to stand up to the Nazi threat or the easy but subtle uses to which Christian doctrine was distorted or put in service of the Nazi enterprise. To the often fruitless and paralyzing feelings of guilt, both Christians and Jews begin to recognize a *common responsibility* to transform those feelings to productive common enterprises. Those enterprises include dialogue, social projects, and mutual understanding to eradicate even the slightest hint that such a vile degradation of the human spirit could ever take place again.

Another feeling common to Christians and Jews in the Auschwitz aftermath is what physician Robert Jay Lifton calls "psychic numbing."[25] Any summary of the holocaust can cause sensitive people to say, "I've had enough—I can't deal with the holocaust anymore. I feel numb, I feel assaulted; my psychic circuit breakers can't bear any more." Obviously, these feelings will affect Christians and Jews differently. Christians may react to learning about the holocaust with distaste and a sense that they must "get on with life" (remember the earlier story of theological academicians who felt that it was "unhealthy" to focus on the holocaust). Just as it is scary for a person who suspects cancer and refuses to seek a full diagnosis, ignoring the holocaust for the Christian may be foolhardy and dangerous. So with good reason it may be that Christians feel reluctant to enter the kingdom of death which is the holocaust. Exploring it may call into question all easy claims of Christian superiority and moral rectitude, to say nothing of the threat to their supersessionist doctrines.

On the Jewish side, psychic numbing may be felt among younger Jews who have heard much more than their Christian counterparts about the holocaust. They may feel suffocated, even overwhelmed by its seeming omnipresence. They recoil from talking about the holocaust because they feel that it is counterproductive to hold it up as the main reference point for modern Jewish life and self-understanding. They claim to have heard too much about Jewish victimhood and not enough about Jewish life. They stiffen with hearing one more call to "never again!" Strangely, this shared feeling— from decidedly different origins—might bring Jews and Christians together to talk about how they can let the pain and tragedy of the holocaust enter their lives *for the sake of the future* and, surprisingly, they may become resources for one another.

A third shared feeling, similar to the second, also affects both sensitive Christians and Jews who are confronted by the holocaust. In a world riddled with too many famines, earthquakes, the nuclear cloud, and numerous environmental threats, "compassion fatigue" (the feeling of being assaulted by too many worthy concerns) quickly settles in and prevents a thoroughgoing study of this earth-shaking event in both our histories. We have already noted, however, that what one risks by not learning about the holocaust is not knowing who one is and not having the ability to create a future where other genocides are impossible. Compassion fatigue, then, is burdensome until one considers the alternatives.

Finally, one candidly has to admit that part of the aftermath of the holocaust remains the suspicion-of-the-other experienced by both Christians and Jews. Edward Flannery has noted that "those pages of history Jews have committed to memory are the very ones that have been torn from Christian (and secular) history books."[26] Jews skeptically wonder whether Christians will ever come to terms with their own history of oppression or with the holocaust. Many Christians harbor deep prejudices about Jews, often fed by their culture or even their religious tradition. Further they suspect that something deep and sinister happened during the holocaust years, yet are unwilling or even unable to face it through study and self-examination. They fear that their own Christianity may be implicated in it. So the shadow of suspicion hangs over both, Christians and Jews, darkened by centuries of mistrust and persecution.

V. Conclusion

We began this chapter by asking what would it be like to lose one's memory. We speculated that this would be the same as losing one's very identity. Additionally, we raised the question about the purpose of learning about any particular moment in history. Not for the sake of some idle dissecting of a past occurrence do we examine any event—here, the holocaust—but rather it is for the sake of the future, for the sake of life itself. We have considered Hitler's final solution within a book concerned about a particular contemporary relationship, the relationship between Christians and Jews. The holocaust stands as the critical episode in this century for our respective self-understandings, Christian or Jew. Only at great risk do either of us proceed into the next century without a thoroughgoing understanding of this event, not only as part of Jewish history—which would be reason enough—but as part of Christian history, and therefore Christian self-understanding. Simply put, then, we have examined the holocaust so that our memory might be complete, so that we can know who we are, and so that we Jews and Christians can be in life-giving relation to one another. And if we Christians do *not* confront this event in our history, we risk losing who we are as a people and who we are in relation to our Jewish brothers and sisters, the first, undiminished love of God's election.

NOTES

[1] Pope John Paul II, Address to the Jews of Australia, November 26, 1986; quoted in *John Paul II: On the Holocaust,* selected and introduced by Eugene J. Fisher (Washington, D.C.: National Conference of Catholic Bishops, 1988), pp. 5–6.

[2] Raul Hilberg, *The Destruction of European Jewry, 1933–45* (Chicago: Quadrangle Books, 1961), pp. 3–4.

[3] See, for instance, Philip P. Hallie, *Lest Innocent Blood Be Shed: The Story of the Village of Le Chambon and How*

Goodness Happened There (New York: Harper & Row, 1979); Peter Hellman, *Avenue of the Righteous* (New York: Atheneum, 1980); Philip Friedman, *Their Brother's Keeper* (New York: Holocaust Library, 1978); Alexander Ramati, *The Assisi Underground: Priests Who Rescued Jews* (New York: Stein and Day, 1978).

[4] Robert Jay Lifton, "The Genocidal Mentality," *Tikkun* 5 (1990): 30.

[5] Adolf Hitler, *Mein Kampf,* trans. by Ralph Manheim (Boston: Houghton Mifflin, 1971).

[6] See, for example, Lucy S. Dawidowicz, *The War Against the Jews 1933–1945* (New York: Holt, Rinehart and Winston, 1975), pp. 33–34.

[7] Jules Isaac, *The Teaching of Contempt: Christian Roots of Anti-Semitism.* Edited by Claire Huchet-Bishop; trans. by Helen Weaver (New York: Holt, Rinehart and Winston, 1964).

[8] Quoted by Robert Jay Lifton, "The Genocidal Mentality," 31.

[9] Elie Wiesel, "Presentation of the Report of the President's Commission on the Holocaust to the President of the United States," in *Against Silence: The Voice and Vision of Elie Wiesel.* Selected and edited by Irving Abrahamson (New York: Holocaust Library, 1985), p. 166.

[10] Etty Hillesum, *An Interrupted Life: The Diaries of Etty Hillesum 1941–1943.* Trans. by Arno Pomerans (New York: Pantheon Books, 1983), pp. 152–53.

[11] Quoted in Eugene J. Fisher and Leon Klenicki, "An Interreligious Service: From Death to Hope," in Elie Wiesel and Albert H. Friedlander, *The Six Days of Destruction: Meditations Toward Hope* (Mahwah: Paulist Press, 1988), pp. 93–94.

[12] See the thoughtful summaries in Marc Saperstein, *Moments of Crisis in Jewish-Christian Relations* (Philadelphia: Trinity Press International, 1989), pp. 38–50, and Richard L. Rubenstein and John K. Roth, *Approaches to Auschwitz: The Holocaust and Its Legacy* (Atlanta: John Knox Press, 1987), pp. 199–228.

[13] See Guenter Lewy, *The Catholic Church and Nazi Germany* (New York: McGraw-Hill, 1964), pp. 295–96.

[14] The literature on this is quite controversial. See, in addition to works already cited, John Morley, *Vatican Diplomacy and the Jews During the Holocaust* (New York: KTAV,

1980); Saul Friedlander, *Pius XII and the Third Reich: A Documentation* (New York: Alfred A. Knopf, 1966); Pinchas Lapide, *Three Popes and the Jews* (New York: Hawthorne, 1967).

[15] Some of the research in this area is hampered by the fact that Vatican archival material from this era is still closed to historians. It is a hopeful sign that Catholic and Jewish scholars are now beginning to have access to this material. As Pope John Paul II promised, "A Catholic document on the Shoah [Holocaust] and anti-Semitism will be forthcoming, resulting from serious [joint Catholic-Jewish] studies." Pope John Paul II, "The Miami Address to Jewish Leaders," *Origins* 17 (1987): 243.

[16] Quoted in Nechama Tec, *When Light Pierced the Darkness: Christian Rescue of Jews in Nazi-Occupied Poland* (New York: Oxford University Press, 1986), p. 165.

[17] Ibid.

[18] A series of laws promulgated at the Nazi party meeting in Nuremberg in September 1935, which essentially segregated the Jewish people from the rest of the German people. Among other things, the laws denied citizenship to those who did not have "German blood" and prohibited marriage between Jews and other Germans.

[19] According to Orthodox Judaism, the number of commandments which God gave to the Jewish people numbered 613.

[20] Quoted in Rubenstein and Roth, *Approaches to Auschwitz*, p. 613.

[21] Elwyn Smith, "The Christian Meaning of the Holocaust," *Journal of Ecumenical Studies* 6 (1969): 421–22.

[22] See Michael B. McGarry, "Contemporary Religious Responses to the Holocaust: The Crisis of Prayer," in *Contemporary Religious Responses to the Holocaust*. Edited by Steven L. Jacobs (Detroit: Wayne State University Press, 1992.).

[23] See John T. Pawlikowski, "Worship after the Holocaust: An Ethician's Reflections," *Worship* 58 (1984): 315–29, and Lawrence A. Hoffman, "Response: Holocaust as Holocaust, Holocaust as Symbol," *Worship* 58 (1984): 333–41.

[24] Michael B. McGarry, *Christology After Auschwitz* (New York: Paulist Press, 1977).

[25] Robert Jay Lifton and Richard Falk, *Indefensible*

Weapons: The Political and Psychological Case against Nuclearism (New York: Basic Books, 1982), pp. 105–06.

[26] Edward Flannery, *The Anguish of the Jews: Twenty-Three Centuries of Antisemitism.* Rev. and updated (New York: Paulist Press, 1985), p. 1.

Discussion Questions

1. How is the holocaust a tragedy of Christian history?

2. The people of the holocaust included perpetrators, victims, rescuers, and bystanders. Imagine yourself as any one of or all of these. What would be some of your feelings? How would you feel about the other people of the holocaust? What would be some of the virtues and vices you might have in any of these roles? (E.g., as a rescuer, you might say you need courage; as a perpetrator, you might need to numb yourself to human pain, etc.)

3. Why must the Jewish people survive after the holocaust? Explain. What role does the modern state of Israel play in the survival?

4. How do Christians survive after the holocaust? What are the four critical dimensions suggested by the author?

5. What are the various shared feelings (of both Jews and Christians) that are part of the aftermath of the holocaust? How do you react to the four presented by the author in this chapter?

For Further Study

Cohen, Arthur A., ed. *Arguments and Doctrines: A Reader of Jewish Thinking in the Aftermath of the Holocaust.* New York: Harper and Row, 1970.

Fackenheim, Emil L. *To Mend the World: Foundations of Future Jewish Thought.* New York: Schocken, 1982.

Frank, Anne. *The Diary of a Young Girl.* New York: Doubleday, 1952.

Hilberg, Raul. *The Destruction of the European Jews.* New York: Homes and Meier, 1985.

McGarry, Michael B. *Christology After Auschwitz.* New York: Paulist, 1977.

Rausch, David A. *A Legacy of Hatred: Why Christians Must Not Forget the Holocaust.* Chicago: Moody, 1984.

Rubernstein, Richard A. and John K. Roth. *Approaches to Auschwitz: The Holocaust and Its Legacy.* Atlanta: John Knox Press, 1987.

Tec, Nechama. *When Light Pierced the Darkness: Christian Rescue of Jews in Nazi-Occupied Poland.* New York: Oxford University Press, 1986.

Wiesel, Elie. *Night.* New York: Farrar, Straus, and Giroux, 1960.

Wyman, David S. *The Abandonment of the Jews: America and the Holocaust, 1941–1945.* New York: Pantheon Books, 1984.

IV.

ROBERT ANDREW EVERETT

The Land: Israel and the Middle East in Jewish-Christian Dialogue

I. Introduction

Perhaps on no other issue are Christians quite as perplexed by the Jewish experience as by the centrality of the land tradition in Judaism and the importance of the state of Israel to Jews today. There is simply no parallel in the Christian experience that couples land and people, religion and politics, piety and society to match that of the Jewish experience. Throughout the Jewish tradition, the land of Zion has been an integral part of the Jewish consciousness as reflected in the unbroken covenant between God and the people of Israel. The geopolitical dimension of Jewish theological self-understanding has often been a stumbling block in the modern dialogue between Christians and Jews, yet, we have reached a point in time when it is no longer possible to think seriously about dialogue without putting this issue at center stage.

II. Covenant and Land

One place to start in thinking about this problem is an idea found in the works of W.D. Davies. For Davies, the land tradition lies at the heart of Judaism, yet it is also the idea which creates what he calls the "scandal of particularity" in Judaism. Arthur Hertzberg holds to a similar view. Both men believe that every religious tradition has some doctrine which makes little sense to those outside of the tradition. For both Davies and Hertzberg, the land tradition of Judaism is just

87

such a doctrine, and they both agree that Christianity's doctrine of the incarnation is also just such a doctrine. Davies says: "To accept Judaism on its own terms is to recognize that near to and indeed within the heart of Judaism is 'The Land.' In this sense, just as Christians recognize the scandal of particularity in the Incarnation of Christ, so there is a scandal of territorial particularity in Judaism. The land is so embedded in the heart of Judaism, the *Torah,* that—so its source, worship and theology attest—it is finally inseparable from it."[1]

Neither Davies nor Hertzberg think that this realization alone will make non-Jews more sympathetic, but it makes it necessary for non-Jews to struggle with this doctrine of Judaism if they really seek to have a serious dialogue with Jews. It also raises the important issue of letting the dialogue partner define his or her own tradition. This is a serious question for Christians in the dialogue. Can they understand this aspect of the Jewish tradition? The enlightenment view of Judaism as "merely" a religion devoid of ethnic and territorial dimensions is simply not a Jewish understanding of the Jewish experience. The events of the twentieth century have almost completely destroyed this "liberal" interpretation of Judaism found in such Jewish thinkers as Spinoza, Mendelssohn, and Cohen. The land issue has become central to Jewish identity in ways unexpected one hundred years ago, but it is not the introduction of something foreign to Judaism. Rather, it is the elevation of a central theme in Judaism which has remained remote but not dead.

The modern Zionist movement is the political expression of this land tradition, although there are many different interpretations of what the Zionist movement represents even among Jews. The refusal of the Zionist leaders to accept Uganda as a Jewish state, and their final insistence on the traditional land of Zion as the future homeland for Jews, is indicative of just how powerful this tradition has been in Judaism, even among Jews who may have broken with traditional religious life. Certainly, the modern dialogue between Christians and Jews can only take place if Christians are willing to listen and take seriously this "scandal of particularity" in Judaism. As the Christian scholar Walter Brueggemann writes: "It is clear that since the recent wars of the State of Israel, Christians cannot speak seriously to Jews unless we acknowledge land to be the central agenda. . . . Unless we address the land question with Jews, we shall not likely understand the locus of meaning or the issue of identity. . . . If Christians could be clear that the gospel entrusted to Christians is also about land, perhaps a new conversation could emerge, but it will not as long as we misunderstand our faith in categories either existentialist or spiritual-transcendental."[2] By this, Brueggemann means that the Christian faith has a social/historical dimension to it as well as concern for one's spiritual well-being.

This question of letting Judaism speak for itself in the dialogue and letting Jews define themselves is a key issue for the German theologian Jurgen Moltmann. He sees the land issue being right at the heart of the dialogue. In his view, Jews must have the right to define themselves. If Christians begin the dialogue with Christian definitions of Jews, then Christians are essentially incapable of dialogue. By demanding this prior definition, Christians begin the dialogue with fixed positions, and the dialogue then becomes a process by which our prior definitions are confirmed. Any attempt to keep the dialogue centered around purely "religious" themes will fail and should fail. Moltmann argues that the modern dialogue must deal with both the holocaust and the state of Israel. He sees the founding of the state of Israel as putting the relationship between Judaism and Christianity on a new level. Christians are no longer confronting Jews who live only in the diaspora (Jews living outside of Israel), but rather they must now deal with Israelis as well. He is well aware that debates rage in the Jewish community as to what all this means for Jews, but Moltmann argues that these debates alone should give Christians pause before they pass judgment on its ultimate meaning for Jews. Nonetheless, he writes that "for the first time in the long history of the Jews, Christians today encounter Jews who are both Jews and Israelis. Therefore, the dialogue from the Jewish side can no longer be purely religious: it must also be political, if it is to be carried on honestly."[3]

Objection could be raised here that the traditional Christian view that the covenant of Israel with God has been superseded (replaced) by Christianity precludes Moltmann's position. But over the last twenty-five years there have been a number of statements by both Protestant and Roman Catholic traditions that reaffirm the Jewish covenant with God and proclaim it unbroken. It is true that some of these documents do not say anything specifically about the land, although many do. But if the Christian community is serious about rethinking its relationship to Judaism, and serious in reaffirming the covenant of Israel with God, it must also face the reality of how the land tradition functions within the Jewish understanding of the covenant. For Paul van Buren, two new facts that the Christian community must deal with are the establishment of Israel and the acknowledgement by the church, starting with the Second Vatican Council, that the covenant between God and the Jewish people is eternal and that Jews today are the living heirs of that covenant. "These two facts create a new situation for the church, for never in its history has it been confronted with Jewish sovereignty in its own land, and not since some time in the late first century has it acknowledged the Jewish people to be Israel in its enduring covenant with God."[4]

It must be clear that affirmation of Israel's covenant with God means being ready and willing to accept the land tradition as a part of that divine promise to Israel from God. Covenant and land go together. The Jewish biblical scholar Harry Orlinsky writes: "The cornerstone, the essence of the exclusive contract into which God and each of Israel's progenitors voluntarily entered, is the Land (*Ha-Erets*). Were it not for Land that God promised an oath to Abraham and to Isaac and to Jacob and to their heirs forever, there would be no covenant. For be it noted that everything in the contract, all the blessings—economic, territorial, political, increase in population, and the like—all these would be forthcoming from God to Israel not in Abraham's native land of Mesopotamia . . . but in the promised land."[5] Orlinsky faults those who would try to malign Jewish nationalism as related to the land while still trying to affirm monotheism. He finds this especially true in the way the prophetic literature has been interpreted by Christian commentators. He writes in response to Bernhard Anderson's attempt to play off the land promise against the nationalism of ancient Israel:

> The overall pejorative use of the term "colored," "proud," and "boast about" in connection with Israel's nationalism hardly derives from the Biblical

view of the covenant between God and Israel; if that contractual relationship doesn't make a most natural and legitimate nationalism, then the monotheism that the covenant constitutes and from which Israel's nationalism derives isn't legitimate either. But nowhere would anyone apply such terms as "colored," "proud," and "boast about" pejoratively to monotheism. The reason is clear enough: whereas the monotheism of the Hebrew Bible—the heart of the New Testament and Christianity and Islam—is perfectly acceptable, the Israelite nationalism of the Bible and its consequences so far as the Land is concerned are not. Furthermore, in accordance with the covenant between God and each of the patriarchs and with the people Israel, which both parties to the contract vowed to fulfill, God gave Israel the Land of Canaan.[6]

For Orlinsky, this is not to be seen as merely a gift, but as an essential sign of the agreement between the people and God.

The centrality of the covenant and land remains true in the prophets, even when they are passing harsh judgment on the people. The very significance of the land is revealed in the punishment of the people for their sins of having their land humiliated and devastated by aliens who defile God's holy land. Yet, in all the prophets, the land theme is as closely tied to restoration themes of hope and deliverance as it is to prophetic critique. The prophets all believed that the outcome of God's judgment would be the return of the Jews to the land. Orlinsky cites Ezekiel as an example. "In accordance with the views of his predecessors, Ezekiel understood the covenant as endless, so that God and Israel would in time resume their contractual relationship in the land of Israel."[7] The most famous example of this is in Ezekiel's vision of the valley of the dry bones (Ez 37:1–14).

The importance of the doctrine of the land is evident throughout the *Tanak* (Hebrew Bible). According to Davies, two elements in the doctrine of the land are central. (1) The land is regarded as promised, or, more accurately, as sworn by Yahweh (God) to the people of Israel. Boundary questions about the actual size of the land vary, but not the promise. (2) There prevailed the conviction that this promised land belonged especially to Yahweh. It is a particular possession among all the lands that God could give to his people. For Davies what is important is: "Out of the combination (nay—fusion) of the three elements which were involved in the promise—God, the people and the land—there emerged what has been regarded as an essential belief of religious Jews of the first century and later, that is, of the indissolubility or eternity of the connection between these realities."[8]

This belief was strong enough that the rabbis continued to center their ideas around the land tradition even though the "sages," the authors and preservers of those sources, had increasingly suspected any disturbing concentration in hopes for the return to the land in messianic context as a delusion, a snare likely to distract their people from the essential task of living in obedience to the Torah. While counseling cooperation with foreign rulers, paradoxically, the rabbis continued to shower their praises on the land, emphatically expressing their concern for it and recognizing the ultimate indissolubility of Israel's connection with it.[9]

The destruction of the land by the Romans in the wars of 66–70 and 133–135 C.E. (common era—the era that Jews and Christians share) could have easily destroyed the land tradition, yet this tradition continued to play a key role in Jewish self-understanding. As Davies states, "There is a kind of umbilical cord between Israel and the Land."[10] Gershon Cohen writes, "By the time Palestine ceased to be the central Jewish community, its centrality had been so impressed upon the Jewish mind that it could not be uprooted."[11] Thus even when Jews were exiled from the land, or, more correctly, even in periods when they lacked sovereignty over the land, the land tradition still played a key role in Jewish self-understanding.

III. Christian Views of the Land Tradition

For Christians, this land tradition has indeed proved to be a puzzle, but a growing number of Christian thinkers seem to believe that this is a part of the Jewish tradition that Christians could benefit from in their own theology. The thinking on this issue is still in its early stages, but it deserves a fair hearing among the churches. Certainly, if dialogue between

Christians and Jews is to mean anything, this issue must be clearly addressed by all of the participants.

Walter Brueggemann has written extensively on this issue in his book *The Land.* His main argument is that Christians need to look more carefully at this aspect of Jewish thinking because the Christian tradition is lacking a clear theology of place. This constantly puts the church in the dangerous position of spiritualizing its teachings. This is a theme that motivates a number of Christian thinkers to deal with this issue. The Roman Catholic scholar Gerald Sloyan argues that this spiritualizing of the tradition is unwarranted by the scriptures, and he argues that while the Gentiles of the early church didn't appreciate this land tradition, that is no reason why the church today cannot work to create a new understanding of the land tradition for itself.[12]

W.D. Davies has written most extensively on this topic.[13] He has traced the centrality of the land to Jews throughout their tradition, and urges Christians to take this aspect of Judaism seriously. He is also clear that there is an ambivalence in Christian thought about the land. Christianity has tended to transcend place, or, to use Davies' term, "christified" places. Nonetheless, like Brueggemann, Davies thinks that Christians would benefit from developing a clearer understanding of place and its importance to theology.

The ambivalence theme is also taken up by John Townsend. He sees the reasons for this to be threefold. (1) The New Testament was addressed primarily to Gentiles, not the people of Israel. (2) The historical place of Jews in the land during the writing of the New Testament was not challenged until the year 135 C.E. (3) It was not in the New Testament writers' interest to discuss themes that could have invited Roman persecution.[14] This silence is not to be read as meaning that the land issue was not important. Townsend points out that Jesus had certain nationalistic overtones in some of his teachings, and that the nationalistic views of the different books of the New Testament vary.

Walter Harrelson finds that the land tradition plays a useful role in Christian theology in reminding the church of its role on earth. The land is not of secondary importance to Harrelson, and he lists five points which illustrate what the attachment to a particular land does for the Christian community:

1. It underscores the need to see all the treasures of earth as gifts of God, gifts that bring with them the same urgent demand that we see in Israel.

2. It makes it harder for Christians to generalize about how one is to live on the land, seeking its justice, struggling for blessing, seeing to the needs of all on the concrete land where we live.

3. It helps to introduce something of the archetypal beauty of life, of the places where revelation occurs, of the central import of the representations of Zion on earth, and thus of the earthly Zion in Israel.

4. It shows us how eschatology provides a spur and an impetus to labor in the direction of God's coming consummation. Remove this understanding of the land and of Zion, and biblical ethics loses one of its most insistent impulses. We must be marching to Zion, not the heavenly one, but the one being fashioned on earth by the power of the transcendent and mysterious God of Israel and of nations.

5. It helps us to construct a picture of the modern State of Israel which stresses the central import of the land of Israel over which Jews can exercise some control, as an element in the heritage of land promised to Israel. As we do so we can rightly stress the obligation entailed by that gift of God, an obligation that does not, however, become heroic and unrealistic, for it is an obligation to a merciful and loving deity to whom all peoples and individuals turn for mercy and forgiveness. The land of Israel partakes of consummation. So also does the Christian community that recognizes that this is the case and associates itself with people and with the land.[15]

For Paul van Buren, the land tradition can be of enormous help to Christians in struggling with the problems of life on earth. Van Buren believes that the land tradition forces Christians to think about historical realities as well as spiritual hopes. The establishment of the state of Israel has brought home to Christians the covenental promise of land. It does not absolutize the state, but it does illustrate the connection between divine promise and human existence. The existence of Israel drives home the point of power and politics as being aspects of human existence that the church cannot ignore any longer. For van Buren, the state of Israel raises a variety of questions for Christians, particularly concerning the proper understanding of the political order, the theological and political significance of power, and the theological and political meaning of the covenant between God and Israel.[16] He believes that the presence of the state of Israel requires the church to reform the ways in which it understands Jewish scripture and to confront the continuing problem of the church's attempt to sever its Jewish roots. The reality of the state of Israel demands that the covenant be rethought now that Jews have returned to the land and established themselves by political and military means. He sees this as a challenge to Christian theology's emphasis on faith by "grace alone."[17] For van Buren, the state of Israel presents Christian theology with a remarkable challenge.

This review of Christian views of the land tradition in Judaism needs to be read in light of the historical facts of Christian antisemitism. While many Christian authors are uncomfortable with the linking of Israel with antisemitism, one needs to be aware of the role the land played in the church's anti-Judaic tradition.[18] One of the major themes of the "teaching of contempt"[19] taught that the Jews were exiled from their land as punishment for their role in the death of Jesus. According to the Christian interpretation of the events, the destruction of the second temple in 70 C.E., and the banishment of the Jews from the land of Israel, are understood as a sign of that curse. The question of the Jewish loss of rule over the land was quite important in the early church. One of the reasons Emperor Julian was so hated by the church stemmed from his desire to rebuild the Jewish temple in Jerusalem. This was an act which would have effectively countered the church's teachings.

A classic example of this polemic is found in Augustine's "Reply to Faustus the Manichean." He wrote that "the unbelieving people of the Jews is cursed from the earth, that is, from the Church, which in the confession of sins has opened its mouth to receive the blood shed for the remission of sins by the hand of the people that would not be under grace, but under the law. And this murderer is cursed by the Church."[20] Augustine adds, "Here, no one can fail to see that in every land where the Jews are scattered, they mourn for the loss of their kingdom, and are in terrified subjection to the immensely superior number of Christians."[21]

Augustine also taught that the role of the Jews in the world was to be a negative witness to Christianity. While warning against Christian violence against Jews, he did teach that Jews were to live in a state of condemnation and misery. They were to be powerless and a living witness to the wrath of God. This "theology of victimization" necessarily precludes any situation in which Jews live in autonomous dignity and control their own destiny. This theological tradition argued that Jewish existence was one of exile: exile from God, the messiah, and the land. The legend of the wandering Jew personified the belief that Jews were both historically and spiritually in exile. The Jews were seen as victims of a divine curse, and the most obvious proof of that curse was their loss of the land.[22]

In the theology of victimization, it was out of the question that Jews could ever again regain their sovereignty over the land of Israel. Historically, it is not true that all Jews were banished from the land. Jews have always lived in the land since the time of Jesus. But the idea of exile had a firm hold on the Christian mind. From a theological viewpoint, it appeared impossible for Jews to ever regain sovereignty of the land because sovereignty implies power. When Pope Pius X told Theodor Herzl that the church could not accept the repossessing of the holy land by the Jews as long as they refused Christ, he was merely reiterating the traditional Christian theology of victimization. For Jews, there could be no power, no sovereignty, no redemption. They could only be victims.

The tenacity of this teaching is illustrated by a statement from Dietrich Bonhoeffer, who on most other issues is really quite free of anti-Jewish bias and was himself a defender of Jews in Nazi Germany, which cost him his life. Yet, he was able to write in 1934, "the Church of Christ has never lost sight of the thought that the 'chosen people' who nailed the redeemer of the world to the cross must bear the curse of its actions through the long history of suffering."[23] The point here is not to condemn Bonhoeffer, but to illustrate how even as sensitive a thinker as Bonhoeffer could repeat this theme without questioning it. But, as David Hartman writes, "The rebirth of the State of Israel has shattered the Christian theological claim of God's rejection of the Jewish people as witnessed by their endless suffering and wandering."[24]

One Christian theologian who has attempted to deal with this issue is A. Roy Eckardt. Eckardt believes that while the theology of victimization continues to be alive in the church, there is a growing movement, which he calls "Christian reformism," that seeks to reinterpret Christianity in such a way that Zionism and the state of Israel are endorsed and supported, both politically and theologically. He is explicit in rejecting what he terms "territorial fundamentalism," the assumption that the Jewish people possess the land absolutely because of a divine fiat, believing that "no human right can ever be so construed as absolute."[25] But he clearly supports the idea that "Israel" is a special event within the spiritual life of the Jewish people *and the Jewish people alone. . . .* On this position, the return of Jews to the Land can perhaps be read as an instance of the laughter of God (Psalm 2:4–6) at those who fabricated the horror tale of Jewish wandering because of the rejection of Christ."[26] Eckardt is aware, however, that breaking the traditional Christian view will prove difficult.[27] The work of Eckardt and the other Christians reviewed thus far shows that this tradition is under attack, but the sway of this tradition over Christian thought continues to be a problem in the dialogue.

W.D. Davies points out that while "much of the theology and history of Judaism in its main expressions points to the Land as of its essence, the history of Judaism, however, seems also to offer serious qualifications of this."[28] This contradiction that Davies points to has enormous consequences for Jewish thought faced with the new reality of political sovereignty and power brought about by the Zionist movement and the establishment of the state of Israel. The contradiction revolves around the centrality of the land in Jewish tradition and the historical fact that most Jews did not and do not today live in the land. The tension that arises from this contradiction is best seen in the exile and return theme in Judaism.

Historically, exile from the land has been as much, if not

more, of an influence on Jewish life and thought than life in the land. While a small *yishuv* (the Jewish settlement in the pre-state land of Israel) of Jews lived in the land, most Jews lived outside. As Davies makes clear, Jews lived in exile, not dispersion. While many Jews choose to live outside of the land, most Jews had no choice. They lived in an "enforced exile." That Jews outside Palestine conceived of their existence not simply as a dispersion but co-exile meant that, wherever they were, they were still bound symbolically, theologically as well as historically, to their home base, to *Eretz Israel* (Land). They were not simply scattered. The Diaspora maintained the notion of its existence as a *galuth*, exile."[29]

For James Parkes, this idea reflects the tension between universalism and particuliarism in Jewish history. Like Davies, Parkes saw this tension religiously developed in the exile and return theme. The land plays an important role in providing the framework within which one important key to Jewish history and survival is to be found. Parkes argues that the exilic experience has always been understood and made bearable by reference to the land of Zion and the hoped for restoration. Parkes believed that the diaspora community and the Jewish community of Israel were intimately connected.[30] Israel, on the other hand, keeps the diaspora community aware of its Jewish identity, and prevents it from total assimilation into the non-Jewish world. The constant interchange of ideas between Israel and the diaspora is, for Parkes, a key to understanding Jewish history.

IV. Jewish Views of the Land Tradition

The historical realities of the exile had profound ramifications for Jewry after the year 70 C.E. The rabbis were not shy about attributing the exile to the sins of the people, but they always framed this idea within the messianic hoped-for restoration, and they incorporated this belief in the Jewish liturgy itself.[31]

Fackenheim characterizes what he calls *Galut Judaism* by the following beliefs.

1. Exile though painful is bearable because it is meaningful.

2. Its meaning is not altogether negative, for though punishment for Jewish sins, a God who punished is, at any rate, not a God that has abandoned or rejected. On the contrary, the punishment is "suffering of love" intended to induce *teshuvah* (conversion).

3. Punishment for Jewish sins, exile is at times viewed also as vicarious atonement for the sins of others.

4. Climatically, exile will not last forever. Whether or not either the suffering or the *teshuvah* is capable of hastening the messianic end, some future Jewish generation will live to see the ultimate Redemption of Israel and all mankind.[32]

David Hartman also discusses this traditional idea as it relates to contemporary events in Jewish history. He writes:

For many centuries before Zionism, Judaic religious consciousness had been characterized by the sense that the every day world was a preparation for a future messianic reality. It was felt that the temporal world does not reflect the full power of God as Creator and Lord of History, nor can it contain the reward promised to the community for allegiance to the covenant. . . . For traditional religious Jews, the instruments for effecting history were prayer, observance of the *mitzvot,* and *Torah* study. The covenental community was not to sully its hands with the uncertainties and political and moral ambiguities of modern nationalism. . . . The Jewish covenental community could leave responsibility for a total social and political order to the nations of the world, while it lived in anticipation of the ultimate triumph of Judaism in the messianic reality.[33]

Hartman believes that this "conservative" instinct was a direct result of the problems Jews had encountered when their political and messianic dreams were put to the test of history. "The central significance attached to the land of Israel, Jerusalem, and the ingathering of the exiles was expressed with passion daily in the life of prayer, but was to be realized only in a messianic kingdom. History had taught the Jews not to attempt to translate those prayers into a program of action."[34] This "conservative" sway still informs certain ultra-orthodox Jews who maintain an vehement anti-Zionist stance on the ground that humans, not the messiah, established the state of Israel. Both Fackenheim and Hartman acknowledge, but reject, this view. As Fackenheim writes, "Events have shattered a venerable tradition, and there are those among the pious who cannot or dare not confront that fact."[35]

If the land tradition in traditional religious Jewish thought was put into a messianic context, then that same tradition came to be marginalized by modern Jewish thinkers.[36] Arnold Eisen argues that the land in modern Jewish thought, which is influenced more by enlightenment themes than traditional religious themes, remained a marginal concern. The religious and political views of the land were colored by the ideas of Spinoza and Moses Mendelssohn. Eisen argues that modern Jewish thought has done three things to the tradition: demystify, resymbolize, and politicize the idea of *Eretz Israel*. He writes:

> The Land . . . has been stripped of the many-layered dress of imagery and significance which had draped it through generations of Jewish thought (demystification). The particular soil prepared for God's chosen people, the unique dwelling place of His glory, has become the universal symbol of human brotherhood and peace, located wherever those dreams of all mankind attain fulfillment (resymbolization). Finally, the Jewish polity has become a nation among the nations, its territory one among many others, to be secured through the real world instruments of political action (politicization).[37]

The changing role of Jews in western society after the emancipation created a "liberal" view that saw assimilation into the diaspora less dangerous than in the time prior to the emancipation. In discussing Moses Mendelssohn's *On Religious Power and Judaism*, which argues a case for the acceptance of Judaism in the modern order, Eisen comments on why the land appears marginal: "The reason is obvious: while the Jewish role in the emerging European order was a matter of immediate concern, the possibility of return to the Land of Israel could safely be left in the realm of fantasy."[38] So while the traditional religionists keep the land central, but ahistorical, the modern liberal idea is to marginalize the land and urge Jews back into history through a much reinterpreted tradition. In commenting on two modern thinkers, Fackenheim writes that "about a decade after the Kishinev pogrom (a term used to refer to physical attacks on Jewish communities, particularly in Russia and Poland) Hermann Cohen in Germany and Kaufman Kohler in America, Jewish thinkers of substance both, had taught that Judaism had been 'denationalized', and that this was a blessing since it made Jews freer to pursue their universal Messianic mission."[39]

If, on the one hand, Cohen rejected the movement back to the land on universalist grounds rooted in a view of Judaism as an "ethical monotheism" devoid of nationalistic pretense, then, on the other hand, Franz Rosenzweig would question Zionism on the grounds that it made Jews too much like others. He argues from a view of Jewish particularism. Sounding very much like a traditional orthodox thinker, Rosenzweig has a very ahistorical understanding of Judaism that assigns the land to a future messianic time. David Novak has recently raised questions about how either Cohen or Rosenzweig could be used by Jews or those seeking to understand Jewish reality today. His interpretation is worth quoting at length:

> As Rosenzweig's own Jewish identity developed, his attitude toward Zionism changed from outright rejection to ambivalence. Nevertheless, for our concern here, Rosenzweig's rejection of Zionism is a necessary corollary of his basic distinction between Jewish self-sufficiency and Christian worldliness. For this reason his anti-Zionism is almost the opposite of that of his teacher Hermann Cohen, and most of the other adherents of Liberal Judaism at that time. They rejected Zionism as contrary to Judaism's true universalism, whereas Rosenzweig—and here he was remarkably close to many of the Orthodox—re-

jected it as contrary to Jewish particularism. That is, it was a Jewish attempt to assimilate collectively rather than individually, to be a nation like all the other nations of the world . . . Rosenzweig was correct that Zionism—in both its secular and even its religious forms—can present itself as a pseudo-Messianism. It can indeed attempt to be seen as a final redemption or its immediate and inevitable potential. One can have strong theological objections to such pretense without, however, being at all opposed to the State of Israel. Nevertheless, Zionism can also be seen, as it was by Rosenzweig's later colleague Martin Buber, as a unique opportunity for the Jewish people to nurture and develop its own singular life and destiny. . . . Furthermore, to simply leave the worldliness of politics to the Christians or to any other group of non-Jews, for that matter, is an invitation to be dominated and thus, a threat to the very physical survival of the Jews themselves. The near destruction of all European Jewry in the middle of this century readily testifies to just that.[40]

V. Modern Zionism

The modern Zionist movement arose out of tension between the traditionalist view of the land and the modern view. No clear boundary can be made. The noted historian Ben Halpern defines Zionism as:

> . . . a nationalist movement differing from others because it reflects the history of a people uniquely identified with a world religion. Its purpose was to restore the dispersed, stateless Jews to sovereign independence in the Land from which tradition taught they had been exiled by God's will as a punishment for their sins. Hence, Zionism was challenged to define itself either as rebellion against the divine decree of exile, or a fulfillment of the divine promise of redemption.[41]

For James Parkes, there are five roots from which Zionism and the state of Israel spring, and they too are a mixture of the traditional and the modern. Parkes, who is a sensitive Christian interpreter of Judaism, has summed up quite nicely the different strains of Jewish thought and experience that helped to develop the modern Zionist movement. He writes:

> The tree of Israel springs from five roots deeply embedded in the experience of the Jewish people. The first and deepest is Judaism as a religion of a community. The second is the messianic hope, intimately connected ever since the destruction of the Jewish state with the expectations of a return to the Promised Land. The third is Jewish history, and the long experience of dispersion and insecurity. The fourth is the continuity of Jewish life in Palestine. The fifth is the unique relationship between the Jewry of Palestine and the whole Jewish people.[42]

Manfred Vogel also identifies five themes regarding Judaism's relationship to the land and their connection to Zionism. They are:

1. A philosophical-religious trend which deals with the covenant and land theme in theological or philosophical categories rather than political or ideological ones.

2. The Zionist ideology which clearly expressed connection between peoplehood and land in cultural and political categories.

3. The cultural autonomist position which emphasized diaspora life over against settlement in Israel.

4. The socialist approach in which the goals of living in the land were framed in the context of socialism.

5. The mystical trend as exemplified by Rav Kook which spoke of the ties to the Land in mystical categories.[43]

Vogel argues that while the category of land is secondary

and derived, "it should be clear that as far as the redemptive vocation, i.e., the specific task of realizing redemption, is conceived, the category of land is no less essential than the category of peoplehood."[44] In Vogel's view, diaspora Judaism was a "truncated form of existence."[45] And while the Zionist impulse drew upon various aspects of Jewish life and thought, the land theme became more and more central in modern Jewish formulations of self-identity, even within a diversity of ideas about what that identity should be.

This mixture of religious and secular themes can often baffle non-Jews when they seek to understand Zionism, and it has provoked serious debate among Jews. Looking for the rationale behind Zionism, one finds that the nineteenth century provided the necessary framework in which the political expression for the Zionist impulse in Judaism could be expressed, but it is a superficial reading of Zionism to see it only as a western version of Jewish nationalism. That Zionism became politically active in the nineteenth century is more an accident of timing than a necessity. The Zionist movement, while in many ways a rebellion against traditional Judaism, still exhibited impulses long in existence within Judaism, and it was the historical situation of Jews that contributed to its appearance at a particular time.

David Hartman sees Zionism to be a movement which sought in many ways to overthrow traditional Judaism and its attitudes on the politics and history of secular Zionism by replacing ". . . the covenental identity of the Jew with a secular political national identity."[46] Hartman, a religious Jew, seeks to affirm Zionism on the grounds that it offers new possibilities for Jews to live according to Torah. With all the risks that Israel poses to the future of convenental Judaism, he writes, "I am nonetheless prepared to build my hopes for Judaism's future on this new reality. For as the tradition teaches, where there is a potential for desecration, there is also a potential for sanctification."[47]

For Hartman the rebirth of Israel has reawakened "new biblical religious passions" in the Jewish world. Things once hoped for only in the future are now a reality—a Jewish state, a rebuilt Jerusalem, Jewish sovereignty.[48] Hartman sees a new agenda for the Jewish community brought on by the rebirth of Israel. History conspired to keep Jews from having to deal with the questions that arise from a relationship between *halakhah* and political power. Up to the emancipation, Jews were essentially a powerless community; after the emancipation they could participate (somewhat limitedly) in the political process, but not as Jews *qua* Jews. The early Zionists saw the problem for Jews living in such a state of ambiguity, and they sought a way for Jews to be "politically normal." With the rebirth of Israel, particularly given its close proximity to the events of the holocaust when Jewish powerlessness proved so catastrophic, the Jewish political situation has changed dramatically. As Hartman says, "In Israel, religious and non-religious Jews have a new sense of power and belonging that they have rarely felt throughout their long sojourn in the diaspora."[49] But this reentry into history and the political arena brings with it new and difficult problems.

Hartman clearly sees that new reality as a mixed blessing. It can bring out the best of the Jewish tradition, but it can also expose some of the "moral and spiritual inadequacies in that tradition." Hartman fully appreciates the need for power, but he is also aware of the problems which come with power. He writes:

> Moral attitudes that one never expected to characterize Jewish behavior can surface in this uninhibited, passionate, and complex Jewish reality. Triumphalist nationalism, lack of tolerance for other faith communities, indifference, and often an open disregard for the liberal values of freedom of the individual, human dignity, and freedom of conscience can be found articulated by would-be religious leaders in Israeli society. A mature appreciation of our liberation struggle requires that we recognize the mixed blessings that freedom and power bring to Jewish living.[50]

In Hartman's view, Zionism's "quest for normalcy should free the Jewish people of any myth about the unique moral and spiritual powers of the Jewish soul."[51] The traditional view was that the Torah challenged Jews to be a holy people, but in Hartman's words, "it does not tell us that we are immune from the moral weakness and failures that affect every human being."[52] Power now forces Jews to an honest appraisal of themselves and their tradition free of the defensive, apologetic stance of a persecuted and vulnerable society. So while political power and sovereignty are not to be dismissed, Israel now forces Jews to think about how they are to live according to *halakhah* within the morally ambiguous world of power and might.

VI. Power and Powerlessness

The debate about power and powerlessness is a crucial one for the Jewish community. The holocaust and Israel are the two major events in modern Jewish history. While the holocaust is in no way causal in the establishment of Israel as a state, the validity of which is support by international law, the two events do spawn a discussion on the necessity of power and security. John Pawlikowski asks the appropriate question when he writes: "Would the Holocaust generate an *ethic of survival* or an *ethic of solidarity*?"[53] Pawlikowski points to two Jewish thinkers who have argued for each position: Irving Greenberg stresses an ethic of survival, while Marc Ellis argues for an ethic of solidarity.

Greenberg argues that the ethics of powerlessness determined Jewish life for nearly two thousand years, but that tradition came to an end in the holocaust. Powerlessness was a temptation for antisemites to kill Jews. Jewish power is now a moral necessity for Jewish survival. Jewish power could only be accomplished by creating a nation for Jews. Greenberg's ethic of survival is not a plea for absolutizing a state, but he does raise in dramatic fashion the new realities forced upon Jews in the modern world. He sees the events of recent history as shattering old ways of thinking. The idea of divine intervention in human history on behalf of those in danger is destroyed by the *shoah* (holocaust). Human beings must take charge of their lives and become responsible for their own survival. And this new condition can only be accomplished through the judicious use of power accompanied by the development of self-correcting mechanisms for preventing unwarranted application of this power.[54] If there is a problem with Greenberg's position, it is that one could too quickly move to a justification of force. The importance of survival can not simply override ethical concerns about the use of force, but the concern for survival is a legitimate one which cannot be easily dismissed or rejected just because force may be needed.

Marc Ellis, however, argues that after the holocaust Jews should be especially sensitive to the plight of the suffering of others and to issues of justice and peace. An *ethic of solidarity* with victims of oppression should be the central issue for Jews, and a determinative factor in how Israel deals with political problems. Ellis is concerned that the empowerment of the Jewish people brings with it the danger of substituting power for morality. He seems to believe that Jewish survival after the shoah can be ensured only by an ethic of solidarity. The problem that Ellis seems to ignore is that there can be no such ethic if Jews do not survive, and Jewish survival continues to be threatened by hostile Arab neighbors who seem reluctant to forgo their vision of Israel destroyed. While Ellis does not advocate a total pacifist position, he does seem to have a difficult time in stating on what grounds Jewish power could be justified since power employed on behalf of survival cannot easily find room for an ethic of solidarity. Yet the ethic of survival devoid of moral boundaries and untempered by concern for those with less power can easily deteriorate into sheer brutality.

The situation in the Middle East today calls for both of these ethical positions to be weighed in making decisions. The split in Israeli politics seems to mirror just this fact. The country seems divided almost down the middle on how to deal with the conflict with the Palestinians. What needs to be remembered is that this conflict must be viewed within the context of the broader Arab-Israeli conflict. Settling the issue with the Palestinians would not settle the wider conflict. Unless one looks at the broader issues involved in the Arab-Israeli conflict, it would be easy to assume that once a solution to the Palestinian question is reached the way to peace would be clear. The fundamental issue remains, however, Arab refusal to recognize the right of Israel to exist. The creation of a Palestinian state does nothing to solve this refusal. While it is nonetheless true that peace cannot be achieved without a solution to the Palestinian problem, it hardly provides the basis for a total peace. Israel would still be faced with the implacable hatred of most of the Arab states. Hence, security and solidarity issues are not easily separated. The great leap from a state of powerlessness to power has created largely unimagined situations for the Jewish nation today. As David Hartman says, "We never dreamed of a Jewish nation that would dehumanize and exploit an entire people. This is not what we prayed for or waited for during the past 2,000 years. . . . To control the Palestinians permanently will justifiably undermine the centrality of Israel for world Jewry. Palestinians will permanently make us feel as strangers and aliens in our own house as long as we are unresponsive to their urgent need for political freedom."[55] But Israel's decisions must not only be based on an ethic of solidarity with the oppressed, but also on the legitimate need to protect the survival of the Jewish state and its inhabitants. The return to history and power by a people for so long victimized is fraught with moral ambiguities and ethical quandaries that Jews have not had to struggle with for centuries.

The conflict between Arabs and Jews in the Middle East does not lend itself to an easy solution. Conor Cruise O'Brien warns that not all political problems can be solved by reason and compromise. Sometimes it takes history itself to wear down the conflict.[56] Both Jews and Arabs see their version of history in the Middle East to be the right one. This chapter cannot deal with the history of that problem. There are many histories already written, but some ideas need to be kept in mind.

When the Jews accepted partition of Palestine in 1948, they accepted on principle a Palestinian state. The immediate Arab attack on the new state of Israel prevented such a state from coming into reality. Arab refusal to recognize Israel's right to exist as a neighbor has been a constant view held by all Arab states, with the recent exception of Egypt. The various wars between 1948 and today have hardened positions. The use of terrorism by groups like the P.L.O. (Palestinian Liberation Organization) and other extremists have made rational discussion difficult. In many ways, the issue is a classic example of a clash between two rights. Both sides thought the British were promising them something quite different from what they got in 1948.

Trying to sort out these complicated and emotional issues is a task daunting to say the least. The issue has not been made any easier by the interference of so many outside powers. Yet it is not impossible to be supportive of Israel's absolute right to exist on political, moral, and legal grounds (always remembering the religious roots of the Jewish attachment to the land), while also being moved by the plight of the Arab people effected by the making of the Jewish state. On this issue, Arthur Hertzberg offers a very useful summary of the problem in his book *Being Jewish in America*.[57]

As Jews and Christians begin to talk honestly with one another, questions about the land and the return to power of Jews in their own land will have to be given top priority in the dialogue. John Pawlikowski sees a number of issues stemming from this theme which will benefit the dialogue. They include the following:

A. Christians must deal with their long-standing theological doctrine of Jews being destined to be wandering people. As we have noted, this doctrine is under attack, but it still can color Christian views about Jews and Israel.

B. Israel can provide for Christians an improved understanding of Judaism's sense of salvation in a communal and historical context which merges nicely with modern Christian attempts to move away from an exclusively otherworldly individualistic conception of redemption.

C. The Jewish experience of the Holocaust and the Jewish affirmation of life and hope after Auschwitz symbolized by a living and vibrant Jewish state can help the Church as it struggles to deal with oppression and injustice. In this regard, the struggles of the Jewish state to deal with both its use of power to survive within a framework of morality and justice provides a living model for the Church.

D. Serious discussion needs to take place about the Christian idea of its universality and the question of political sovereignty. As Christianity loses its dominant place in many cultures, how will it deal

with its new "minority" status? Pawlikowski
wants to ask whether Christian "universality" is
all that different from Jewish "particularlism."

E. The ways in which the Jewish mystical tradition
has dealt with the Land tradition can help Christians to once again be put back in touch with a
sense of the sacramentality of the earth, and the
possibilities of living a holy life within history.

F. The Christian in dialogue can press the Jew on
the relation of sovereignty and power to the Land
tradition. Can Zionism have a universalist
thrust? What is the place of minorities in the Jewish state?

G. Finally, what is the relationship between antisemitism and anti-Zionism? Not all criticism of
Israel is antisemitic. Israel is a country that
thrives on criticism of the government. But it is
possible to make some rules. Pawlikowski sets
forth this rule of thumb: "If the critic of Israeli
policy makes it clear that he/she is still committed to the survival of the state, whatever its short-
coming, then whether that criticism is valid or
not, the person cannot be termed antisemitic. But
if, as is true in many cases, a criticism of Israeli
policy leaves the distinct impression that Israel
has forfeited its right to exist because of some policy failure, then the criticism might with good
justification be placed in the antisemitic
category."[58]

VII. Conclusion

It is clear that any dialogue that ignores the issue of the
land or the state of Israel will be a truncated dialogue. A central theme in Judaism will be neglected. Given that this issue
causes much unease among Christians, its neglect would
mean that Christians were not confronting their own traditional views about Jews and Jewish existence in an honest
fashion. The dialogue would become a fraud. Hence, despite
its political overtones and its potential for creating dis-ease,

the land and Israel must be a priority for the modern Jewish-Christian dialogue.

I have tried to show in this chapter the wide range of issues and concerns which the land tradition of Judaism raises today for both Christians and Jews. Over the last twenty-five years, the dialogue between Christians and Jews has grown in ways quite unimagined in any prior time period. The dialogue has been a healthy thing for both religious communities. Since they share so many common traditions, ideas, and scriptures, there is always much to talk about. But the dialogue still can encounter tough going when the question of the land comes up. The reasons for this are fairly clear from what we have seen in our discussion.

For Jews, the land tradition and the state of Israel rank as first priority for any interfaith discussion. Life after the holocaust has become one in which the question of Jewish survival is of paramount importance. For most Jews, Israel is a key to any discussion about Jewish existence after the holocaust. We have seen that there is hardly any monolithic Jewish point of view as to what that Jewish existence looks like. The debate between Irving Greenberg and Marc Ellis is a perfect illustration of this point. But, for the Christian engaging in dialogue for the first time with Jews, it may well come as a surprise to find the question of Israel so central to Jewish concerns. The simplistic separation of religion and politics so common in the mind of many Christians is immediately challenged by the Jewish demand to discuss the political and social realities of Israel. The importance of the Zionist movement to most Jews cannot be doubted, yet the variety of Zionist positions may make it difficult for Jews to clearly express to their Christian friends what exactly they mean by Zionism. It is just this uncertainty that makes it important for all participants to engage in *dialogue* rather than *monologue.* The person on the other side of the table may not have the faintest ideas about what initially is being discussed. Jews cannot expect that their Christian counterparts are as familiar with Zionism and Israel as Jews are, although it is not a given that Jews are all that familiar with these facts either.

The Christian participant in dialogue needs to not only listen to Jews speak about the land and its importance to Judaism, but he or she needs also to listen to those Christian

theologians who have begun to struggle with the meaning of
the land for Christians and with those aspects of the Christian tradition that make it difficult for Christians to appreciate this tradition. Israel is not usually high on the theological
agenda of churches, and when it is, at least within "Mainline
Protestantism" to which I belong, Israel is often raised in a
critical discussion over some aspect of Israeli government policy. Within evangelical or fundamentalist Christianity, Israel
sometimes gets more approval, but it comes within a theological context that many Jews find uncomfortable. It is often the
case, therefore, that any discussion of the land tradition by
Christians involves a wholesale reexamination of the "teaching of contempt" within the Christian tradition, as well as
listening to Jews explain why the land is so important.

The importance of Israel to Jews today stems not only
from the centrality of the land tradition in Judaism, but also
from the real fears that Jews have for survival after the holocaust. For Christians to dismiss these fears as misplaced
concern is to commit the worst mistake one can make in dialogue—not taking the other partner seriously. This does not
mean that Christians must give *carte blanche* to everything
Israel does as a nation. Clearly, Israelis are not afraid to criti-
cize their own government. But it is incumbent upon Christians to make their criticism within a supportive context that
does not imply any wish for the state to go away. There are
many Christians who are sincerely concerned about the Palestinian situation, and Jews need to be able to hear that concern. But if Christian concern for Palestinians is to carry any
moral weight, Christians must be willing to be as critical of
Palestinian and Arab refusal to recognize the right of Israel to
exist as they are of Israeli policy.

Jewish survival is a central concern for Jews today, and
Christians need to come to grips with this fact. All the nice
theological discussions we can have will mean nothing if
there are no Jews with whom to talk. The discussion about
the land and Israel is probably the most difficult component
of the modern-day dialogue. It causes tempers to flare and
exchanges can become quite heated. There is always the
temptation to avoid this issue for fear that it will make everyone uncomfortable. True dialogue, however, should make everyone uncomfortable. True dialogue means that we discuss
our most intimate beliefs with people outside our community.

Anyone engaged in dialogue is always taking a risk of being changed, of having long held beliefs challenged, and hearing of hurts we may have inadvertently caused to others. Dialogue may produce more doubt than assurance. Yet, true dialogue is a unique opportunity to grow and change with someone else. And in the end, one may become a better person whose faith has been tested and strengthened.

If the dialogue between Christians and Jews is ever to produce a new relationship, great risks will have to be taken. Troubling questions of the past must be confronted, and new present realities need to be discussed. It is not enough to have good intentions. Hard work must be done to learn about the other one's traditions and beliefs. That is why it is so important to become aware of what has been said in the past about the land, and what is being said about it today. Any dialogue that refuses to deal with this issue is incomplete, and, as we have seen, there is much to be learned. If the dialogue between Jews and Christians is to proceed, there is no question but that the land tradition and the state of Israel will remain at the heart of the discussion.

NOTES

[1] W.D. Davies, *Jewish and Pauline Studies* (Philadelphia: Fortress Press, 1984), p. 71.

[2] Walter Brueggemann, *The Land* (Philadelphia: Fortress Press, 1977), p. 193.

[3] Jurgen Moltmann, *The Crucified God: The Cross of Christ as the Foundation and Criticism of Christian Theology* (San Francisco: Harper, 1990), p. 194.

[4] Paul van Buren, *In Faith and Freedom* (Elmsford: Pergamon Press, 1988), p. 119.

[5] Harry Orlinsky, "The Biblical Concept of the Land of Israel," in *The Land of Israel: Jewish Perspectives,* edited by Lawrence Hoffman (Notre Dame: University of Notre Dame Press, 1986).

[6] Orlinsky, "Biblical Concept," p. 42.

[7] Ibid. 48.

[8] Davies, *Jewish and Pauline Studies,* p. 50.

[9] See Gershon Cohen, "Zion in Rabbinic Literature," in *Zion in Jewish Literature,* edited by Abraham Halkin (New York: Hertzl Press, 1961), pp. 38–64.

[10] W.D. Davies, *The Territorial Dimension of Judaism* (Berkeley: University of California Press, 1982), p. 36.

[11] Cohen, "Zion in Rabbinic Literature," p. 52.

[12] Gerald Sloyan, "A Theology of the Land of Israel," unpublished paper presented to the Israel Study Group, pp. 27–28.

[13] See *The Gospel and the Land: Early Christianity and Jewish Territorial Doctrine* (Berkeley: University of California Press, 1974) and *The Territorial Dimension of Judaism*.

[14] John Townsend, "Israel's Land Promise under the New Covenant." Unpublished paper.

[15] Walter Harrelson, "The Land in Tanakh." Unpublished paper presented to the Christian Study Group on Jews and Judaism, 1986.

[16] Paul van Buren, *In Faith*, p. 121. See also Chapter Six in his *A Christian Theology of the People Israel* (New York: Seabury, 1983).

[17] van Buren, *In Faith*, p. 124.

[18] Rosemary Ruether's latest book, *The Wrath of Jonah* (New York: Harper & Row, 1989), is a clear example of how a Christian writer ignores the antisemitic bias of the church when looking at the Jewish state and its meaning. If one reads her previous works on antisemitism and the church, it is possible to see that even when she deals with the anti-Jewish tradition she remains ambivalent on the question of Jewish nationalism and the land tradition.

[19] The "teaching of contempt" is a phrase given to the anti-Jewish teachings of the church by Jules Isaac in his book *The Teaching of Contempt: Christian Roots of Anti-Semitism* (New York: Holt, Rinehart and Winston, 1964). This book has had an enormous impact on many Christians since it was published.

[20] Augustine, "Reply to Faustus the Manichean," in *Disputation and Dialogue*, edited by Frank Talmage (New York: Ktav, 1975), pp. 29, 31.

[21] Ibid. 31.

[22] See Robert A. Everett, "A Reply to Hyam Maccoby," in *The Origins of the Holocaust: Christian Antisemitism*, edited by Randolph Braham (Boulder: Social Scientific Monographs, 1986).

[23] Dietrich Bonhoeffer, *No Rusty Swords* (London: Collins, 1965), p. 222.

[24] David Hartman, *A Living Covenant* (New York: Free Press, 1985), p. 280.

[25] A. Roy Eckardt, *Jews and Christians: The Contemporary Meeting* (Bloomington: Indiana University Press, 1986), pp. 74, 78.

[26] Ibid. 79.

[27] Ibid. 74, 78.

[28] W.D. Davies, *Territorial Dimension*, p. 116.

[29] Ibid. 117.

[30] James Parkes, *Israel and the Diaspora* (London: Jewish Historical Society of England, 1952).

[31] Emil Fackenheim, *What Is Judaism?* (New York: Summit Books, 1987).

[32] Ibid. 237.

[33] Hartman, *A Living Covenant*, p. 286.

[34] Ibid.

[35] Fackenheim, *What Is Judaism?* p. 238.

[36] See Arnold Eisen's "The Land in Modern Jewish Thought," in *The Land of Israel* (South Bend: University of Notre Dame Press, 1986) for an excellent review of the issues. Arthur Hertzberg's *The Zionist Idea* (New York: Atheneum, 1971) also gives a comprehensive survey of the issues involved.

[37] Eisen, "The Land," p. 264.

[38] Ibid.

[39] Fackenheim, *What Is Judaism?* p. 235.

[40] David Novak, *Jewish-Christian Dialogue* (New York: Oxford University Press, 1989), pp. 111–12.

[41] Ben Halpern, "Zionism," in *Contemporary Jewish Religious Thought* (New York: C. Scribner's Sons, 1987), p. 1069.

[42] James Parkes, *Israel and the Diaspora*, p. 3. See my article "A Christian Apology for Israel: The Thought of James Parkes," *Christian-Jewish Relations* 72 (1980), 50–64.

[43] See Manfred Vogel, *A Quest for a Theology of Judaism* (New York: University Press of America, 1987), Chapter Ten. See also John Pawlikowski, *What Are They Saying About Christian-Jewish Relations?* (Mahwah: Paulist Press, 1980), pp. 112–13.

[44] Ibid. 199.

[45] Ibid.

[46] Hartman, *A Living Covenant*, p. 287.

[47] Ibid.

[48] Ibid. 278.

[49] Ibid. 293.

[50] Ibid. 294.

[51] Ibid. 296.

[52] Ibid.

[53] John T. Pawlikowski, "Ethical Issues In the Israeli-Palestinian Conflict: One Christian's Viewpoint," in *Beyond Occupation: American Jewish, Christian, and Palestinian Voices for Peace* (Boston: Beacon Press, 1990), p. 166.

[54] Irving Greenberg, *The Jewish Way: Living the Holidays* (New York: Summit Books, 1988).

[55] Quoted in "Israel in Gaza, Israelis Speak Out," *Tikkun* 3 (1988) 19.

[56] Connor Cruise O'Brien, *The Siege* (New York: Simon & Schuster, 1986), pp. 654ff.

[57] (New York: Schocken Books, 1979), pp. 263–64.

[58] Pawlikowski, *What Are They Saying About Jewish-Christian Relations?* p. 127.

Discussion Questions

1. What do you see as the role of the "land" in Jewish-Christian dialogues? What role does your own native land play in your life?

2. What is the relationship between the covenant with God and Israel to the gift of the land?

3. How can the modern Jews of the modern state of Israel, who began a country of, by, and for refugees, have helped to perpetuate another large class of Palestinian refugees?

4. Do Christians have a tendency to spiritualize the concept of the land whereas Jews concretize it? What does this mean in regard to Jewish-Christian dialogue?

5. What is the role of the stereotype of the "wandering Jew" to the land? Is there a theology of victimization here?

For Further Study

Brueggemann, Walter. *The Land: Place as Gift, Promise, and Challenge in Biblical Faith.* Philadelphia: Fortress, 1977.

Davies, W.D. *The Territorial Dimension of Judaism.* Berkeley: University of California, 1982.

Drinan, Robert F. *Honor the Promise: America's Commitment to Israel.* Garden City: Doubleday, 1977.

Eckhardt, A. Roy and Alice L. Eckardt. *Encounter with Israel: A Challenge to Conscience.* New York: Association, 1970.

Hartman, David. *A Living Covenant.* New York: Free Press, 1985.

Heschel, Abraham Joshua. *Israel: An Echo of Eternity.* New York: Farrar, Straus, and Giroux, 1967.

Hoffman, Lawrence A., ed. *The Land of Israel: Jewish Perspectives.* Notre Dame: Notre Dame Press, 1986.

Parkes, James. *End of An Exile: Israel, the Jews, and the Gentile World.* Marblehead: Michah, 1982.

Rudin, James. *Israel for Christians.* Philadelphia: Fortress, 1983.

Sachar, Howard J. *A History of Israel: From the Rise of Zionism to Our Time.* New York: Knopf, 1979.

V.

MARY CHRISTINE ATHANS

Antisemitism? or Anti-Judaism?

I. Introduction

"Anti-Semitic attack injures 2 in Brooklyn." This headline in the *National Catholic Reporter* (October 20, 1989), is a reminder that antisemitism is painfully alive in the United States as we approach the end of the twentieth century. The incident is reported as follows:

> Two 19-year-old Jewish students were hospitalized and three Brooklyn teenagers charged with first-degree assault after an October 10 anti-Semitic attack in Brooklyn.

> A fight began after 18-year-old Anthony Sorrentino allegedly called Brooklyn College student Steven Weisburg a "kike" as he and a fellow student Joshua Fogel left a party at Hillel House, a Jewish student center. Sorrentino was joined in the attack, according to the police, by 16-year-old Joseph Guben and 17-year-old James E. Hynes.[1]

In the same issue another headline shouts: "Boston suburb plagued by anti-Semitic attacks" which included spray-painting of swastikas on homes, mailboxes, and shops on the eve of Yom Kippur. Roman Catholic Bishop Robert A. Gonzalez is quoted as saying that the attacks were "particularly deplorable and insidious since they appear to have an element of desecrating the high holyday of Yom Kippur."[2] According to Leonard Zakim of the Anti-Defamation League, the number of antisemitic incidents reported in Massachusetts in the summer of 1989 was greater than the number for all of 1988.³ Desecration of synagogues, the marches of the Ku Klux Klan, the emergence of the "skinhead" movement all graphically depict a hatred of Jews which has never completely subsided even after the atrocities of World War II.

In reflecting on these incidents there are key questions to be addressed. First of all, what is antisemitism? What is anti-Judaism? How do we define each, and how do we distinguish between the two?

Second, how did these phenomena emerge in human history? Is it possible for Jews and Christians to understand each other today if they are not aware of the history of anti-semitism and anti-Judaism over the past two thousand years? Knowledge of the history of Jewish-Christian relations is the solid ground on which a new approach to mutual understanding can be constructed. For that reason, the majority of this essay will be devoted to a history of antisemitism.

Third, what is the relationship of antisemitism and anti-Judaism to that monumental event of the twentieth century which Jews refer to as "the shoah," and which the world in recent years has named "the holocaust"? Although the topic of the holocaust will be discussed elsewhere in this volume, there is need to reflect at least briefly on the painful question: "If Christians had really been *Christian* over the centuries, would the holocaust have occurred?"

Last, given the history of the relationship of Jews and Christians, is there reason for hope that our understanding of one another will improve in the future? Although there is still need for improvement, the remarkable changes which were ushered in by the Second Vatican Council of the Roman Catholic Church (1962–1965) give us reason for optimism in Jewish-Christian relations as we approach the twenty-first century.

II. Definitions

What is meant by "antisemitism"? This term is really a misnamed and invented word. "Semitic" is a designation for a family of languages, not a racial description—a factor unknown to or discounted by the journalist Wilhelm Marr who coined the expression "antisemitism" in Germany in 1879. In the nineteenth century racial theories emerged as a result of the writings of the biologist Charles Darwin and his hypothesis of "the survival of the fittest." Other writers applied Darwin's ideas to society which led to an emphasis on "racial purity"—the presupposition being that northern Europeans were superior to Mediterranean peoples and those of darker skin. Jews were categorized as "Semites"—inferior beings who were a threat to the life and culture of Europe. Antisemitism became the accepted expression for hostility toward or discrimination against Jews generally for "racial" reasons. Although the word is used today exclusively for anti-Jewish attitudes and actions, it is important to note that Arabs are Semites, too.

Currently the term "anti-Judaism" (religious antisemitism) is becoming more common because it is specific to hatred or discrimination against Jews because of their religion. It identifies theology as the base for the rejection of Jews; for example, Jews became victims of hostility because they did not accept Jesus as the messiah, or they had "killed Christ." In this post-holocaust era, many Christians have been confronted with a new awareness that the almost two thousand years of hatred for Jews that preceded the holocaust had its roots in Christian theology and its location largely in the Christian churches. This anti-Judaism created the atmosphere in which the nineteenth century racially-oriented antisemitism (with its counterparts in economic, social and political antisemitism) flourished and eventually led to Hitler's attempt at Jewish genocide in Europe in the mid-twentieth century.

Although antisemitism has become a generic word, it is important to note that sub-groups within the category can, in subtle ways, mask the reality of what is really antisemitic behavior. Stereotypes of Jews as money manipulators, or as absentee landlords who extract the last dime from the poverty-stricken in the slums, or as international bankers involved in a conspiracy are all part of "economic antisemitism." Fear of Jews in government, particularly as they might be aligned to communism, or as a force for division and hatred in modern Israel, are part of "political antisemitism." This does not mean that people cannot question or disagree with political decisions in Israel. However, anti-Zionism—hatred for Jews not as religion or as a race, but as a nation—

is frequently a cloak for antisemitism. (See the chapter on Israel for further discussion on this topic.)

III. History of Anti-Judaism and Antisemitism

To understand Christian anti-Jewish attitudes one must explore the New Testament, the writings of the fathers of the church, the medieval canons of the church councils against the Jews, and the tracts of Martin Luther on the Jews during the reformation.[4] The entire story is too lengthy to be explained here, but some historical background and a few illustrations of the rhetorical extremes of these periods will help us to understand what caused Jews to fear for their lives then, and why some Jews are fearful even today.

It should be stated that the phenomenon of antisemitism existed in the world prior to the Christian era. Jews always considered themselves a unique people set apart from those who worshiped false gods. In their experience of exclusivity —especially in celebrating the sabbath, ritual circumcision, and observance of dietary laws—a wall of separation grew up between themselves and other peoples of the eastern Mediterranean region. An example would be the Hellenistic Jews who accepted the Greek language and culture, but who retained their Jewish religious beliefs and practices. They were sometimes absorbed into another world from a cultural point of view, but never religiously. It was as if they had erected a "spiritual fence" around themselves so that they could fulfill the commandments of God. This was resented by others with whom they refused to have contact.

Perhaps the most complicated factor in interpreting the ground of Christian antisemitism is the language of the New Testament. In 1965 Gregory Baum wrote a volume with the controversial title, *Is the New Testament Anti-Semitic?*[5] This was a catalyst for an ongoing dialogue on the relationship of antisemitism to the gospels which will be discussed elsewhere, but it is important to note that authors such as Samuel Sandmel, A. Roy Echardt, Rosemary Radford Ruether and others have challenged the Christian churches to examine the scriptural roots of antisemitism, something unheard of in earlier centuries.

Christians with a more literal approach to scripture believe that the Jews were responsible for the death of Christ. The prophecies of doom occasionally mentioned in the Christian scriptures (e.g. Lk 19:41–44) state that the Jews ultimately would suffer as a people for what they did. The destruction of Jerusalem in 70 C.E. (the "common era"—that period of time that Jews and Christians share) and the subsequent dispersion of the Jews was interpreted as a punishment for the crucifixion of Jesus. Emphasis has been put on the supposed "degenerate" condition of Judaism at the time of Jesus; these interpreters believe that it was the fault of the Jews that they did not recognize Jesus as the messiah. The conclusion of many literalist Christians was that the Jews were a "deicide" people. Because they had "killed Christ," the God-Man, they had "killed God." These are only a few examples of the accusations against the Jews that find their roots in some interpretations of the New Testament.

Scripture scholars who are less literal in their interpretations have given us new insights into the New Testament. This is a result of recent discoveries such as the Dead Sea Scrolls, coupled with more scientific approaches to the study of scripture, and the historical-critical method. Many of the anti-Jewish writings in the Christian scriptures were composed by members of the Christian community who were converts from Judaism and were distraught over the separation between the church and the synagogue in the later first century. When the Jewish Christians did not fight with the other Jews against the Romans at the time of the fall of Jerusalem (70 C.E.), they were expelled from the synagogue. In their anger at "their mother" (Judaism), and in competition with the Pharisees for new converts, "the Jews" in the gospel of John, and "the Pharisees" in the synoptic gospels (Matthew, Mark and Luke), became the targets for animosity in the early Christian community.[6] Scholars believe that this antagonism is responsible for some of the hostile language in the New Testament regarding the Jews.

With this break between the church and the synagogue at the end of the first century church leaders found themselves confronted with new and challenging questions about the relationship of Christianity to Judaism. Gnosticism, a movement which emphasized the separation of body and spirit and the inferiority of material things, was dominant in that period. An extreme adaptation of Gnosticism to Christianity was labelled Marcionism. The followers of Marcion in the second century of the common era taught that the God of the New Testament was entirely different than the God of the Old Testament—who was interpreted as a God of law, angry and judging. Marcion wanted the books of the Old Testament excluded from the church's list of scriptures. Although Marcionism was condemned, the residue of this heresy (an opinion or doctrine contrary to church dogma) became a source for the frequent Christian misinterpretation that the God of the Old Testament is a God of fear and anger, and only the God of the New Testament is a God of love. Christians often forgot that Jesus was quoting from the Hebrew scriptures (Dt 6:4–5; Lev 19:18) when he stated that people should love God with mind, heart, soul and strength, and love one's neighbor as oneself (see Mk 12:29–31). As Christianity developed in the second century, the church became more separated from Judaism.

Within the next two centuries the gap between the church and the synagogue became a chasm. In the fourth century Christianity was established as the religion of the Roman empire. The Romans, who had conquered the Jews, became Christians—adding insult to injury for the Jews. Jewish converts to Christianity were exhorted against participating in Jewish festivals or attending synagogue services. St. John Chrysostom—a prominent bishop and theologian of the church known as "the golden-mouthed orator"— preached a series of eight sermons against the Jews during the High Holy Days in Antioch c. 386–387 C.E. The following excerpt is indicative of the tenor of these *Adversos Judaeos* sermons:

> I know that a great number of the faithful have for the Jews a certain respect and hold their ceremonies in reverence. This provokes me to eradicate completely such a disastrous opinion. I have already brought forward that the synagogue is worth no more than the theater. Here is what the prophet says, and the prophets are more to be respected than the Jews: "But because you have a harlot's brow, you refused to blush" (Jer. 3:3). But the place where the harlot is prostituted is the brothel. The synagogue therefore is not only a theater, it is a place of prostitution, it is a

den of thieves and a hiding place of wild animals . . .
not simply of animals, but of impure beasts. . . .
They say that they too worship God; but that is not
so. None of the Jews, not one of them is a worshipper
of God. It was the Son who told them: "If you knew
the Father, you would know me also, but you know
neither me nor my Father" (Cf. John 8:19).

As the sermon progressed, Chrysostom became more severe
in his ridicule of the Jews:

Since they have disowned the Father, crucified the
Son, and rejected the Spirit's help, who would dare to
assert that the synagogue is not the home of demons!
God is not worshipped there; it is simply a house of
idolatry. . . . The Jews live for their bellies, they
crave for the goods of the world. In shamelessness
and greed they surpass even pigs and goats. . . . The
Jews are possessed by demons, they are handed over
to impure spirits. . . . Instead of greeting them and
addressing them as much as a word, you should turn
away from them as from the pest and a plague of the
human race.[7]

Scholars tell us that Chrysostom was distraught because
Christians who had converted from Judaism to Christianity
continued attending services in the synagogues especially
during the High Holy Days. He was trying to dissuade them
from this practice. No matter what qualifying statements
might be suggested regarding the motive for these sermons, it
is difficult to understand such violent rhetoric from a theologian and saint of the church.

John Chrysostom was not alone in rejecting and berating
the Jews. Hilary of Poitiers, Cyril of Jerusalem, and Gregory
of Nyssa, to name a few, denounced the Jews from the pulpit.
Ambrose, bishop of Milan, defended the burning of a synagogue by a mob in Callinicum in Asia Minor in 386 C.E. Emperor Theodosius wanted to assist in rebuilding it, but Ambrose threatened him with excommunication if he would
do so.

Throughout the middle ages legends materialized about
the Jews that were insidious. Because the vision of the Chris-

tian empire was paramount, one who did not confess Jesus as the Lord could not be a citizen. Jews were not allowed to own property or exercise the usual political and civil rights. They had to live in a separate place, the "ghetto," and were cut off from communication. They were not only considered inferior beings, but because "the Jews" were considered to be responsible for the crucifixion of Jesus, they were called "Christ-killers."

There had been prescriptions against the Jews in Roman civil law. Later these were incorporated into church law and passed on to the other nations in Christendom. The teachings of the church councils made the restrictions very clear as will be noted in the following:

> Prohibition of intermarriage and of sexual intercourse between Christians and Jews, Synod of Elvira, 306.

> Jews and Christians not permitted to eat together, Synod of Elvira, 306.

> Jews not permitted to employ Christian servants or possess Christian slaves, 3rd Synod of Orleans, 538.

> Jews not permitted to show themselves in the street during Passion Week, 3rd Synod of Orleans, 538.

> Burning of the *Talmud* and other books, 12th Synod of Toledo, 681.

> Jews obliged to pay taxes for the support of the church to the same extent as Christians, Synod of Geneva, 1078.

> Jews not permitted to be plaintiffs or witnesses against Christians in the courts, 3rd Lateran Council, 1179.

> Jews not permitted to withhold inheritance from descendants who had accepted Christianity, 3rd Lateran Council, 1179.

> The marking of Jewish clothes with a badge, 4th Lateran Council, 1215.

> Construction of new synagogues prohibited, Council of Oxford, 1222.

Compulsory ghettos, Synod of Breslau, 1267.

Christians not permitted to sell or rent real estate to Jews, Synod of Ofen, 1279.[8]

Due to the massive illiteracy of the majority of the people in the middle ages, ignorance, superstition and fanaticism allowed myths about Jews to flourish. They were accused of ritual murder, poisoning wells, and sorcery. Myths regarding "the demonic Jew" were perpetuated by pamphlets, tracts, plays, woodcuts, and sculptures which frequently portrayed the antichrist as the Jewish messiah. Because baptism was a ritual in which Christians believed that Satan was renounced and indeed "driven out" of an individual, some drew the conclusion that those who were not baptized—namely, the Jews—were still inhabited by the devil and were therefore to be shunned.[9]

In the art and architecture of the later middle ages, the constantly recurring theme of the rejection of the Jews is evident. The figures of two women—*Ecclesia* (representing the church), and *Synagogua* (representing the synagogue) were sometimes sculpted in stone on either side of the crucified Jesus on the portals of cathedrals. *Ecclesia* was portrayed receiving the blood of the crucified savior in a cup; *Synagogua* was usually blindfolded, sometimes with the broken tablets of the ten commandments in her hands. These architectural portraits communicated a theology of the rejection of the Jews even to the unlettered masses of people during that period.[10]

The goal of the crusades in the medieval period—the "holy wars" of Christendom—was to free the holy land from the Muslims who were seen as infidels. It occurred to some crusaders as they were en route through Europe to the Middle East that the Jews were "infidels" in their midst. The result was the massacre of Jews and the looting and burning of flourishing Jewish communities in the Rhineland, France, Bohemia, and Palestine during the first three crusades. Many Jews were forced to choose between baptism and death.[11]

Some popes and bishops in the medieval period did make efforts to protect the Jews. Innocent IV (1247), Gregory X (1272), and Martin V (1422) among others protested against the charges of ritual murder—the legend that the Jews needed Christian blood for the celebration of certain festivals, particularly Passover.[12] Various bishops in France and Germany tried to defend the Jews during the massacres at the time of the crusades.[13] As a whole, however, Jews were isolated, expelled from some nations, brought before the inquisition in others, and often persecuted in the dominantly Christian culture. Although some Jews did accept baptism in order to avoid persecution, they often continued their Jewish practices secretly.

The Jews came to play a key role in the economy, partly because of their contact between the Christian west and the trade routes held by the Muslims, and also because of the church's teaching prohibiting usury (the lending of money with an interest charge for its use). Unable to belong to the guilds, and therefore excluded from many occupations more "acceptable," Jews became the moneylenders of Europe— the economic agents and the economic scapegoats for the European ruling class. All of this contributed to the negative portrayal of the Jew in western Christendom.[14]

At the beginning of the reformation Martin Luther was convinced that the primary reason that Jews had not accepted Christianity was because of the "papists" (a derogatory word which described those Christians who adhered to the authority of the pope) who had distorted the Christian message. In the tract *That Jesus Christ Was Born a Jew* (1523), Luther stated:

> Perhaps I will attract some of the Jews to the Christian faith. For our fools—the popes, bishops, sophists, and monks—the coarse blockheads! have until this time so treated the Jews that to be a good Christian one would have to become a Jew. And if I had been a Jew and had seen such idiots and blockheads ruling and teaching the Christian religion, I would rather have been a sow than a Christian.[15]

By 1543, however, Luther's frustration regarding the sparsity of Jewish conversions was evident in his vitriolic statement entitled *Concerning the Jews and Their Lies*. He asked: "What then shall we Christians do with this damned, rejected race of Jews?" Some of his suggestions are as follows:

First, their synagogues or churches should be set on fire. . . . And this ought to be done for the honor of God and of Christianity in order that God may see that we are Christians. . . .

Secondly, their homes should likewise be broken down and destroyed . . . they ought to be put under one roof or in a stable, like gypsies, in order that they may realize that they are not masters in our land. . . .

Thirdly, they should be deprived of their prayer-books and Talmuds in which such idolatry, lies, cursing, and blasphemy are taught.

Fourthly, their rabbis must be forbidden under the threat of death to teach any more. . . .

Fifthly, passport and traveling privileges should be absolutely forbidden to Jews. . . .

Sixthly, they ought to be stopped from usury. . . .

Seventhly, let the young and strong Jews and Jewesses be given the flail, the ax, the hoe, the spade, the distaff, and the spindle, and let them earn their bread by the sweat of their noses as is enjoined by Adam's children. . . .

To sum up, dear princes and nobles who have Jews in your domains, if this advice of mine does not suit you, then find a better one so that you and we may all be free of this insufferable devilish burden— the Jews.[16]

Although there were some exceptions, such as Spain and Portugal where Jews were considered to have *mala sangre* (bad blood)—the concept that became the basis for Spanish racism—most of the discrimination and persecution against Jews was theologically based until the modern period.

The enlightenment in the seventeenth and eighteenth centuries was characterized by the "rule of reason"—a new enthusiasm regarding all that was rational with an emphasis on science and empiricism. Human beings were to be affirmed for their rationality and educability, not for their blood lineage or status in society. "Liberty! Equality! Fraternity!"

became the slogan of the period. Democratic and republican forms of government were heralded as the appropriate political systems for rational beings. The "rights of man," the inevitability of progress, and an optimistic view of the world were convictions which were espoused by philosophers such as Locke, Rousseau, and Montesquieu, literary figures such as Voltaire, and the encyclopedist Diderot. Deism, the religion of the period, accepted the existence of a very impersonal God. Rationalists, however, questioned the divinity of Jesus and the authenticity of the scriptures.

The culmination of the enlightenment in Europe was the French Revolution (1789)—a traumatic experience for Christians, and a liberating one for Jews. The Catholic Church in France saw its property confiscated, nuns and priests sent to the guillotine, and a "goddess of reason" enthroned during the reign of terror. For Jews, however, the French Revolution meant freedom and emancipation. Because all people were given "rights" as citizens, Jews suddenly found themselves with basic rights to vote, own property, acquire an education, and hold political office. As a result of the French Revolution Jews received citizenship in the nation, and Judaism was accepted as a religion. Separation of church and state and religious liberty achieved for the Jews the status of free persons in society. As Jews emerged from their ghettos, however, many became assimilated into society and some converted to Christianity. Unfortunately Jewish political emancipation which allowed for religious freedom did not wipe out the development of a rationalist antisemitism that was championed by some of the enlightenment figures: Voltaire, Rousseau, and Diderot. If reason was the rule by which knowledge should be judged, then the Hebrew scriptures were just as subject to criticism as the New Testament. The very possibility of God's revelation to humanity was questioned not only in the Jewish and Christian scriptures, but also in the implications which these held for society and culture.[17]

With the end of the French Revolution and Napoleon (1815), kings and queens were restored to their thrones and a century of tension and revolution ensued. The monarchy, the military and the church tended to form alliances. They saw as their enemies those who espoused democratic/republican forms of government, socialists, communists, and Jews—all of whom they believed were trying to undermine the values of western Christendom. A new kind of cultural and political antisemitism evolved.

Advances in science, particularly in the work of the biologist Charles Darwin who wrote *The Origin of Species* in 1859, contributed to racial theories which became distorted as they were reinterpreted by others into the pseudo-science of racism. With "the survival of the fittest" came an emphasis on "purity of race." The presupposition was that the "Nordic race" was superior. Warnings were issued against crossbreeding with those of "inferior races" such as the Jews who were supposedly inferior physically, morally, and culturally. Writers such as Count J.A. de Gobineau, Edouard Drumont, Housten Stewart Chamberlain, and Madison Grant fanned the fires of antisemitism in the late nineteenth and early twentieth century.

Political and social conditions of the Jews in eastern Europe worsened. Pogroms (organized massacres) against the Jews in Russia broke out in the 1880s after the assassination of Czar Alexander II. Because some Jews were associated with liberal movements, all Jews became targets for anti-revolutionary activity. Russian soldiers massacred entire communities. The pogrom at Kishinev in 1903 was barbarous and protests against inhumanity were heard around the world. These events were not without a religious dimension. Holy Week (the week prior to Easter Sunday) was a particularly painful time for Jews. Christians in small towns in Poland and Russia would sometimes descend upon the ghettos after services on Good Friday and stone the homes of the Jews who had "killed Christ." There is more truth than fiction to some of the pathetic scenes from "Fiddler on the Roof."

Racial and political antisemitism exploded in France at the turn of the century in the experience known as the Dreyfus affair in which a Jew, Captain Alfred Dreyfus of the French army, was accused of spying for the Germans. Although he was acquitted of the charges in 1906, the antisemitism that the situation evoked during those years reached a fever pitch and left deep wounds in France for decades.

Jewish-Christian relations in the United States were unique. Although Jews first came to New Amsterdam (later

New York) in 1654, their numbers remained meager, and at the time of the American Revolution there were only about 2,000 in the newly formed United States. These Jews were among the first to enjoy the religious freedom guaranteed by the Bill of Rights of the United States Constitution. Jewish settlers in this early period were mainly Sephardic (Spanish-speaking), and were located largely in Philadelphia, New York, Rhode Island and the Carolinas.

The second wave of Jewish immigration was from German-speaking lands during the years 1820–1880. Many came as a result of the revolutions in Europe and the reaction against the enlightenment. Limitations were put on the earlier emancipation; for example, in 1836 a Bavarian law limited the number of Jews who could contract marriage, and this inspired a mass immigration to America. By 1880 the Jewish population reached approximately 250,000—the majority coming from a German cultural background. Many of these Jews were accepted as German-Americans who practiced Judaism and often belonged to German-American clubs in their areas. Although there are some examples of discrimination, and Jews were not allowed to hold high offices in some states until late in the nineteenth century (New Hampshire, 1876), there were also examples of courtesy and cooperation as Jews and Christians established new communities in America.

With the advent of the east European immigrations (1880–1924), however, large numbers of Christians and Jews from eastern Europe and the Mediterranean nations flooded the east coast of the United States. Russian and Polish Jews, Italian and Polish Catholics, Greek and Russian Orthodox Christians all arrived with customs and costumes alien to the predominantly Anglo-Saxon culture. Protestant Americans feared that this invasion of foreigners might "pollute" the environment of a "Christian America" and a new wave of xenophobia (fear and hatred of foreigners) broke out over the land. "Social Darwinism" emphasized white superiority over blacks, Asians, eastern Europeans and Jews. Even educated and wealthy Jews were not considered for positions for which they were qualified. They were not allowed to own property in "restricted" areas, belong to exclusive clubs, practice on the staffs of particular hospitals, or attend prestigious schools. College quotas emerged. (These types of discrimination continued in some geographical areas until 1960 and later.) Stereotypes of Jews in novels and the theater grew apace.

In 1905 the famous forged document *The Protocols of the Elders of Zion* appeared.[18] It described an alleged Jewish conspiracy to dominate the world and establish a Jewish state. This contributed to the paranoia of those who were convinced of a Jewish international monetary conspiracy and of Jewish connections to socialism and communism—a fear that was enhanced by the accusation that the Jews had instigated the Bolshevik Revolution in 1917 and inaugurated the reign of communism in eastern Europe. Portions of *The Protocols* were published by the industrialist Henry Ford in his newspaper *The Dearborn Independent*, and later republished by him under the title *The International Jew*,[19] all of which contributed to the suspicions of the "100% Americanists" that Jews were a racial, a religious, and a revolutionary peril.[20]

The post-World War I period in the United States, the so-called "roaring twenties," began with a sense of optimism, but as the decade progressed a variety of crises evolved: the unpopularity and failure of prohibition; government scandal; the closure of immigration; fear of communism; the fundamentalist/modernist uproar relating to the Scopes trial which centered on creationism, evolution and the Bible; the rise of the Ku Klux Klan; the beginning of the Depression. In this period of isolationism the United States raised protective tariffs and rejected the League of Nations. Another wave of xenophobia swept over the nation. Blacks, Catholics and Jews were targeted, especially by the Ku Klux Klan, for harassment and terror.

Perhaps one of the best known of the so-called "demagogues of the Depression" was the famous "radio priest" of the 1930s–1940s—Father Charles E. Coughlin.[21] Born, educated and ordained in Canada, Coughlin moved to Detroit in 1923. In 1926 he was assigned by Bishop Michael Gallagher to build a new parish in the suburb of Royal Oak, Michigan, to be named after the newly-canonized St. Thérèse of Lisieux (known affectionately to Catholics as "The Little Flower"). In an effort to raise money to build a church he negotiated with WJR in Detroit, and his first radio program aired on October 11, 1926.

Coughlin's first radio addresses were sermons. With the advent of the depression, however, he spoke more to the economic frustrations of the people. By 1930 CBS radio picked up his program nationally, and within months his "Golden Hour of the Little Flower" had an estimated forty million listeners. In due time, short wave from Philadelphia carried his program all over the world. It was said that his voice was second only to President Franklin D. Roosevelt in recognition and popularity during the "radio days" of the 1930s–1940s.

Coughlin became an early supporter of Franklin D. Roosevelt in his campaign for the presidency in 1932. After the election, however, the "radio priest" felt that his advice was not accepted and that he was not sufficiently appreciated. In due time he became embittered. In an effort to unseat Roosevelt, Coughlin helped to form the Union Party which was roundly defeated in the Roosevelt landslide in 1936. During those years Jews became a focal point in his radio addresses and in his newspaper *Social Justice.* Coughlin who had earlier coined the slogan "The New Deal Is Christ's Deal" was later more inclined to equate the New Deal with "the Jew Deal." He accused the Jews of being responsible for the international monetary crisis, and at the same time for collaborating with the communists to overthrow Christianity and the western democracies. His derogatory remarks and innuendo regarding Jews was enhanced by the quality of his voice and manner of his speech.

In 1938 Coughlin's antisemitism took a more radical turn. He became obsessed with a focus on the Jews as responsible for everything problematic and evil in the world. He began to base his antisemitic utterances on the writings of an Irish theologian, Father Denis Fahey, and adopted Fahey's theological framework as a religious justification for his vicious attacks against the Jews, particularly in his radio addresses in the fall of 1938. In a letter to Fahey on March 5, 1941 Coughlin stated: "While anti-Semitism is to be abhorred in so far as it is related to hatred for the Jews as individuals and racials, nevertheless, anti-Judaism, which means opposition to the Judaic concept of life, is not to be so condemned."[22] In emphasizing a theological basis for the rejection of the Jews, antisemitism was becoming anti-Judaism again.

As late as 1942 Coughlin was still defending Hitler as "a

defense mechanism against communism." Coughlin stirred the flames of suspicion and fear, and many Catholics and Protestants were only too ready to accept his appraisal of Jews. Although some church leaders had disassociated themselves from Coughlin over the years, many Catholics presumed that the well-known priest in clergy garb was speaking for the church. Finally, in 1942, Coughlin was "silenced" by his superior Archbishop Edward Mooney, and he dutifully served the rest of his years either as a pastor or in retirement until his death in 1979.

The world had been aware of Hitler's persecution of the Jews during the 1930s but few believed that he would resort to genocide. When World War II ended and the death camps were discovered, many people were in a state of shock and disbelief. One would have hoped that antisemitism might have died in the aftermath of Auschwitz—the Nazi death camp famous for its annihilation of Jews.

After World War II there was a rise in the fear of communism, and once again Jews were associated with international conspiracies. Jews were also accused of controlling the media, particularly films, in an effort to communicate socialistic and materialistic ideas to young people in society. Legal issues became the battleground for differences between Catholics and Jews. Court cases relating to separation of church and state focused on Bible reading and prayer in the public schools, released time programs for religious education, bus transportation for those attending parochial schools, and the constitutionality of laws regarding birth control, abortion, and interreligious adoption. Jews were fearful of Christian efforts to proselytize, particularly in the schools, but were accused by Christians of being anti-God, imbued with secularism, and against prayer.

The 1950s, however, was also an era of religious revival when the power of positive thinking was proclaimed by the Reverend Dr. Norman Vincent Peale and Bishop Fulton J. Sheen. Second and third generation Jews and Catholics moved to suburbia, and churches and synagogues, schools and community centers were under construction everywhere. In 1955 the sociologist Will Herberg published the first edition of his classic *Protestant—Catholic—Jew* in which he suggested that the United States had become a kind of "triple melting pot."[23] Assimilation did not seem to be the answer; rather it was important to identify oneself as belonging to one of the three acceptable American religious traditions: Protestant, Catholic or Jew.

The Protestant scholar Martin Marty in his volume *The New Shape of American Religion* described the 1950s as follows: "On the national level religion-in-general, realized pluralism, and a religion of democracy had graduated into the status Protestantism once held." He also believed that a kind of "Living-room Deism" had evolved with its "universal and corrosive credo: 'After all, we're simply in different boats heading for the same shore.'"[24] True, life in suburbia allowed for dialogue and interaction between Jews and Christians. For many Jews, however, it was a new crisis in assimilation often highlighted by a decision as to whether one should have a Christmas tree or a "Hanukkah bush."

In 1960 antisemitic vandalism became epidemic. Some eight hundred incidents were reported by the Anti-Defamation League that year. It was decided that to understand more fully the dimensions of antisemitism in the United States an extensive research project should be undertaken. Under the leadership of Charles Y. Glock, director of the Survey Research Center at the University of California at Berkeley, a team of scholars committed themselves to obtaining statistical data and analyzing what became known under the general title *Patterns of American Prejudice.* Possibly the best known of the seven volumes, *Christian Beliefs and Anti-Semitism,* concluded that there was a significant relationship between antisemitism and the widespread belief that Jews were responsible for the death of Jesus.[25] The study had a substantial impact. It is noteworthy that the results were distributed to the bishops and theologians at the Second Vatican Council who were preparing the *Declaration on the Relationship of the Church to Non-Christian Religions* (sometimes known under its Latin title *Nostra Aetate*) with its very important Article 4—the statement on the Jews.[26]

IV. Antisemitism and the Holocaust

The key question remains: "If the Christians had really been *Christian* over the centuries, would the holocaust have occurred?" Was the holocaust the result primarily of racial antisemitism, or were there religious roots as well? Jewish and Christian scholars, interfaith activists, and church and synagogue dialogue groups have analyzed and agonized over this matter both with depth and in pain. The results strongly suggest that the culmination of years of simplistic biblical interpretation, anti-Judaic pronouncements, legislation by the churches, and the behavior of Christians as noted above laid the groundwork for the events of the Nazi era. While it is true that the basic orientation of the Nazi ideology was atheistic, the Christian writings and proclamations of the centuries provided fertile soil in which the hatred of Jews could grow. The abiding contempt for Jews which had been inculcated in Christians over the centuries served Hitler's purposes well. Ultimately this contributed to an environment in which some irrational leaders attempted a "final solution" and the majority of Christians responded passively in silence.

V. Is There Reason for Hope?

Possibly the most hopeful event of Jewish-Christian relations in almost two thousand years was the Second Vatican Council of the Roman Catholic Church (1962–1965). With the inspiration and leadership of Pope John XXIII and Pope Paul VI a new spirit of openness and dialogue pervaded the religious world. As mentioned above, Article 4 of the *Declaration of the Relationship of the Church to Non-Christian Religions* (which included the statement on the Jews) made an enormous impact in recognizing the "common spiritual heritage" of Jews and Christians.[27] Adapting the words of the apostle Paul the document states: "the Jews remain very dear to God, for the sake of the patriarchs, since God does not take back the gifts he bestowed or the choice he made."[28]

In a further section of the Declaration the rejection of the Jews is refuted. "It is true that the church is the new people of God, yet the Jews should not be spoken of as rejected or accursed as if this followed from holy scripture."[29] Most importantly the fathers of the council declared:

> ... the church reproves every form of persecution against whomsoever it may be directed. Remembering, then, her common heritage with the Jews ... she deplores all hatreds, persecutions, displays of

antisemitism leveled at any time or from any source against the Jews.[30]

Commentators have suggested that this reproof includes the many writings and decrees against the Jews throughout the history of the church.

Although some felt that the Declaration had not been forceful enough in specifically rejecting the accusation of "deicide" and in neglecting to recognize contemporary Judaism and the state of Israel, still others have suggested that in no other area has the Catholic Church so completely reversed its teachings from earlier centuries.

Protestant denominations which formed the World Council of Churches in Amsterdam in 1948 presented a report entitled "The Christian Approach to the Jews" to their First Assembly for serious consideration and appropriate action. The document made the following statement on antisemitism:

> We have failed to fight with all our strength the age-old disorder of man which anti-Semitism represents. The churches in the past have helped to foster an image of the Jews as the sole enemies of Christ, which has contributed to anti-Semitism in the secular world. In many lands virulent anti-Semitism still threatens and in other lands the Jews are subjected to many indignities.[31]

The following challenge was issued:

> We call upon all the churches we represent to denounce anti-Semitism, no matter what its origin, as absolutely irreconcilable with the profession and practice of the Christian faith. Anti-Semitism is sin against God and man.[32]

At the Third Assembly of the World Council of Churches at New Delhi, India in 1961, the above statements were reiterated and the Assembly renewed its plea that the member churches "resist every form of anti-Semitism." It added:

> In Christian teaching, the historic events which led to the Crucifixion should not be so presented as to

impose upon the Jewish people of today responsibilities which must fall on all humanity, not on one race or community. Jews were the first to accept Jesus and Jews are not the only ones who do not yet recognize Him.[33]

Various Protestant denominations have also produced documents regarding their relationships with the Jews and statements against antisemitism.[34]

However, documents from official church bodies—both Catholic and Protestant—or from scholarly dialogues can be somewhat detached unless they make contact with people in the local congregations. The late 1960s and 1970s saw the growth of what has been called "grass roots" ecumenism. Protestant churches, Catholic churches and synagogues formed clusters and corporate ministries and worked together in education and social justice. "Living Room Dialogues" became popular. A new appreciation of the Hebrew scriptures, of the Jewishness of Jesus, and of the Jewish roots of Christian ethics and liturgy opened the eyes of both Jews and Christians to new areas of understanding.

A major breakthrough was the development of joint prayer services. Frequently this was the interfaith thanksgiving service—an American feast day when Catholics, Protestants and Jews could all pray together. Constructing prayer services for these occasions was a challenge. In one particular experience in Phoenix, Arizona the celebration was centered around "the sounds of our faith": the shofar for the Jews, Angelus bells for the Catholics, trumpets for the Protestant reformation. The service concluded with the breaking of bread which had been baked according to a kosher recipe by a retired Presbyterian gentleman and blessed in Hebrew by a Catholic nun.[35] The contrast of that gathering and the viciousness of Christians toward Jews over the centuries left little doubt that progress had been made in the effort to obliterate antisemitism.

In a follow-up study to the project *Patterns of American Racism* it was encouraging to discover that the 1980s had a more educated and tolerant public regarding Jewish issues. Education had clearly provided benefits for all. One such example is the National Workshops in Christian-Jewish Relations held every eighteen months in various cities in the

United States. These have not only provided opportunities for those committed to improving Jewish-Christian relations to gather to hear scholars and practitioners, and to dialogue and develop relationships, but special efforts have been directed toward creating programs for Jewish, Catholic, and Protestant seminarians so that the clergy of the future will be better able to educate their congregations.

Although the above study was basically positive, the trend was negative in a few areas. Black attitudes toward Jews were more hostile, revolving around three issues: Jewish power, Jewish business practices, and Jewish loyalty to Israel. A linkage between antisemitism and anti-Israel attitudes was found to exist for the first time in a study of this nature.[36]

Education, dialogue and interaction have contributed to the bettering of conditions between Christians and Jews in America. But occasions such as the visit of former President Ronald Reagan to the cemetery at Bitburg, Pope John Paul II's acceptance of Kurt Waldheim's invitation to visit Austria, and the controversy over the Carmelite convent at Auschwitz remind us that antisemitism is not far below the surface in many parts of the world.[37] Jews are fearful of a united Germany and of the hostility which seems to be growing in the Soviet Union. As one rabbi reflected after an enjoyable and productive clergy meeting with priests and ministers who were his friends: "I look around the table at each of those fellows and I ask myself: 'Would he hide me in his cellar if it happened again?' "[38]

Is it antisemitism? or anti-Judaism? or both? Edward Flannery reminds us: "Anti-Semitism is the longest and deepest hatred in human history."[39] He contends that antisemitism and anti-Judaism are different in kind, but historically they form a continuum. "Modern racist antisemitism, as exemplified in its purest culture by the Nazi regime, would not have been possible without centuries of anti-Judaic and anti-semitic precedents."[40] There is an irrational inexplicable dimension to antisemitism and anti-Judaism which sociologists, psychologists, philosophers and theologians will continue to probe. Antisemitism will only be eradicated, however, when Jews and Christians come to deeper understandings of each other and the faith they each proclaim. Only then can they build a trust that allows for each to love and worship

God in the unique covenants he has extended to them, and love our neighbors as ourselves.

One might conclude that, knowing of the extraordinary prejudice exerted against the Jews over the centuries, Christians need to be contrite and especially sensitive in regard to the results of these experiences for many Jewish people in our world today. Pope John XXIII offered the following prayer for reflection:

> We are conscious today that many, many centuries of blindness have cloaked our eyes so that we may no longer see the beauty of Thy chosen people nor recognize in their faces the features of our privileged brethren.
>
> We realize that the mark of Cain stands upon our foreheads. Across the centuries our brother Abel has lain in the blood which we drew, or shed tears we caused by forgetting Thy love.
>
> Forgive us for the curse we falsely attached to their name as Jews. Forgive us for crucifying Thee a second time in their flesh. For we know not what we did. . . .[41]

Only by acknowledging and accepting the past with all the pain it entails, and building trust, will Jews and Christians be able to walk into a future with a sense of freedom and hope.

NOTES

[1]*National Catholic Reporter* (October 20, 1989), p. 4.
[2]Ibid.
[3]Ibid.
[4]See Edward H. Flannery, *The Anguish of the Jews: Twenty-Three Centuries of Anti-Semitism,* rev. and updated ed. (New York: Paulist Press, 1985), and A. Roy Eckardt, *Elder and Younger Brothers: The Encounter of Jews and Christians* (New York: Charles Scribner's Sons, 1967).
[5]Gregory Baum, *Is the New Testament Anti-Semitic?* rev. ed. (Glen Rock: Paulist Press, 1965). The original study was published in 1961 under the title *The Jews and the Gospel.*

[6]See Raymond Brown, *The Gospel According to John*, 2 vols. (New York: Doubleday, 1966).

[7]From the *Patrologia Graeca*, Vol. 48, Columns 847, 848, and 852, as quoted in Gregory Baum, *Is the New Testament Anti-Semitic?* p. 18.

[8]Raul Hilberg, *The Destruction of European Jews* (New York: Harper and Row, 1961), p. 5. One cannot help but note that some of these same restrictions were imposed by Hitler in Nazi Germany in the 1930s.

[9]See Joshua Trachtenberg, *The Devil and the Jews: The Medieval Conception of the Jew and Its Relation to Modern Anti-Semitism*, 2nd ed. (New Haven: Yale University Press, 1983).

[10]Wolfgang S. Seiferth, *Synagogue and Church in the Middle Ages: The Encounter of Jews and Christians* (New York: Charles Scribner's Sons, 1967), pp. 12–14.

[11]Leon Poliakov, *The History of Anti-Semitism* (New York: Schocken Books, 1974), Chapter 4.

[12]See Edward A. Synan, *The Popes and the Jews in the Middle Ages* (New York: Macmillan, 1965).

[13]See Flannery, *The Anguish of the Jews*, Chapter 5.

[14]The character of Shylock in William Shakespeare's *The Merchant of Venice* would be an illustration of this attitude.

[15]F.E. Talmage, ed., *Disputation and Dialogue: Readings in the Jewish-Christian Encounter* (New York: KTAV, 1975), p. 33.

[16]Ibid. 35–36.

[17]If the Jewish and Christian scriptures could not be proved by reason, did that not cast doubt on the value of the ten commandments?

[18]For a further explanation of why the document was forged, see Flannery, *The Anguish of the Jews*, pp. 192–193.

[19]*The International Jew, The World's Foremost Problem* (Dearborn: Dearborn Publishing, 1920).

[20]John Higham, *Strangers in the Land: Patterns of American Nativism 1860–1925* (New York: Atheneum, 1974), preface to the second edition, n. p. (p. 2).

[21]David H. Bennet, *Demagogues in the Depression: American Radicals and the Union Party, 1932–1936* (New Brunswick: Rutgers University Press, 1969). See also Sheldon Marcus, *Father Coughlin: The Tumultuous Life of the Priest of the Little Flower* (Boston: Little, Brown and Company, 1973).

[22]See my article "A New Perspective on Father Charles E. Coughlin," *Church History* Vol. 56 (June 1987), 224–235.

[23]Will Herberg, *Protestant—Catholic—Jew: An Essay in American Religious Sociology* (New York: Doubleday and Company, 1960). The theory was first proposed by Ruby Jo Kennedy. See pp. 32–34.

[24]Martin Marty, *The New Shape of American Religion* (New York: Harper and Brothers, 1958), p. 86.

[25]Charles Y. Glock and Rodney Stark, *Christian Beliefs and Anti-Semitism* (New York: Harper and Row, 1960; Harold E. Quinley and Charles Y. Glock, *Anti-Semitism in America* (New Brunswick: Transaction Books, 1983). This volume summarizes the seven volumes in the earlier study and includes updated material from the 1980s.

[26]Austin Flannery, ed., *Vatican Council II: The Conciliar and Post Conciliar Documents* (Northport, NY: Costello Publishing Co., 1975, 740–742.

[27]Ibid. 741.

[28]Ibid.

[29]Ibid.

[30]Ibid.

[31]Helga Croner, ed., *Stepping Stones to Further Jewish-Christian Relations: An Unabridged Collection of Christian Documents* (New York: Paulist Press, 1977), p. 70.

[32]Ibid.

[33]Ibid.

[34]Ibid. 85–149. See also Helga Croner, ed., *More Stepping Stones to Jewish-Christian Relations: An Unabridged Collection of Christian Documents 1975–1983* (New York: Paulist Press, 1985).

[35]See my article "Ecumenism in the Valley of the Sun," *Next Frontier* (Phoenix: North Corporate Ministry, 1976), 9–16.

[36]See Quinley and Glock, xiii–xxxii.

[37]In May 1985 former President Ronald Reagan while on a state visit to West Germany laid a wreath in the German cemetery at Bitburg where some Nazi officers were buried. This provoked an outcry not only from Jews but from other U.S. citizens as well.

In June 1988, while under a cloud of suspicion regarding his activities as a Nazi officer during World War II, Kurt Waldheim, president of Austria and formerly secretary-general of the United Nations, invited Pope John Paul II for a state visit. Many people were critical of the pope for accepting the invitation.

In the fall of 1989, the nuns at a Carmelite convent at Auschwitz failed to move their residence in accord with an agreement reached earlier by Jewish and Catholic officials who had decided that the convent should be located a few miles from the site of the former concentration camp which was a place of special veneration to Jews. When this occurred a group of Jews protested; a few scaled the fence at the convent and seemingly were making efforts to break into the building. This caused an outcry on the part of Jews and Catholics around the world. Cardinal Jozef Glemp, leader of Polish bishops, made statements which stirred up antisemitic sentiments from the past.

[38]Rabbi B. Charles Herring after a meeting of the North Phoenix Corporate Ministry Clergy Council at the time of the Yom Kippur War in the fall of 1973.

[39]Flannery, *Anguish of the Jews,* p. 284.

[40]Ibid. 290.

[41]Pinchas E. Lapide, *The Last Three Popes and the Jews* (London: Souvenir Press, 1967), frontispiece. Quoted from *The Catholic Herald,* May 14, 1965.

Discussion Questions

1. What is the difference between "antisemitism" and "anti-Judaism"? Have you ever experienced prejudices toward your own racial, religious, or ethnic background?

2. In light of the historical connection between some Christian teachings and anti-Judaism, what do you think Christians should say to Jews before inviting them to engage in a dialogue?

3. Is the New Testament antisemitic? Explain. What is the relationship of the charge by Christians that Jews were responsible for the death of Jesus to anti-Judaism?

4. How do you as a twentieth century Christian or Jew react to the anti-Jewish statements of John Chrysostom, church councils, and Martin Luther presented in this chapter?

5. Is anti-Judaism the same as any other racial or religious prejudice? If not, how is it different? If it is, then what does anti-Judaism have in common with óther forms of prejudice?

For Further Study

Davies, Alan T., ed. *Antisemitism and the Foundations of Christianity.* New York: Paulist, 1979.

Flannery, Edward H. *The Anguish of the Jews: Twenty-Three Centuries of Anti-Semitism.* Rev. ed. New York: Paulist, 1985.

Isaac, Jules. *The Teaching of Contempt.* New York: Holt, Rinehart, and Winston, 1964.

Marcus, Sheldon. *Father Coughlin: The Tumultuous Life of the Priest of the Little Flower.* Boston: Little, Brown and Company, 1973.

Parkes, James. *The Conflict of the Church and Synagogue: A Study in the Origins of Antisemitism.* New York: Atheneum, 1969.

Poliokov, Leon. *The History of Anti-Semitism.* (Four volumes.) New York: Charles Scribner's Sons, 1967.

Quinley, Harold E. and Charles Y. Glock. *Anti-Judaism in America.* New Brunswick: Transaction Books, 1983.

Ruether, Rosemary Radford. *Faith and Fratricide: The Theological Roots of Anti-Semitism.* New York: Seabury, 1974.

Sandmel, Samuel. *Anti-Semitism in the New Testament?* Philadelphia: Fortress Press, 1978.

Williamson, Clark M. *Has God Rejected His People? Anti-Judaism in the Christian Church.* Nashville: Abingdon, 1982.

VI.

PHILIP L. CULBERTSON

The Seventy Faces of the One God:
The Theology of Religious Pluralism

Samuel Taylor Coleridge, the nineteenth century English poet, observed: "He who begins by loving Christianity, better than truth, will proceed by loving his own sect or church better than Christianity, and end in loving himself better than all."[1] This same assumption—that a true faith is inquiring, flexible, and unafraid—was recently reaffirmed by Anglican Bishop David Jenkins who echoed Coleridge by insisting that "To know God is to be bound to question everything."[2]

Any number of religious doctrines and issues could be addressed within an essay on the theology of pluralism. For example, we could discuss the relationship between humanity and God: Is humanity so full of sin that it cannot help itself, needing God to step in to the rescue (as some parts of Christianity claim), or is humanity inherently rational and dignified, capable of choosing to cooperate with God through a structured responsive style of life (as some parts of Judaism claim)? Other examples within the world of pluralism would include the question of whether God is directly involved in the daily lives of those who worship God, whether there is such a thing as human resurrection, and, if so, when it occurs—at death or at the last judgment—and what is the character of the afterlife—eternal sleep, eternal revelry, or eternal prayer? Because the subject is so large and complex, this essay will attempt to illustrate the sort of questions which need to be asked, by focusing on one limited portion of the discussion: whether there is truth outside of Christianity and Judaism, and whether there is salvation outside of Christianity and Judaism.

145

I. Introduction

For most of its history, Christianity has lived with the self-affirming assumption that it and it alone contained the full revelation of the will of God, in the birth, life, death, and resurrection of Jesus Christ. This was particularly true at times and locations wherein Christianity was the officially recognized religion of a political government. Yet frequently in such periods and places, peoples of other religions have continued to practice their faiths alongside Christianity, and there is no time in the history of Christian consciousness that it has been completely unaware of the failure, or even refusal, of particular peoples to adopt Christianity. The most obvious example of an "other" religion confronting Christianity has been Judaism; even when Jews were expelled from Christian countries for decades at a time, Christianity remained painfully aware of their existence, and perturbed by Judaism's adamant rejection of what Christians generally considered to be the obvious and exclusive truth.

Although the "triumphalist" voice of Christianity—the one which claims that Christianity fulfills and thereby displaces all other religions of the world as the ultimate revelation of God's truth—has been the majority religious voice throughout most of western history, there have been minority voices in every age, even within the church, who persisted in raising embarrassing questions. Why, they ask, if God loves all creation, should God limit revelation to one system of belief? How could a loving God offer only one way to salvation, when so many people in the world have such little chance of engaging it, or even knowing it exists? If Genesis 1:31 is correct, that God created men and women as "very good," how do we justify any claim that sin is the natural human condition? If human beings are already created in the image of God (Gen 1:26–27), from what do they need rescuing? If God is such an all-knowing God, it must have been obvious from the beginning that humanity would fail repeatedly; why then did God not create us perfect? And if we are not created perfect, then whose job is it to repair that condition: the omnipotent God's, or ours in our human fallibility?

These and many similar questions have plagued religious faiths from the beginnings of time. Christianity has attempted answers, often called doctrine or dogma, and has usually failed to come up with answers which have convinced the entire Christian community, or have stood the challenges of time. And always within that struggle for definitive answers have been minority voices that have questioned whether Christianity could provide answers that would satisfy everyone in the whole world—indeed, whether God was ever willing to limit God's freedom by entrusting all revelation to only one human type or system of ideation.

II. Models of Covenant

The history of these embarrassing challenges lies in the Jewish scriptures (the Old Testament). In Exodus 3:14, Moses asks God to reveal the divine name to him; God replies: "I Am that I Am." Theologian Martin Buber has pointed out that the Hebrew word for "that"—*asher*—means "whatever."[3] In other words, God's earliest self-revelation to Moses includes the implication that God will not allow himself to be limited to any specific revelation, but "will be whatever God wishes to be." Exodus 33:19 contains a similar insistence by God proclaiming unlimited freedom. There Moses tries to convince God to let him have a peek at God's physical form. God refuses, offering instead to let Moses know God's goodness, answering: "I will be gracious to whom (*asher*) I shall be gracious, and I shall have compassion on whom (*asher*) I shall have compassion." God refuses to limit himself to human rules of fairness, or human demands to gain power over God by limiting where or how God can operate. God's self-definition includes both unpredictability and uncontainability.

These two passages from Exodus should not be understood as a rejection of the human need for security. God clearly wishes to enter into some particular kind of relationship with Moses, usually referred to as a "covenant." Covenants in the Bible are difficult to describe, but many of them have certain characteristics in common: they are initiated by God, they have a promise and a sign attached to them, and there is little sense that they are dependent upon a specific human response for them to retain their validity.[4] Theologian Donald Dawe has suggested that the covenants in the Jewish scriptures are particularizations within the larger covenant which God makes with Noah in Genesis 9:15—that God loves all of humanity so much that God will never again destroy people, no matter what they do.[5] It is within this larger permanent universal covenant that God offers the special covenant to Abraham and his descendants (Gen 15 and 17): a more particular covenant within the context of a broader covenant. Within that particularized Abrahamic covenant, we might understand two "sub-covenants" which are even more particular: the covenant of Moses at Sinai (Exodus 19 through 24; Deuteronomy 5 through 7), and the covenant of Christ on the cross.

This is, of course, only one way to look at the complicated subject of covenant. Many other models have been offered, though mostly by Jewish or Christian thinkers, since these are the two world religions that concentrate so heavily on theology of covenant. According to the multi-covenant theory, God has made a number of covenants with those whom God has chosen, including covenants with Noah, Abraham, Isaac, Jacob, David, and Jesus. None of these covenants precludes or replaces any earlier one. Rather, each covenant is offered and accepted in specific times and places for specific purposes. This multi-covenant theory has been set forth by both Christian and Jewish theologians, including Father Maurice Gilbert, S.J. and Rabbi Irving Greenberg. Other theologians, both Jewish and Christian, hold that there are two separate but completely equal covenants. For example, Coert Rylaarsdam would argue that the two covenants—which he terms the covenant with Israel and the covenant with David, or mutual pact vs. eschatology—run in constant tension through both the Hebrew scriptures (the more accurate and respectful name for what Christians sometimes call the Old Testament) and the New Testament (those various books ultimately accepted by Christians as most accurately conveying the faith and memory of the first followers of Jesus). Anglican theologian James Parkes sees a dual covenant of "Sinai and Calvary"—the community vs. the individual—at work in both Testaments. A more traditional division is held by others: that the covenant with the Jewish people and the covenant with the Christian people are separate covenants, intended for each specific group, and that since each is valid only for a particular group, the two covenants are neither interchangeable nor competitive. Among those holding such a position is the Yale historian Jaroslav Pelikan.[6]

A third group of theologians holds that God has made a single covenant, first with the Jewish people, which was then expanded to include the Gentiles without jeopardizing the priority of the Jews. Biblical support for this position has often come from Paul's epistle to the Romans, especially chapters 9–11, in which he speaks of Christianity being "grafted" on to Judaism, branch to root. A recently-emerging model of single-covenant theology, most notably in the writings of Anglican and Roman Catholic theologians, such as Paul van Buren and John Pawlikowski, relies less on Paul's letter to the Romans and more on the promises to Abraham in Genesis 12, 17, and 22. In Genesis the original covenant between God and Abraham is worded in such a way as to imply that from the beginning God intended the covenant with the Jewish people to be expanded to include the Gentiles.

Contemporary Jewish theologian Michael Wyschogrod has pointed out how our natural human tendency is to compete for a parent's love, hoping that we are each loved more than our siblings. Covenant perceptions, then, tend to be competitive. Wyschogrod points out that consuming relationships with God do not necessarily proceed according to our limited human logic. When we truly encounter God, "nothing can be controlled, no certainty of result can be preordained." He continues:

> The election of Israel is thus a sign of the humanity of God. Had [God] so willed it, [God] could have played a more godly role, refusing favorites and loving all his creatures impartially. [God's] love would then have been a far less vulnerable one because impartiality signifies a certain remoteness, the absence of that consuming passion that is a sign of need of the other. . . . Those not elected cannot be expected not to be hurt by not being of the seed of Abraham, whom God loves above all others. The Bible depicts clearly the sufferings of Esau. . . . The consolation of the gentiles is the knowledge that God also stands in relationship with them in the recognition and affirmation of their uniqueness. The choice, after all, is between a lofty divine love equally distributed to all without recognition of uniqueness, and real en-

counter, which necessarily involves favorites but in which each is unique and addressed as such.[7]

III. Taming God's Truth

The point is that we all have the human tendency to look at God through our particular covenantal relationship, and forget that our own covenant is part of a larger covenant promised by God to all of creation. A critical condition of this larger covenant is that God remains free to do as God wills, rather than as we will. Some theologians have used the metaphor of a telescope. The great nineteenth century American preacher Phillips Brooks applied the same metaphor to the scriptural truth: The Bible is like a telescope. If one looks through the telescope, then one sees worlds beyond; but if one looks at the telescope, then one does not see anything but that. The Bible is a thing to be looked through, to see that which is beyond, but most people only look at it; and so they see only the dead letter.[8] If we look at our own covenant, it will always appear to be the supreme manifestation of truth. If we look through our own covenant, we see that it is too small to contain all of God's truth. Our own covenant is without doubt a particularly important incarnation of truth, but it does not define or limit truth.

Perhaps this untameability of God's truth is the point of the biblical account of the tower of Babel (Gen 11:1–9)—our human temptation to create a monolithic vehicle that will contain all truth and all revelation is doomed to failure, because it contradicts the rich variety which God has built into creation from its inception. Indeed, such diversity is of itself characteristic of God's endless creative potential.

God's radical insistence on freedom to be in charge of creation, and therefore also the distribution throughout the world of God's own truth, is reflected in the New Testament as well. The parable of the laborers in the vineyard (Mt 20:1–15) is often understood as an allegory for the relationship between God and creation.[9] In that parable, the owner of a vineyard hires a group of workers early in the morning, some more at mid-day, and some more at the end of the day. When the time comes for the workers to receive their day's wages, the owner of the vineyard pays each person the same, no matter how many hours during the day each had worked. The

laborers who worked the entire day complain: should they
not get more for their work during the long hot daytime hours
than those who worked only a few hours in the cool of dusk?
To their angry and self-protective challenge, the owner of the
vineyard replies: "Surely I am free to do what I like with my
own money? Why be jealous because I am generous?" This
teaching of Jesus not only echoes the freedom of God suggested in the above analysis of Exodus 3:14 and 33:19, but
also reminds its hearers of the words of the prophet Isaiah
(55:8): "My thoughts are not your thoughts, and neither are
your ways my ways, says the Lord."

The existence of God's truth outside of any particular covenant or specific revelation is not the only issue at hand here.
Even those Christians who have been willing to admit that
God's truth cannot be contained by the Christian revelation
alone have still raised the question of whether salvation is
possible outside of Christianity. Supported by a literal reading of John 14:6, "I am the way, the truth and the life; no one
comes to the Father but by me," many Christians have argued that while God's truth may be available outside Christianity, God's truth is not of itself sufficient unto salvation,
for only Christ can offer salvation. Alternatively, God's truth
is available outside Christianity in part, but salvation is possible only with the fullest truth as revealed in Christ. However,
we must always be careful not to fall into the trap of arguing
one part of the Bible against another. The Bible speaks simultaneously with many voices, and all of them are understood
by Christianity as the one voice of God. To claim that one
biblical opinion is true and another is not is to run the danger
of listening only to God's voice when we like what is being
said. The point here is to remember that God's voice has not
spoken as definitively or finally on the subjects of revelation
and salvation as many Christian exclusivists are tempted
to claim.

The moral of the parable of the laborers in the vineyard,
then, appears to argue against exclusivist claims of salvation
in Christ. God will decide who is worthy of salvation, whether
within the Christian revelation or not. This alternative interpretation is further supported by Matthew 25:31–46, in
which salvation is not dependent upon faith in Christ, but
upon whether or not a person has been attentive to issues of
social justice. Another expression of support is contained in

Romans 10:18–11:36, in which Paul delivers his most mature thinking considering salvation, without connecting the salvation of the Jews with faith in Christ, but rather assuming that their salvation is the logical outcome of the promises given to their forebears.

Much of the discussion of both Christianity and paganism in relation to rabbinic Judaism falls into the categories of "idolatry" or "heresy."[10] The boundaries of Jewish communal identity appeared at times fluid, and at times more restricted. On the one hand, Christianity is often condemned in rabbinic documents as a perverse violation of God's will for humankind and a tragic misunderstanding of the scriptural heritage; on the other hand, the Babylonian *Talmud*, redacted c. 500 C.E. (common era, or the entire period of history in which Christianity flourished alongside Judaism), could also claim in *Tractate Megillah* 13a: "Anyone who repudiates idolatry is called a Jew," and righteous Gentiles would be guaranteed a place in the world to come. As well, varieties of religious experience and perception were recognized as being within the sphere of orthodoxy. According to the Babylonian *Talmud, Tractate Yoma* 74b–75a, at Sinai each person tasted the manna according to his or her individual perception. Torah (in its larger definition including scripture, commentary, and tradition) was the primary vehicle for God's revelation, but that revelation contained expectations for non-Jewish behavior as well. Thus the salvation of those outside Judaism was provided for, as long as their behavior conformed to the stipulations of the developing torah. But in general, as the power of Christianity increased, even to demanding censorship of rabbinic texts, Judaism was in such an increasingly precarious position that it could not always speak frankly of its own understanding of the role—positive or negative—of non-Jews within the larger scheme of God's truth.

IV. Church Fathers and God's Activity

Origen is among the most important formative thinkers of the early church, often referred to as the patristic period. Born in Alexandria, Egypt, in about 185 C.E., he was a deeply spiritual man, a skillful preacher, and a prolific writer. In his commentary on the gospel of John (1:39), he speaks of all creation as being infused with the *logos spermatikos,* that is, the seminal Word of God, most often identified in Christian tradition with Jesus (see Jn 1:14–17). In other words, for Origen, truth existed outside of Christianity—indeed spread throughout all creation—but even when that truth was discovered outside of Christianity, it was still Christian in character, for all truth is synonymous with God's pre-existent Logos, most fully expressed in the incarnation (God's voluntary assumption of human form). But though truth was available outside Christianity, salvation was not. Origen (*In Jesu Nave* 3, 5) and his contemporary Cyprian (c. 300) are generally identified as the authors of the famous dictum "outside the church, there is no salvation." Once this later doctrine was formulated, it exerted a significant influence on the continuing development of Christian thought, at least until the mid-twentieth century.

Two hundred years later, Augustine of Hippo (354–430), theologian and biblical exegete, was somewhat more generous in his judgment. For him, God's revelation was of one piece, existing "from the very beginning of humankind" (though the truest form of it was Christianity!) and the "saving grace of this religion . . . has never been refused to anyone who was worthy of it" (*Retractationes,* 1, 13, 3; *Epistola* 102, 2). According to Augustine's *Confessions* (Chapter 12), although the most comprehensive form of truth might be Christianity, truth could be neither limited to the Bible nor limited by the Bible, and truth always bore with it the possibility of salvation. In other words, Augustine remained aware of the availability of salvation outside of Christianity, though he ultimately understood salvation as God's place to determine freely, and not the church's. In his treatise *On Christian Doctrine* (2.40.60 and 2.18.2), he does not consider the influence of Greek philosophers and rhetoricians as a hindrance to his search for truth; rather he sees the Greek classical disciplines as a valuable vehicle for God's revelation in the non-Christian world. Out of deep respect for his own classical education, Augustine seems to suggest that educated Hellenists (i.e. the Greeks and Romans of the classical world) are already included within the company of saints. Augustine is convinced that wherever he might find truth, there he has found God and God's people.

Both Origen and Augustine were significantly influenced

by the same two dilemmas which have reemerged for us in our contemporary pluralistic society: how could they claim the ultimacy of the Christian revelation and still respect the truth of their secular studies, and how could a truly loving God ordain such an exclusive system of faith that it would deny salvation to the large numbers of people in the world who could not or would not hear of Jesus Christ?

V. The Medieval and Reformation Periods

The question of salvation outside of Christianity is not of particular interest to the great shaper of scholastic Roman Catholicism, Thomas Aquinas (1225–1274). In general, his theology should be categorized as "creationist"—that is, concerned with God's identity and God's relationship to humanity—rather than "redemptionist"—that is, concerned with the work of Christ. In his massive systematization of theology, the *Summa Theologica,* Aquinas develops so many themes that upon occasion they seem contradictory. His universe is tidy and hierarchical, and filled to overflowing with God's love. In discussing Jews and Judaism, Aquinas grants them special status within God's effective revelation of truth, and asserts that through *halakhah* (Jewish "legal" observance), they have acquired a special character of holiness.[11] Above all, Aquinas asserts that God hates nothing that has been created, wills the good of every person, and desires that no one be excluded from salvation. Truth cannot be separated from God, and creation cannot be separated from God, and therefore truth cannot be separated from creation. While recognizing that there is truth outside of Christianity (Adam and Eve and the patriarchs understood the basic tenets of Christianity, even though they lived before the revelation in Christ), he adapts Augustine's argument that all truth is a reflection of God's Logos, so that truth outside of Christianity is still of the mind of Christ the Logos. For Augustine, as for his predecessors, the institutionalized religion of Christianity is often too limited to contain God's fullest self-revelation.

One significant influence upon Aquinas was the Jewish philosopher, physician and theologian Maimonides (1135–1204). In the course of developing his own foundational approach to Jewish thought, Maimonides wrote of the relationship between Christianity and Judaism, holding forth three somewhat conflicting opinions about the value of Christianity within the larger scheme of salvation as Judaism understood it: (a) that Christianity is an evil system designed to destroy all but itself; (b) that Christianity is a form of idolatry, based on a mistaken anthropomorphic ("humanizing") conception of God (as if God could have a Son!); or (c) that Christianity was a valid form of non-Jewish monotheism, by which love and respect for the God of Israel was carried to the nations of the world.[12] His later disciples, most notably Meiri and Rabbenu Tam, granted Christianity an even more respectable place by picking up on Maimonides's third argument, saying that Christianity was the logical expansion of the Seven Noahide Laws originally intended by God as a means for Gentile salvation.

Throughout much of the medieval period in Europe, the questions of truth and salvation outside of Christianity seem hardly to have been addressed. Membership in society was co-terminous with membership in the church, and since non-Christians had limited political rights, their concerns had limited theological authority. Jews and Muslims who lived in Christian countries were small enough in number or separated enough from church interests that few shapers of Christian thought concerned themselves with the ultimate disposition of non-Christians.[13] On the occasions when Christianity did encounter another faith system, it often was extremely cruel to those non-Christian adherents, unless their faith could be "raided" to satisfy some Christian need. This utilitarian approach explains how the church hierarchy of the period could turn a blind eye to popular persecution of Jews, and yet the theologians and academicians of the church could study openly with brilliant Jewish teachers, or could search rabbinic writings for insight.[14] Surely, these Christian theologians assumed, whatever truth lay outside of Christianity was there only for the ultimate purpose of serving and justifying the accuracy of Christian exclusivist claims.

It may be claimed that the reformation was so obsessed with whether the various emerging types of Christians could each be saved that there was little energy left over to worry about the salvation of non-Christians. One of the great shapers of reformation theology was Martin Luther (1483–1546) of Germany. In a now-notorious development, Luther

was convinced that with his challenge to Roman Catholicism, Jews would at last be attracted to Christianity and join
him in his struggle toward the reformation of certain abuses
within popular Catholic piety. When he discovered that his
reforms were not attracting mass conversions by Jews, he
turned on them in disillusionment, and wrote a bitter anti-
Jewish diatribe now contained in his collection entitled *Table Talk*. The foundational cry of Lutheran theology, beginning with the reformation, has been "Justification by faith,"
a slogan often understood as a disclaimer of "legalistic" religion including Judaism. Of course such justification by faith
was available only through Christ, for Christ was God's gift of
grace to fallen humanity. But Luther's theology is not narrow
or rigid as it is sometimes portrayed in the popular mind.
Theologian Paul Althaus has summarized Luther's more mature thinking by citing Luther's own distinction that Christ is
the "effective" expression of God's will, but not the "exhaus-
tive" expression of God's will. For, as Althaus points out,
Luther believed that God's word is not identical to the totality
of God; in addition to the received revelation, God retains
complete freedom over everything. God does many things
that are not necessarily shown us through God's word. God
also wills into being many things that transcend the limitations of our human perception of God's word.[15]

With the ages of rationalism and enlightenment, some of
the same questions of the patristic period reemerged. As the
printing press made knowledge widely available, as explorers
brought back more and more stories of foreign societies, and
as the Copernican revolution challenged the church's grasp
on infallible revelation, Christianity could no longer ignore
that the world was populated by so many non-Christians.
One of the most sophisticated English-language theologians
of the sixteenth century was Richard Hooker, at first a university lecturer, but for most of his life the minister of a local
congregation. For Hooker, God was the author of natural law,
and nothing which God authored could be devoid of God's
truth. This meant that sufficient truth was available to humanity outside of Christianity, often simply through the ordered beauty of creation, God's perfect handiwork, but as
well through the natural sciences. In his most famous book,
Treatise on the Laws of Ecclesiastical Polity, Hooker wrote:

There is in the world no kinde of knowledge, whereby any part of truth is seene, but we justlie accompt it pretious, yea that principall truth, in comparison whereof all other knowledge is vile, may receive from it some kinde of light. Whether it be that Egyptian and Chaldaean wisedom Mathematicall, wherewith Moses and Daniell were furnished; or that naturall, morall, and civill wisdom, wherein Salomon excelled all men; or that rationall and oratoriall wisedom of the Graecians, which the Apostle Saint Paule brought from Tarsus; or that Judaicall, which he learned in Jerusalem sitting at the feet of Gamaliell, to detract from the dignitie thereof, were to injurie even God himselfe, who being that light which none can approch unto, hath sent out these lights wherof we are capable, even as so many sparkls resembling the bright fountain from which they rise.[16]

Through his eloquent prose, we learn that Hooker found undeniable sources of truth variously in Christianity, mathematics, philosophy, law, and other such revelations to non-Christian minds.

Hooker also argued that the intention of the church was to teach a doctrine of inclusivity, rather than promote an exclusive society of the pure or the elect. Because of God's limitlessness and gracious generosity, salvation was too powerful to be contained within Christianity alone. Any Christian who said to any other creature or person within creation "I need thee not" had usurped God's self-willed power to determine the inter-relatedness of the whole world, and thus the salvation of its entirety.[17] His contemporary, the philosopher John Locke (1632–1704), argued in his *Letter on Toleration* that the true church can be found only where there is tolerance, including religious freedom for non-Christians.[18]

VI. The Twentieth Century

No century has been more aware of religious pluralism and the multiplexity of God's revelation than our own. As has been observed, "Pluralism is the sociological 'blessing' of the late 20th century, a true providential novum in which old

forces of domination are collapsing."[19] Christians are suddenly aware that hatred from one religious group to another
produces terror, destruction, and death. Rapidity of change
has called into question the function of tradition within religious faith. Mass media have brought the horrors of religious wars in Northern Ireland, Pakistan, and Lebanon into
our living rooms. In an increasingly mobile world, we no
longer speak of Islam as an abstract non-Christian faith; we
must talk instead of the flesh-and-blood Muslim who lives
next door to us. And perhaps above all, the atrocities of the
holocaust have raised new questions about the relationship
between God and exclusive claims to truth and salvation.
Some Christians have even become aware of ways in which
Christian exclusivist theological language was used to justify
the mass murders of Nazi Germany.

Raul Hilberg, historian of the *shoah* (holocaust), points
out that in its early conversionary zeal the church was quick
to say to the Jewish people: "You cannot live among us as
Jews." The continuing presence among those early Christians of a religion that refused to recognize Jesus as messiah
was threatening, and religious pluralism was perceived as
inherently opposed to the Christian missionary imperative.
In the medieval period, beginning particularly in 1492 with
the expulsion of Jews from Spain, the church could justify its
continuing fear of Judaism simply by shortening the previous
sentence, to "You cannot live among us." In Germany of the
1930s, the sentence could be shortened once again—"You
cannot live"—in justification of Hitler's program.[20] In this
manner, Hilberg would trace the roots of Christian complicity
in the *shoah* to Christianity's early missionary imperative
which assumed that all humanity was so enslaved in sin that
it could only be rescued unto salvation through the Christian
message.

Brave new theological voices have begun to be heard in
our century, calling into question certain unexamined assumptions by offering generous and more gracious interpretations of humanity's relationship with the loving God. In
general, the positions of contemporary Christian theologians
can be divided into three: exclusivist, the traditional Christian position which holds that the only path to God is through
Jesus Christ; inclusivist, the mediating position, which holds
that truth is available outside Christianity, though salvation

is not; and pluralist, an emerging position becoming more widely held, which is exploring new theological ground in order to affirm that God can be reached adequately by more than one way.

One of the contemporary voices most respectful of "otherness" was Jewish theologian Martin Buber (1878–1965). In his important book *I and Thou,* he argues that humanity cannot know God, who has created us first by calling us "thou," until we learn to say "thou" back to God, rather than "it." Similarly, no human relationship is truly reflective of the divine character, or even of God's vision for human character, unless it contains the mutual dignity of each person calling the other "thou," rather than he, she, or it. All ways in which we name each other, label each other, define or judge each other, and determine the "place" of another in order to serve our own needs, destroys the "thou" in which we find the presence of God. As Buber wrote, ". . . the separated *It* of institutions is an animated clod without soul, and the separated *I* of feelings an uneasily fluttering soul-bird. Neither of them knows [personhood]: institutions know only the specimen, feelings only the 'object'; neither knows the person, or mutual life. Neither of them knows the present: even the most up-to-date institutions know only the lifeless past that is over and done with, and even the most lasting feelings know only the flitting moment that has not yet come properly into being. Neither of them has access to real life. Institutions yield no public life, and feelings no personal life."[21]

In Buber's thought, to approach another person without the prior assumption that he or she is as equally worthy or assured of God's love and salvation as we are is to fail ever to know that person, but only to make that person into an object for our personal self-service or self-exaltation. Indeed, one could question how any person could be addressed as "thou" were it presumed that he or she were already outside the pale of salvation. How can I "love my neighbor as myself" if I do not help create a space wherein my neighbor, in all his or her particularity, can stand together with me in God's presence?

Buber's book has had an immeasurable influence not only on theology, but on psychology and philosophy as well. Unfortunately, his influence was not sufficient to prevent the Nazi war machine's murder of twelve million people, each an *it* in the eyes of the powers of darkness. (As Ernst Troeltsch deduced: when my way is the only way, your way becomes fair game for my weapons of exploitation or dominance.[22]) In more recent times, a whole school called relationship theology has developed, drawing heavily on Buber's theories.

Another critical voice in twentieth century theology is that of Paul Tillich (1886–1965). Son of a Lutheran pastor, Tillich was born in Germany, and he emigrated to New York at the outbreak of World War II. In his foundational work entitled *Systematic Theology*, he argues that the "spiritual presence" pervades every world religion, though to varying degrees. God's revelation is a kind of "ground of being" out of which spring the particular manifestations of God within particularized cultural and historical contexts. Wherever this grounding "presence" is found, no matter the form or content of the world religion, there is also the opportunity for the re-creation of each person as a "new being," and each new being has available the possibility of salvation, because he or she now is a product of God.[23] Since every new being reflects a springing forth of God's revelation, for the fullness of that revelation to be known, humanity has to be in dialogue, each with the other. Tillich insisted that for partners of two religions to understand and talk to each other, they had to enter that dialogue respecting the values of both systems equally as "real" revelations of God.[24] The "demonic element" in any religion is that which seeks to make itself and its creeds, codes, and cults more important than the revelation and experience it is meant to serve, a judgment closely related to the earlier writings of Immanuel Kant and Arnold Toynbee.[25] The ultimate purpose of each and every world religion is to point its adherents toward the true "spiritual presence," rather than to the externals of the religion itself. This same call "to replace ecclesiocentrism with theocentrism" is typical of many contemporary theologians, including the later writings of Hans Küng.[26]

Though approximately contemporaneous with Tillich, Karl Barth (1886–1968) developed a more conservative, evangelical approach to the Christian faith. "Let God be God" is often identified as the underlying theme for his entire corpus of writings. The *shoah* was a turning point in the theology of Barth. Prior to the war, his theological position concerning Judaism had shown a significant tension, and on occasion he reverted to an understanding of Judaism as the darkness necessary in the world so that the illumination of Christ might appear to shine even brighter.[27] On this basis he could oppose the Nazi genocide, but for reasons which made non-Christians valued only insofar as they served to prove the truth of Christianity. Following the war, and once aware of the horrors of the Nazi holocaust and its Christian theological justifications, he changed his position radically, and wrote with intensity of Christianity's obligation to protect Jews and Judaism from any sense of obliteration for their own sake, rather than Christianity's. In his most mature work, Barth struggled through an analysis of the epistle to the Romans, including those passages in chapters 9–11 which use the metaphor of an olive tree and an engrafted wild branch to describe Christianity's relationship with its parent, Judaism. In another moving essay, he concluded: "Without any doubt the Jews are to this very day the chosen people of God in the same sense as they have been so from the beginning, according to the Old and New Testaments. They have the promise of God; and if we Christians from among the Gentiles have it too, then it is only as those chosen with them, as guests in their house, as new wood grafted on to their old tree."[28]

Though Barth himself never says so overtly, the implication in his later work is that Christianity could not continue to exist if Judaism as a living world religion were to disappear, just as no engrafted branch could live once the rootstock were dead. But by way of the root/branch metaphor, Barth's mature theology suggests an interdependence of Christians and Jews, which would mean that if Christianity's traditional goal to convert all the people of the world were ever to be achieved, Christianity would then itself die from asphyxiation. In his *Church Dogmatics*, he argues a complicated syllogism which affirms the possibility of salvation outside of Christianity:

(a) God is known only where God's word exists.
(b) God is known outside Christianity.
Hence,
(c) God's word exists outside Christianity.
(d) Jesus Christ is the one word of God.
(e) Jesus Christ is God's word of salvation.
Hence,

(f) God's one word is the word of salvation.
(c) God's word exists outside Christianity.
(f) God's one word is the word of salvation.
Hence,
(g) Salvation exists outside Christianity.[29]

Indeed, at a 1966 meeting of the Vatican Secretariat for Christian Unity, Barth summarized in his own words the growing Christian understanding that centuries of theological isolation and assumed superiority were drawing to a close: "There exist today many good relations between the Roman Catholic Church and many Protestant Churches, between the Secretariat for Christian Unity and the World Council of Churches; the number of ecumenical study groups and working groups is growing rapidly. The ecumenical movement is clearly driven by the Spirit of the Lord. But we should not forget that there is finally only one genuinely great ecumenical question: our relations with the Jewish people."[30]

A third Christian theologian of import in the mid-twentieth century was H. Richard Niebuhr (1894–1962), brother to the equally famous theologian Reinhold Niebuhr. As an American Protestant, Niebuhr was confronted at an early age by the religious pluralism that has always been such a cherished value in our country. Perhaps because his theology was so shaped by the unique dynamism of the American religious experience, he held that Christianity must itself be always in a continuous process of conversion, in the midst of a continuous state of revolution. Niebuhr justified his foundational theological argument by citing the constant new hope for tomorrow which the resurrection promises. Any faith which feared change also feared resurrection; a faith which looked solely to the past and tradition ("we've always done it that way"), rather than remaining open to the newness of the future, could not claim itself as Christian. But commitment to change is not enough in itself: the Christian must also be ready to let go, and to trust God to be in control. The revelation of God is not ours to possess; Christians are called only to constant repentance and conversion, but not to judgment or control of others, for in respect to Jesus Christ, "we live not before or after, but in the midst of a revolution."[31] Niebuhr's theories suggest an interesting correlation to the process theologies, as developed by Alfred North Whitehead, Karl Rahner, Norman Pittenger, and Schubert Ogden.

One of the most important contemporary theologians to have devoted his recent work almost exclusively to religious pluralism is Paul van Buren. In the past decade, van Buren has completed a three-volume systematic theology based on what he calls "the Jewish-Christian Reality."[32] Taking the holocaust extremely seriously, van Buren has attempted to find a way to speak of God, from within the Christian tradition, in a manner that does not belittle or do violence to other religious traditions, particularly to Judaism.[33] Van Buren's metaphor for pluralism, reminiscent of another contemporary Christian theologian of pluralism, Raimundo Panikkar,[34] is that we are all journeying to God along a broad path. (Panikkar uses the image of a mountain peak which can be reached by many different trails.) Along the way we meet others who are on the same journey, but for whom the path behind and before may not exactly match ours. We assist and support each other along the way if we are willing to share with each other where we have been and what we believe yet to lie before us. In such sharing, each of us is strengthened and enabled to find God more easily.[35] Since sharing includes telling our stories of faith, the foundational principles of van Buren's theology are quite compatible with recent developments in story or narrative theology.

VII. Church Documents

Christian theologians are not alone in having made critical strides in our century. Official church documents, now representing several of America's largest Christian denominations, have established a sensitivity to God's truth and salvation outside of Christianity as official church policy. At least four major American denominations—the Roman Catholic Church, the United Church of Christ, the Episcopal Church, and the Disciples of Christ—have official denominational policy statements on the relationship between Judaism and Christianity, and a fifth—the Presbyterian Church USA—has such a policy pending further study.

The Second Vatican Council, in 1965, issued a document called *Nostra Aetate,* as a part of the larger conciliar *Declara-*

tion on the Relationship of the Church to Non-Christian Religions. Included within *Nostra Aetate* was the now famous statement ". . . God holds the Jews most dear for the sake of their forebears; God does not repent of the gifts he makes or of the calls he issues." The document draws to a close with this charge to the Catholic faithful throughout the world, including those who belong to the largest Christian denomination in the United States: ". . . this sacred synod wants to foster and recommend that *mutual understanding and respect* which is the fruit, above all, of biblical and theological studies as well as of fraternal dialogues."[36] Other documents of Vatican II reassert the basic theological assumption that Christians do not carry God's grace anywhere in the world, but rather that God is present everywhere already, waiting simply to be discovered. This dogma is usually referred to as "prevenient grace."[37]

In 1987, the General Synod of the United Church of Christ, America's eleventh largest denomination, passed into policy the following statement: ". . . the United Church of Christ . . . affirms its recognition that God's covenant with the Jewish people has not been rescinded or abrogated by God, but remains in full force, inasmuch as 'the gifts and promise of God are irrevocable' (Rom 11:29)."[38] One year later, in 1988, the General Convention of the Episcopal Church legislated an official policy on its relation with Judaism. Beginning by quoting a previous resolution which affirmed that ". . . the Jews remain precious to God for the sake of the patriarchs, since God does not withdraw the gifts he has bestowed or revoke the choices he has made (Romans 11:28–29),"[39] the policy statement continues:

> Christians believe that God's self-revelation is given in history. In the Covenant with the Jewish people at Mt. Sinai, the sacred law became part of our religious heritage. Christians see that same God embodied in the person of Jesus Christ, to whom the Church must bear witness by word and deed. It would be false to its deepest commitment if the Church were to deny this mission. The Christian witness toward Jews, however, has been distorted by coercive proselytism, conscious and unconscious, overt and subtle. The Joint Working Group of the Roman Catholic Church

and the World Council of Churches has stated: "Proselytism embraces whatever violates the right of the human person, Christian or non-Christian, to be free from external coercion in religious matters." Dialogue can rightly be described as a mutual witness, for witness is a sharing of one's faith conviction without the intention of proselytizing. . . .[40]

In 1989 the Disciples of Christ, America's fifteenth largest denomination, at its General Assembly adopted a resolution which declared that ". . . God's covenant with the Jewish people has not been broken, and God has not rejected God's people. Judaism is a living witness to God's continuing dealings with humanity."[41] A fifth denomination, the Presbyterian Church USA, introduced a resolution at its General Assembly 1987 which includes the following declaration: "We affirm that both the church and the Jewish people are elected by God for witness to the world and that the relationship of the church to contemporary Jews is based on that gracious and irrevocable election of both. . . . Hence, when speaking with Jews about matters of faith, we must always acknowledge that Jews are already in a covenantal relationship with God."[42] This resolution has not yet been passed by the General Assembly of the Presbyterian Church USA, but is under further study.

What the statements of these five denominations, representing approximately sixty-two million American Christians, have in common is that they all affirm that nothing has happened in history to negate, abrogate, break, or even threaten God's continuing covenanted relationship with the Jewish people. These official denominational documents do not suggest that the covenanted relationship between God and the Jewish people is deficient, or needs fulfillment or completion. They all assert Christianity's belief in the saving power of Christ, and hold that in some way the function of Christ in relationship to Judaism remains for us "a mystery."[43] They reject, either implicitly or explicitly, any coercive, devious, or manipulative attempts to convert Jews to Christianity, calling instead for a dialogic relationship between equal partners in one covenanted relationship with God. Dialogue demands ultimate respect from one partner to the other, and as well demands that each partner be vulnerable enough to the other's revelation that neither will emerge from the dialogue without their own faiths both affirmed and created anew.

VIII. Conclusion

A repeated theme of this essay has been Christianity's search to find ways of speaking of God that do not limit God to the boxes of human language and perception. Anthropomorphism, or picturing God as though endowed with a human body and as acting and feeling like a human being, is generally discouraged in most contemporary theologies as an example of the ways in which our human perceptions cause us to miss the richness of God's self-disclosure by confusing God with ourselves. Yet anthropomorphism is part of both the Jewish and Christian traditions, and as long as we understand it as metaphorical rather than real, it can still prove useful. Such a useful metaphor comes from within rabbinic tradition, and dates from the literature of the period between the Hebrew scriptures and the New Testament. In the intertestamental Book of Enoch, in the Babylonian *Talmud*, Tractate, and elsewhere, we find the torah described as being one true revelation with "70 faces."[44] Perhaps we might be so bold as to speak of God in the same manner.

Of course there is only one God. Christianity, Judaism, and Islam, as well as certain movements within other world religions, recognize this to be the case. But we seem to perceive God in so many different or even competitive ways that sometimes we lose sight of God's one-ness. Perhaps the image of God as having one face, which due to our human limitations appears in seventy different manners, is helpful for us. To some God's face is black, to others yellow, to others brown, red, or white. To some God's face looks female, to others male. To some God looks young and ever-changing, to others God looks elderly and wise with tradition. To some God looks like a story-teller, to others God looks lovingly authoritarian. The one God with seventy faces is always only one, and yet always looks different to the wide variety of humanity. But no matter how different God may look to me than to my neighbor, God is still one, and it is ultimately that one God whom we all seek. If we understand that the one God loves all and desires the salvation of every human being, then perhaps we can stop competing and start listening to each other. If we understand that no matter how different God's face may seem to me or to you, that each one of God's faces is true because God is one, then perhaps we can begin to grasp that God is larger than any human system yet devised, and that only when we cherish each individual revelation of the nature of God can all the pieces be put together to give us a hazy glimpse of God's majesty. When each piece is equally important, then my defense of Christian revelation is just as important as my neighbor's defense of his or her revelation. All are part of the truth, and each may prove a path to salvation.

NOTES

[1]Samuel Taylor Coleridge (1772–1834), *Aids to Reflection: Moral and Religious Aphorisms XXV.*

[2]David Jenkins, *The Contradiction of Christianity* (London: SCM, 1976).

[3]Martin Buber, *The Prophetic Faith* (New York: Macmillan, 1949), p. 164.

[4]See Philip Culbertson, "New Christian Theologies of Covenant," *The Reconstructionist* 51 (1985): 15–19, 32.

[5]Donald G. Dawe, "Christian Faith in a Religiously Plural World," in *Christian Faith in a Religiously Plural World,* edited by Donald G. Dawe and John B. Carmen (Maryknoll: Orbis, 1978), pp. 19–20.

[6]Jaroslav Pelikan, *Jesus Through the Centuries* (New Haven: Yale University Press, 1985), pp. 14, 19.

[7]Michael Wyschogrod, *The Body of Faith: Judaism as Corporeal Election* (New York: Seabury, 1983), pp. 62–64. Uniqueness does not insist upon exclusivity; see John Hick, *God and the Universe of Faiths* (New York: St. Martin's Press, 1973), pp. 113–14.

[8]Phillips Brooks, as quoted in Frederick Houk Borsch, ed., *Anglicanism and the Bible* (Wilton: Morehouse Barlow, 1984), p. 222.

[9]Rabbinic tradition ordinarily rejects the interpretation of parables as allegories, though Christianity, under the influence of Hellenism, has a long tradition of interpreting sacred texts allegorically. It can be claimed that an allegorical interpretation of any parable of Jesus is a violation of the spirit in which it was taught. See Moses Maimonides, *Guide of the*

Perplexed, 6b–7a, in Shelomo Pines, ed. (Chicago: University of Chicago Press, 1963), pp. 11–12. See also Philip Culbertson, "Reclaiming the Matthean Vineyard Parables," *Encounter* 49 (1988): 257–83.

[10]See the various essays in *To See Ourselves as Others See Us: Christians, Jews, "Others" in Late Antiquity,* edited by Jacob Neusner and Ernest S. Frerichs (Chico: Scholars Press, 1985), esp. chapter 10.

[11]Thomas Aquinas, *Summa* I-II, q. 98, art. 5. In general, questions 98–107 develop his respectful arguments concerning the value of God's revelation to the Jewish people. At II-II, q. 10, art. 12 he argues that the forced baptism by Christians of Jewish children is a violation both of the Christian faith and of natural justice.

[12]See David Novak, *Jewish-Christian Dialogue: A Jewish Justification* (New York: Oxford University Press, 1989), pp. 9ff, 66–68.; David Burrell, *Knowing the Unknowable God: Ibn-Sina, Maimonides, Aquinas* (Notre Dame: University of Notre Dame Press, 1986); and David Hartman, *Maimonides: Torah and Philosophic Quest* (Philadelphia: Jewish Publication Society, 1976).

[13]See Jacob Katz, *Exclusiveness and Tolerance: Studies in Jewish-Gentile Relations in Medieval and Modern Times* (New York: Behrman House, 1961).

[14]For examples, see Frank E. Talmage, *Disputation and Dialogue* (New York: Ktav, 1975), and also Pinchas Lapide, *Hebrew in the Church* (Grand Rapids: William B. Eerdmans, 1984).

[15]Paul Althaus, *The Theology of Martin Luther* (Philadelphia: Fortress, 1966), pp. 276–284, as cited in Peter A. Pettit, "Christ Alone, the Hidden God, and Lutheran Exclusivism," pending publication.

[16]Richard Hooker, "Laws of Ecclesiastical Polity III.8.9," in *Hooker's Works,* edited by John Keble, Seventh Edition (Oxford: At the Clarendon Press, 1888), I:370–71.

[17]Richard Hooker in *Hooker's Works,* III.617.

[18]John Locke, *Epistola de Tolerantia: A Letter on Toleration,* ed. by Raymond Klibansky, trans. by J.W. Gough (Oxford: At the Clarendon Press, 1968).

[19]Peter Gorday, "Raimundo Panikkar: Pluralism Without Relativism," *The Christian Century* 106 (1989): 1147.

[20]Raul Hilberg, *The Destruction of European Jews* (Chicago: Quadrangle, 1961), pp. 3–4. Robert McAfee Brown, in *Elie Wiesel: Messenger to All Humanity* (Notre Dame: University of Notre Dame Press, 1983) draws two conclusions from the holocaust: (1) that God is more concerned with how we treat human beings than with what we think about God, and (2) how we treat human beings will indicate what we think about God.

[21]Martin Buber, *I and Thou*, 2nd ed., trans. by Ronald Gregor Smith (New York: Scribner's Sons, 1923, 1958), p. 44.

[22]Ernst Troeltsch, *The Absoluteness of Christianity* (Richmond: John Knox, 1971), pp. 114–15.

[23]Paul Tillich, *Systematic Theology*, (New York: Harper and Row, 1951–63) vol. 1, pp. 160–62; vol. 2, pp. 191–94; vol. 3, pp. 148–50 and 254–56; also Tillich's *The Future of Religion*, edited by Jerald C. Brauer (New York: Harper and Row, 1966) p. 181.

[24]Paul Tillich, *Christianity and the Encounter with World Religions* (New York: Columbia University Press, 1963), pp. 62ff; see also "Missions and World History," in *The Theology of Christian Mission*, ed. by Gerald H. Anderson (Nashville: Abingdon, 1961), pp. 281–89. Edward Schillebeeckx, in *Christ: The Sacrament of Encounter with God*, trans. by Paul Barrett (New York: Sheed and Ward, 1963), p. 151, insists that Christian notions of salvation now need completion from Jewish sources: "Judaism has preserved certain key notions of human salvation that were blotted out in the Church after its split with the Synagogue."

[25]Immanuel Kant, *Religion within the Bounds of Pure Reason*, trans. by Theodore Greene and Hoyt Hudson (New York: Harper and Row, 1960), p. 108; Arnold Toynbee, *An Historian's Approach to Religion* (New York: Oxford University Press, 1956), pp. 264, 274–77.

[26]Hans Küng, *On Being a Christian*, trans. by Edward Quinn (Garden City: New York: Doubleday, 1976); also "The World Religions in God's Plan of Salvation," in *Christian Revelation and World Religions*, edited by Joseph Neuner (London: Burns and Oates, 1967), pp. 31–47. In *Does God Exist? An Answer for Today* (New York: Random House, 1978), pp. 627ff, he states forthrightly that salvation is available to Jews, without a belief in Christianity, because the God we

worship is one and the same. See also James Sanders, *From Sacred Story to Sacred Text* (Philadelphia: Fortress Press, 1987), especially chapter 9.

[27]See for example Barth's hair-raising arguments in *Church Dogmatics* (Edinburgh: T & T Clark, 1957) II, pp. 205–13, entitled "The Judgment and the Mercy of God." However, later in the same work (p. 286), he insists that even though Christianity has superseded Judaism, Christians must express constant humility in the face of Jews, who were first-chosen and remain elect.

[28]Karl Barth, *Against the Stream: Shorter Post-War Writings 1946–52* (London: SCM Press, 1954), pp. 199–200. A recently published collection of Barth's works suitable for beginning students of his theology is Clifford Green, *Karl Barth: Theologian of Freedom* (San Francisco: Harper and Row, 1990).

[29]Carl E. Braaten, "Salvation Through Christ Alone," *Lutheran Forum* 22 (1988): 10.

[30]*Freiburger Rundbriefe*, 27, 1976, cited in *Handreichung*, 39, 102, *Evangelische Kirche im Rheinland*.

[31]Richard Niebuhr, quoted in Carlyle Marney, "The Language of Revelation," *The St. Luke's Journal of Theology* 16 (1973): 17.

[32]Paul van Buren, *Discerning the Way: A Theology of the Jewish Christian Reality* (New York: Seabury, 1980); *A Christian Theology of the People Israel* (New York: Seabury, 1983); *Christ in Context* (San Francisco: Harper and Row, 1988).

[33]Among other Christian theologians who are working to develop a theology which will take the tremendum of the holocaust into serious account are Roy and Alice Eckardt, Michael McGarry, Franklin Littell, John Pawlikowski, Eugene Fisher, David Tracy, Peter von der Osten-Sacken, Clemens Thoma, Robert Everett, Clark Williamson, and Rebecca Chopp. Jewish theologians would include Richard Rubenstein, David Hartman, Michael Wyschogrod, Eliezer Berkovits, Shemaryahu Talmon, Eugene Borowitz, Irving Greenberg, Emil Fackenheim, and Arthur Cohen.

[34]See Raimundo Panikkar, *The Unknown Christ of Hinduism*, rev. ed., (Maryknoll: Orbis, 1981), p. 19, 24. The same image of "journey of faith" appears in Vatican II's *Lumen Gentium*, chapter 7. Two of the finest summaries of various

contemporary Christian theologies of religious pluralism are Paul Knitter, *No Other Name? A Critical Survey of Christian Attitudes toward the World Religions* (Maryknoll: Orbis, 1985); and David Tracy, *Plurality and Ambiguity: Hermeneutics, Religion and Hope* (San Francisco: Harper and Row, 1987).

[35]Paul van Buren, *Discerning the Way.* In his book *A History of Christian Missions* (Baltimore: Penguin, 1964), p. 456, Anglican theologian Stephen Neill affirms the position paper of the World Council of Church's Conference on Faith and Order, entitled "Rethinking Missions": "The task of the missionary today . . . should not be conversion—the drawing of members of one religious faith over into another or an attempt to establish a Christian monopoly. Cooperation is to replace aggression. The ultimate aim, so far as any can be described, is the emergence of the various religions out of their isolation into a world fellowship in which each will find its appropriate place."

[36]As found in *The Documents of Vatican II*, edited by Walter M. Abbott (New York: Guild Press, 1966), pp. 660ff.

[37]See Michael McGarry, "Interreligious Dialogue, Mission, and the Case of the Jews: A Response to Cardinal Josef Tomko," forthcoming in *Christian Mission and Interreligious Dialogue*, edited by Paul Mojzes; the same argument is found in Edward Schillebeeckx, *The Christ: The Experience of Jesus as Lord* (New York: Seabury, 1980), p. 646 and elsewhere; and Karl Rahner, *Theological Investigations*, vol. 5 (Baltimore: Helicon, 1966), pp. 115–34.

[38]See George Cornell, "2 denominations shedding abrasive view of Judaism," *AP Press Release*, July 18, 1987. See also Denise Dombkowski Hopkins, "God's Continuing Covenant with the Jews and the Christian Reading of the Bible," in *Prism* 3 (1988): 60–75.

[39]General Convention 1979 of the Episcopal Church, Resolution A-44.

[40]General Convention 1988, Resolution B-004a. This same understanding of Anglicanism's non-proselytizing relationship with Judaism was affirmed at the Lambeth Conference in its resolution "Jews, Christians and Muslims: The Way of Dialogue." See also Peter Steinfels, "A Leap Toward Closing the Basic Gap between Christians and Jews," in *The New York Times*, July 24, 1988.

⁴¹General Assembly 1989, Resolution 8946.

⁴²See text in the official reports of General Assembly 1987; see also John Kelsay and David Levenson, "Double-Talk or Dialogue? Presbyterians Encounter Judaism," in *The Christian Century*, 105 (1988): 638–40.

⁴³*Nostra Aetate*, from the Vatican conciliar Declaration on the Relationship of the Church to Non-Christian Religions, found in *Stepping Stones to Further Jewish-Christian Relations*, compiled by Helga Croner (New York: Stimulus Books, 1977), pp. 1–2. See also Philip Culbertson, "Is There Room for Evangelism in the Christian-Jewish Dialogue?" *Shofar* 8 (1990): 38–53.

⁴⁴The source is the Book of Enoch, particularly Otiyot de Rabbi Akiba, and other related midrashim, and needs also to be connected to Jeremiah 23:29. See for example Charlesworth *Old Testament Pseudepigrapha* I, 246–47; Beit Ha-Midrash II, 116; Batei Midrashot I, 354. The earliest medieval connection seems to be R. Azriel (RaABaD) to Hagiga, as cited in Tishbi, *Peirush le Rabbi Azriel*, p. 79 [136–137].

⁴⁵In Panikkar's words, the advaitic, or non-dualistic, structure of the experience of dialogue is revealed when pluralism is taken seriously: there can be no absorption of my experience into yours or yours into mine; there can only be the grounding of both experiences in a new common experience. See Gorday, "Raimundo Panikkar," p. 1149.

Discussion Questions

1. What is meant by the "triumphalist" voice of Christianity? Explain your answer in relationship to the "embarrassing" questions mentioned in the Introduction.

2. Why does God's self-definition include *both* unpredictability and uncontainability? Explain.

3. What are the common characteristics of covenants in the Bible? What theory of covenant do you believe in and why?

4. Why is it better to look *through* our own covenant rather than *at* our own covenant when looking at God?

5. What are some differences between the excerpts of the

five denominational statements about the relationship of Christians and Jews?

For Further Study

Culbertson, Philip. "New Christian Theologies of Covenant." *Reconstructionist* 51 (1985): 15–19, 32.

Dawe, Donald G. and John B. Carmen, eds. *Christian Faith in a Religiously Plural World.* Maryknoll: Orbis, 1978.

Hopkins, Denise Dombkowski. "God's Continuing Covenant with the Jews and the Christian Reading of the Bible." *Prism* 3 (1980): 60–75.

Knitter, Paul. *No Other Name? A Critical Survey of Christian Attitudes Toward the World Religions.* Maryknoll: Orbis, 1985.

Küng, Hans. *The Incarnation of God.* New York: Crossroad, 1987.

Novak, David. *Jewish-Christian Dialogue: A Jewish Justification.* New York: Oxford University Press, 1989.

Pawlikowski, John T. "Jews and Christians: The Contemporary Debate." *Quarterly Review* 4 (1984): 23–36.

Rylaarsdam, J. Coert. "The Two Covenants and the Dilemma of Christology." *Journal of Ecumenical Studies* 9 (1972): 249–70.

Van Buren, Paul M. *A Theology of Jewish-Christian Reality.* (3 vols.) New York: Seabury, 1980, 1983; New York: Harper and Row, 1987.

Wyschogrod, Michael. *The Body of Faith: God in the People Israel.* New York: Harper and Row, 1989.

VII.

JOHN T. PAWLIKOWSKI

Jesus—A Pharisee and the Christ

I. Introduction

Jesus of Nazareth lived and died as a believing Jew. More-over, as the church historian Franklin Littell has compel-lingly reminded us, if Jesus had been alive during the time when the Nazis were exterminating Jews in Europe he would have gone to the gas chambers with his people. Yet many Christians have been conditioned to regard Jesus as essen-tially anti-Jewish in the fundamentals of his teaching and preaching. As the 1985 Vatican *Declaration on Jewish-Christian Relations* tells us, "Jesus was and always re-mained a Jew. . . . Jesus is fully a man of his time, and his environment—the Jewish Palestinian one of the first cen-tury, the anxieties and hope of which he shared."[1]

While Jesus' precise relationship to the complex Jewish society of his day may never be determined exactly for lack of ample documentation, it is becoming increasingly clear to many biblical scholars that his positions most closely resem-bled those of the Pharisees whose strong commitment to the doctrine of the resurrection (over against the Sadducees) is highlighted in the New Testament. The Pharisees were a Jew-ish movement with several centuries of history behind them, mostly on the fringes of Jewish society. Their origins were probably in the Hellenistic Jewish communities outside Pal-estine. By the time of Jesus they were emerging as a major force for religious renewal in Judaism, focusing on family rit-uals, lay leadership, reinterpretation of the tradition, and the synagogue. Their chief rivals, the Sadducees, meanwhile controlled the temple and the temple priesthood, thereby serving as the de facto local political authorities in Roman occupied Palestine. Their religious worldview centered on strict observance of ritual laws, the Jerusalem temple and its priesthood, and the sacrificial cult. The Pharisees eventually gained almost total control of the Jewish community after the destruction of the temple during the Jewish war with Rome (64–70 C.E., "common era"—the era Jews and Christians share) totally undercut the basis for the Sadducean movement.

The above-mentioned Vatican Declaration picks up on this growing scholarly consensus as it enumerates several key points of belief, such as the notion of God as Father of all and the priority of the commandment of love (on which Jesus and the Pharisees appear to have virtually identical stances). The statement also points to evident similarities between Jesus and the Pharisees in the way they read and interpreted the Hebrew scriptures. Finally, the Declaration calls our attention to the fact that, despite the evident disagreements between Jesus and some segments of the Pharisaic movement, there is almost no mention of the Pharisees in the gospel accounts of Jesus' passion and death.[2] It is vital to focus on Jesus' Pharisaic roots because so much of what we call christology had its origins in themes associated with Pharisaism.

II. Distinguishing Characteristics of Pharisaism

Who were these Pharisees, so long regarded by Christians as Jesus' chief antagonists, and now increasingly viewed—as a result of new research—as the Jewish movement with which Jesus most clearly identified? Contemporary scholars have not arrived at any consensus regarding the origins of Pharisaism. What we do know for certain is that the Pharisees suddenly appear as a vibrant group after the Maccabean revolt (164 B.C.E.—the period before the "common era" of Jews and Christians) in the *Antiquities,* the Jewish historian Josephus' account of his people's changing political and religious fortunes. It is clear from his account that, whatever the origins of the Pharisees, they had established themselves by this time as a major force generating a quiet, yet far-reaching, revolution within the Jewish community. According to the Jewish historian Ellis Rivkin, the Pharisees saw themselves as commissioned by Moses himself and standing very much in the tradition of the prophets of Israel. They were thoroughly committed to the preservation of Jewish law, not only in its written form but also in its ongoing interpreted version (oral law).[3]

As the Pharisees grew in numbers and influence, and as the political situation of the Jewish people deteriorated following the Roman conquest of Palestine (63 B.C.E.), the movement came face-to-face with the question of Jewish survival. The Pharisees concluded that this issue had to be resolved in the context of traditional Jewish teachings, but with a decided openness to the contemporary situation. In other words, if the Jewish people were to survive and prosper amid significant political changes, then they must adopt a flexible approach to their religious heritage.

The Pharisees continued the understanding of the Jewish covenant that had emerged with the prophets and the reforms introduced in the book of Deuteronomy. Basic to this interpretation of the covenant was the sense that justice and worship must be integrally linked together. Worship of God by itself was insufficient in terms of fulfillment of the covenantal obligations. The Pharisees also reaffirmed the sense of Jewish peoplehood and mission. The reign or kingdom of God would not appear in its fullness until the day when justice and mercy dominated the social order. And this *day of the Lord* would come about only if and when people began working together as a community with a sense of mission to weave the ideals of justice and mercy into the fabric of human society.

Anyone with even the barest knowledge of biblical history must be aware that the ideals of the exodus covenant did not attain full expression in Jewish society during the biblical period. Prophets appeared on the scene time and time again to warn the people that they faced suffering and national destruction if they failed to take seriously the obligations Israel had accepted to bear as part of its mission of chosenness. Though at times the biblical prophets concerned themselves with the appearance of idol worship among the Israelites, their pre-eminent target was the people's violation of the covenantal demands of justice and mercy. The prophets' rate of success was low, however, as the entire population of Israel gradually fell under the sway of foreign conquerors, a fate the prophets clearly attributed to covenantal abuse.

Yet another effort to counteract covenantal failure was initiated by King Josiah (640–609 B.C.E.) who launched the reform of the Sinai/exodus tradition that has been preserved for us in the book of Deuteronomy. He too failed in this attempt, though the process he set in motion was to have a decided impact on later Jewish society and on the early Christian church. What Josiah began to recognize was that the ideals of the covenant would never materialize short of some basic changes in the social structures and patterns of Jewish life.

This was the legacy inherited by the Pharisees. Their leaders looked back and reflected on Israel's past experiences and traditions in the light of the new challenges facing Jews in their own time. The Pharisees had a deep reverence for the original covenantal tradition. And they surely admired the prophetic endeavor to make its ideals a reality in the everyday life of the community. But they also detected what they judged to be a fatal flaw in the prophetic approach. The prophets generally confined themselves to moving words that appealed directly to people's conscience in a generalized way. The bitter experience of the Babylonian exile (597–537 B.C.E.) was clear enough evidence for the prophets that such generalized appeals to conscience, in the end, did not do the job. Something more was definitely required. The Pharisees sensed that King Josiah was probably on the right track in his attempt to introduce structural reform in the Jewish community along with renewed personal commitment to covenantal values.

Of major concern to the Pharisees was the dominance of cult in the prevalent interpretation of covenantal religion. This cultic orientation had even been enhanced after the rebuilding of the second temple in Jerusalem and the general reforms of Jewish life described in the books of Ezra and Nehemiah.

The Pharisees did not see these second temple reforms as offering any permanent solution for covenantal faithfulness. A different direction was unquestionably necessary in their estimation. The Jewish people, after all, were once again under foreign occupation. This time it was the Romans who had become their political masters. The morale of the Jews had fallen to a very low point and there existed genuine threats to the loss of total national identity as a result of both physical force and the lure of assimilation into the general culture. The temple priesthood in the meantime had become tarnished by corruption to the point where the best interests of the Jewish community as a whole were often sacrificed for priestly self-interest. This was particularly true in Jerusalem.

These social realities forced the Pharisees to the conclusion that only a major social revolution involving the basic institutions of Jewish life could ultimately transform the situation. In their mind, such a social revolution need not be of the violent kind preached by the Zealots, a Jewish political movement espousing the violent overthrow of Roman control over Palestine. Rather, it must involve fundamental changes in the approach to the Torah, in the understanding of religious leadership, in the definition of the temple and in the shape of the community's worship. Gradually, but persistently, the Pharisees set out to realize these goals.

The Pharisees first turned their attention to the task of strengthening the people's devotion to Torah, the heart and soul of the original covenant with God. Believing that the written Torah (basically the first five books of the Hebrew scriptures which Christians call the Pentateuch) had become for many a dead letter, they introduced the notion that the interpretation of Torah had to be continually renewed and readjusted within the framework of the changing experience of the covenantal community. They rejected the claims of the Sadducees that only the priestly class could alter Torah teaching. Jewish scholar Stuart Rosenberg puts it well:

> Out of the hands of the priests, the rabbis took a fixed and unyielding tradition that had become congealed in words and cultic practice, and gave it over to the whole people. What is more . . . they ordained that all who would study and master that tradition might teach it, expound it, and ultimately even amplify it.[4]

The Pharisees insisted that the original 613 commandments found in the written Torah remain in effect. But the commandments had to be carefully rethought in light of new human needs and other realities facing the Jews of the Pharisees' time. The priestly tradition looked upon these Torah precepts primarily in terms of cultic observances. They were seen as the means of sanctifying God. The Pharisees, on the other hand, were convinced that the Torah had to provide as well for the sanctification of ordinary human life. The Pharisees thus decided to integrate the general moral teachings of the prophetic tradition with the obligations prescribed in the Torah. In this way they hoped that every ordinary, human action could become sacred if it were understood—as the Pharisees believed it should be—as an act of worship. The loving deed, what in Hebrew is termed the *mitzvah*, was given a status in some ways surpassing that of temple worship. This new Pharisaic vision of Jewish existence paved the way for the survival—at times even the flourishing—of the community well after the destruction of the Temple in the Roman war (64–70 C.E.) precluded all possibility of a temple-centered lifestyle.

The Pharisees developed what Rosenberg has described as "rituals of interpersonal behavior."[5] The written Torah was quite specific and detailed in its provisions regarding temple sacrifice and priestly responsibilities. But the exact meaning of Torah commands such as "Honor your father and your mother," or "Love your neighbor as yourself," or "Remember that you were once slaves in the land of Egypt" was not so clear. Drawing out the implications of such commandments for the people of their own time was a major preoccupation of the Pharisees. Many of the responses they provided would prove to outlast their own time, thereby transforming oral Torah into a treasured legacy of the people Israel. Through judicious application of the oral Torah, the Pharisees were able to deepen, humanize, and universalize the biblical tradition. As the priests had devoted themselves to the codification (arrangement in a systematic form) of cultic legislation, so the Pharisees focused their attention on the "codification" of love, loyalty, and human compassion. The Pharisees' ultimate goal was to render these human virtues as inescapable religious duties for each and every member of the Jewish community.

This Pharisaic concern with oral Torah makes evident that the movement held that anyone committed to following the covenantal ideals must be prepared to move beyond mere generalized verbal commitments. This move would entail specific actions that would begin to dismantle the injustices generated by unjust social structures. The rabbis firmly believed that religious people had to foster concrete plans for eradicating unjust practices in a society. Only in this way would the people fulfill their divinely designated roles of co-creators. Only thus would the messianic kingdom of justice and peace be brought closer to realization.

The Pharisaic revolution also saw the slow emergence of a new religious figure in Judaism—the teacher. This position of teacher or rabbi differed from that of the earlier prophetic and priestly roles in Judaism, though the rabbinic class never directly challenged the biblical prerogatives of their predecessors. This new teaching role was a direct consequence of the emphasis on oral Torah in Pharisaic circles spoken of previously. Rabbis fulfilled a twofold role in the community: interpreting Torah and, even more importantly, specifying the generalized precepts of the Pentateuch and prophetic writings into concrete obligations that would meet the needs of the Jewish community of their day. In other words, the rabbis were principally engaged in applying the oral Torah.

Rabbis, it should be emphasized, played no specific role in community worship at the outset. Their principal task was instructional, not liturgical. If we examine the issues with which they dealt, we will discover that a high percentage of them fall under the category of social responsibility. What needs emphasizing here is that a non-cultic figure, whose main responsibility was to address the social needs of the people, gradually replaced the temple priest as the chief religious representative of the Jewish faithfulness to the Torah. The criteria for judging an authentic rabbi went far beyond oratorical skills in synagogue debates or depth of wisdom in legal decisions. Did they show mercy and compassion? Were they able and willing to heal the sick? These are the criteria the Talmud sets for rabbinic evaluation.

The third important aspect of the Pharisaic revolution was the emergence of the institution that eventually came to be called the synagogue. It is not likely that the Pharisees directly created the synagogue. Historians are divided about its exact origins. Some feel that the synagogue grew up gradually as a by-product of the social transformation launched by the Pharisees, while others believe its roots go back to pre-Pharisaic times. Whatever the actual facts, the synagogue became a centerpiece of the Pharisaic movement, spreading throughout Palestine and the cities of the Jewish diaspora (Jews living outside the land of Israel).

As a Pharisaic institution, the synagogue became the focal point of the community in its many dimensions. Originally the emphasis definitely was not on the synagogue as a place of worship. Prayer always did have a place in the overall synagogue scheme. But, unlike the temple, worship was not its central focus. It became not merely a "house of God," but far more the "house of the people of God."

The rabbis utilized the synagogue to present their interpretations of how the generalized Jewish commandments were to be concretely observed in their time. The synagogue also became a place of communal assembly. Law courts carried out their duties within it, strangers to the community were welcomed and given shelter, and help for the poor was made available. In time the synagogue had become the supreme focus of Jewish life. As the historian Albert Reville has shown, it was also destined to parent both the Christian church and the Muslim mosque.[6]

A fourth distinguishing characteristic of the Pharisaic movement was its emphasis on table fellowship. Jacob Neusner believes that table fellowship was the way in which the Pharisees hoped to alter the power center in the Jewish community of their days, shifting authority gradually away from the temple priest to the community of Israel as a whole.[7] The majority of the Pharisees had concluded that there was no reasonable chance of challenging the oppressive Roman colonial occupation for the foreseeable future. So they decided to concentrate instead on relationships within their own community.

By making table fellowship a central part of Jewish life, the Pharisees intended to extend to all the people the duties previously prescribed only for the temple priests. In the eyes of the Pharisees the temple altar in Jerusalem could be replicated at every table in the household of Israel. A quiet, but far-reaching, revolution was at hand. The previous basis for power and authority in Israel, birth into a priestly family, was eroding under the weight of the Pharisaic vision. There was no longer any basis for assigning the priestly class a totally unique level of authority. As Neusner puts it,

> The Pharisees thus arrogated [to claim without right] to themselves—and to all Jews equally—the status of the Temple priests, and performed actions restricted to priests on account of that status. The table of every Jew in his home was seen as being like the table of the Lord in the Jerusalem Temple. The commandment, "You shall be a kingdom of priests and a holy people," was taken literally: everyone is a priest, everyone stands in the same relationship to God, and everyone must keep the priestly laws.[8]

One final aspect of Pharisaism needs to be brought into the picture at this point—its underlying theological perspective. A careful examination of the Pharisaic movement will reveal that the ultimate power behind its revolution lay in a fundamentally new understanding of the basic God-human person relationship. The Pharisees saw God not only as creator, giver of the covenant, an all-consuming presence, and much more, but in a special way as the Father of each individual. The Pharisees believed that, in light of this universal divine fatherhood, everyone had the right to address God in a direct and personal way, not merely through the temple sacrifices offered by the priests. A new sense of intimacy between God and every human person was arising in Judaism, thanks to the Pharisees. Ellis Rivkin sums up this development:

> When we ask ourselves the source of this generative power, we find it in the relationship the Pharisees established between the One God and the singular individual. . . . The Heavenly Father was ever present. One could talk to Him, plead with Him, cry out to Him, pray to Him—person to Person, individual to Individual, heart to Heart, soul to Soul. It was the establishment of this personal relationship, an inner experience, that accounts for the manifest power of Pharisaism to live on.[9]

One consequence of this new heightened sense of each

person's direct relationship with God among the Pharisees was a belief that would come to distinguish their movement from other Jewish groups of the period. That belief centered on the notion of the resurrection of each individual person from the dead. It was a conviction that brought the Pharisees into heated controversy with the Sadducees who adamantly rejected this view. The notion of resurrection constituted the Pharisees' ultimate affirmation of the fundamental dignity and uniqueness of every individual. Those whose lives were marked by justice would rise once the messiah had come and would enjoy a perpetual union with God. This belief was clearly a result of the process of "oral Torah" spoken of previously. There is little, if any, basis for it in the Hebrew scriptures.

III. The Pharisees' Influence on Jesus

At this point it would be important to confront a question that inevitably arises when Christians hear the kind of basically positive description of the Pharisaic movement that has just been presented here. Anyone well-versed in the writings of the New Testament is quite familiar with the sections of the gospels, especially in Matthew, that make the Pharisees appear as the archenemies of Jesus and his preaching. How, then, do we maintain a basically positive connection between the teachings of Jesus and those of Pharisaism in the face of this supposed scriptural evidence? The problem does not lend itself to easy resolution. This is due partly to the difficulty of knowing whether the stories of Jesus' controversies with the Pharisees reflect actual events in his own day or are rather insertions of the early Christian community resulting from intensive conflicts with the Pharisaic rabbis over converts and over membership in the Jewish community.

Within a framework of basic caution about our ability today to reconstruct fully Jesus' actual outlook upon the Pharisaic movement, three possible approaches to those texts in the New Testament that show Jesus and the Pharisees in intense conflict may be suggested. The first approach maintains Jesus as in conformity with the general Pharisaic willingness to modify Torah legislation for the sake of the well-being of the individual so long as the basic identity and existence of the Jewish community is not seriously threatened. The difficulty arises when Jesus began to challenge laws that the Pharisees regarded as critical to the preservation of the religious identity of the people. At the same time the people were facing continued threats from the Hellenizers—the culturally Greek members—in the community who urged Jews to assimilate into the broader Roman society of the time.

A clear example of this occurs in the gospel of Mark (Mk 2:23–28; 3:1–6) when on a sabbath day Jesus goes into a field and gathers grain for his disciples to eat and then follows that with the healing of a man with a withered hand in a synagogue. While Jesus justifies his first action with a principle well-honored within Pharisaism—the sabbath was made for people, not vice versa—and while the Pharisees continued to hold the traditional Jewish belief that the provisions of the Torah could be suspended when one is faced with the need to save a life, there is little doubt that the Pharisees saw Jesus' activities in the difficult circumstances of the time as posing a threat to the overall life of the Jewish community. For the Pharisees had made observance of the Torah a centerpiece of their effort to counteract the destructive influence of the Hellenizing Jews in their midst. On other occasions Jesus seemed to share fully the Pharisees' concern about preservation of a distinctive Jewish identity in order to safeguard the basic mission entrusted by God to the people of his covenant. In some areas scholars have noted that Jesus seems even more strictly observant than the Pharisees (Mt 19:21–22), perhaps exceeding even the Dead Sea Scroll community[10] (a group of Jews, opposed to what they regarded as a corrupt temple in Jerusalem, who went out to the Judean desert to live a monastic-type life). But in this particular instance Jesus decided to carry the general Pharisaic concern with the special dignity of the human person to its ultimate limit. While he may have been aware of the danger in doing so, he obviously felt that this principle was so central to the whole of his mission that it needed to be highlighted in dramatic fashion. The Pharisees obviously thought otherwise. The point then is, as the Christian scholar James Parkes stressed, neither was totally right or wrong despite the inevitable conflict in their viewpoints.[11] Each started from different, though equally valid, premises in judging the situation.

Though his focus is more directly on the conflicts between Jesus and the Pharisees in the gospel of Matthew rather than in Mark, Anthony Saldarini also sees them as basically the result of differing approaches to the defense of Jewish society ". . . from the many non-Jewish political and social pressures which surrounded it." Since both assumed leadership roles in their day their opposition to one another is "reasonable and expected."[12] Hence Saldarini feels that Matthew has portrayed the actual relationship between Jesus and the Pharisees rather accurately.

The second possible explanation of the gospel hostility toward the Pharisees results from our enhanced understanding of the Talmud which has collected the teachings of the Pharisees and their rabbinic heirs. In the Talmud we find reference to some seven categories of Pharisees. Five of these Pharisaic groups are viewed negatively, while the other two, the "Pharisees of awe" and the "love Pharisees," receive a positive evaluation overall. The "love Pharisees," whose chief figure was the great Rabbi Hillel, espoused love as the central feature of Jewish faith. This list of Pharisaic types clearly shows us that the movement encompassed a wide range of viewpoints, and, more importantly, that *internal* disputes, often of the heated variety, were not unusual. With this background information we could argue that Jesus, in his gospel disputes with "the Pharisees," was engaging in an internal critique—that was not unknown in Pharisaic circles—rather than condemning the movement in global fashion.

The difficulty in determining for certain whether the condemnations of the five negatively-viewed groups in the Talmud actually come from the time of Jesus or were framed much later on leaves some scholars with serious doubts. Their doubts call into question whether the above explanation is a solution to the dilemma concerning the gospel conflicts between Jesus and "the Pharisees." Jewish New Testament authority Michael Cook is among these scholars. He would prefer a third approach, namely stressing the positive connections between many of Jesus' central teachings and those of Hillel in particular. In light of these evident connections, Cook says, we are automatically forced into a suspicious stance regarding these texts of conflict.[13] Surely Jesus would not denounce totally a movement with which he had so much in common. Hence, either he was speaking in a very limited context or the conflict stories represent the situation in the latter part of the first century when the gospels were composed rather than Jesus' own situation. By the last third of the first century, the Christian community—now formally expelled from the synagogue—was engaged in intense competition with Jews for converts. Hence it is understandable how Matthew may have projected the turmoil of his own era into his narrative of Jesus' encounters with the Pharisaic movement.

IV. Shared Convictions of Jesus and the Pharisees

In light of the aforementioned, there is little doubt any longer that Jesus and the Pharisees shared many central convictions. It is to these that we now turn.

Their first common point is their basic approach to God. As was already stressed, the Pharisees elevated the notion of God as *Father* to a central place in their theological outlook. So did Jesus. Story after story of the gospels has Jesus addressing God with this title, and Jesus' central prayer begins by invoking God as "Our Father" (Mt 6:9–13). And the overall effect of this stress on divine fatherhood was fundamentally the same for Jesus as for the Pharisees. It led both to an enhanced appreciation of the dignity of every person and ultimately to the notion of individual resurrection.

Ellis Rivkin has spoken of the Pharisees mounting a *hidden* revolution. Clearly this was the case. They kept a relatively low profile despite the many substantive changes they introduced into the basic fabric of Jewish society and its patterns of worship. They also maintained a deep attachment to the earlier Jewish tradition in the Hebrew scriptures, commonly called by Christians the Old Testament. Jesus was thoroughly schooled in the teachings of the Old Testament, or simply "the scriptures," as he referred to these sacred texts. They were in no sense a foil or prelude for his own teachings. They stood rather at the very core of his message. Without these scriptures Jesus' message remains truncated and incomplete.

Christian scripture scholar James Sanders has spoken in even stronger terms about how any divorce between the New Testament and Hebrew scriptures mutilates the soul of Jesus' sacred word to us. "Without Torah (i.e. Old Testament)," he says, "the Christian gospel is hollow, gutless, and nothing but a form of hellenistic Palestinian cynicism."[14] And Cardinal Carlo Martini of Milan, Italy, a biblical scholar, echoes much the same notion when he insists that Christianity's roots are profoundly enmeshed in Judaism. "Without a sincere feeling for the Jewish world, therefore, and a direct experience of it, one cannot fully understand Christianity. Jesus is fully Jewish, the apostles are Jewish, and one cannot doubt their attachment to the traditions of their forefathers."[15]

Jesus also shared with the Pharisees a general reluctance to antagonize the Roman occupying authorities in Palestine. He definitely was not a Zealot challenger to the political domination of Rome despite the claims of a few scholars that he engaged in overt political activity.[16] He told people to abide by the laws of Caesar unless they directly contradicted their religious convictions. In deciding to invade the temple precincts where he overturned the tables of the money-changers in rather dramatic fashion he did venture beyond parameters that most Pharisees seemed unwilling to cross. We shall return to this episode shortly.

Jesus clearly picked up on three other central features of Pharisaism as well—oral Torah, the new role of the teacher, and the synagogue. Throughout the gospels we find Jesus offering interpretations of the scriptures, sometimes novel, sometimes exceeding even progressive boundaries, whose similarity to Pharisaic oral Torah is unmistakable. Jesus was quite evidently thoroughly familiar with the way the Pharisees sought to inject new life into the Jewish tradition through oral Torah, and he put the method to frequent use in his own ministry. His own public stance in the community also closely parallels the evolving role of the Pharisaic teacher which eventually became more structured within the framework of the rabbinate.[17] Ample evidence exists that Jesus and his apostles, and the early Christian community, modeled themselves on the synagogue which the Pharisaic movement had elevated into prominence in Jewish life.

Finally, the New Testament provides us with plenty of support on how deeply Jesus embraced the table fellowship notion of Pharisaism. In the end he selected this setting for one of the most critical moments of his entire ministry—the celebration of what the Christian community has traditionally called "the first eucharist." It was in the context of future table fellowship meals that his disciples would continue to experience that direct and special contact with his Father that he had manifested in his person and ministry.

V. Differences Between Jesus and the Pharisees

But, despite the profound linkage between Jesus and the Pharisaic movement, some important differences appear. And it is these differences that give specific shape to the unique dimensions of Jesus' message.

A difference, as noted expert in Christian-Jewish relations Clemens Thoma emphasized, is that Jesus' personal sense of intimate union with the Father went considerably beyond anything the Pharisees were willing to acknowledge up to that time. According to Thoma, Jesus ". . . did experience this God in a uniquely close and intimate way."[18]

A few scholars have questioned this claim, arguing that Jesus' use of the term "Father" for God does not seem to differ in any substantial ways from that common to the Judaism of his day. One such scholar is Dieter Zeller. He feels that Jesus' approach to God as Father basically remained within the established Pharisaic framework. The "new" dimension in Jesus' understanding came rather in the way he explained access to the divine presence. For Jews, even the Pharisees, it ultimately remained linked to the particular history of the people. But Jesus, as Zeller understands his teaching, redefines God's nearness. He frees it from excessively nationalistic interpretations and makes it more direct and personal. This is a trend, it might be noted, already apparent in Pharisaic writings. Within the context of God's intimate presence with all persons Jesus demands, in the name of God the Father of Israel, ". . . a loving openness for the socially oppressed, which overcomes all religious appearances of group egotism."[19]

While Zeller makes a perfectly valid point about the availability of God's intimate presence outside the parameters of Israel's particular history in Jesus' teaching, nonetheless he is not altogether convincing on the more basic point about whether Jesus' sense of union with the Father went beyond standard Pharisaic understandings. Scholars like Thoma in the end make the better case that there is a unique quality to Jesus' approach to God as "Father." However, the difference is not to be found solely in the way Jesus understands the fatherhood of God, but from a variety of Jesus' actions and sayings. Such an action is his willingness to forgive sins. While this is interpreted in earlier gospel accounts far more within the context of freeing people from obligation of the Torah, by the time we come to the later accounts it is clearly a matter of Jesus assuming a divine prerogative for himself as he forgives people's sins. Even the most progressive Pharisees of the time recoiled against the idea of anyone but God forgiving sins. Jesus then even goes one step further by sharing this power of forgiveness with his faithful disciples. He thereby emphasized the proximity to the divine presence that he shared in a special way. But equally he stressed that those who believed could somehow share this closeness to God through him. This is one aspect of his teaching that brought him into conflict with the Jewish community as a whole, including the Pharisees.

A second area where Jesus' teaching shows distinctiveness involves the vision of individual human persons and their role in the process of human salvation. As we saw previously, the Pharisees had definitely enhanced Judaism's appreciation of the status and worth of the individual believer. But they did this within the framework of the continuing primacy of the people Israel as the focal point of salvation. Jesus never abandoned the commitment to community that was inbred in his Jewish heritage. On the contrary, he emphasized it on many occasions. But he also made a special effort to push the fundamental dignity of the individual person to new limits, as when he healed on the sabbath. Even more importantly, as Zeller said above, in a significant way he made realization of human dignity far more central to human salvation than national identity. Community in general and the destiny of Israel as a people remained critically important to him. But they could never take a back seat to the attainment of personal dignity.

Jesus brought into focus this commitment to individual dignity in at least three other significant, and related, ways. The first is his general affirmation of the worth and status of the outsider, even one's enemy. Donald Senior has termed this teaching as Jesus' scandalous doctrine of *enemy love.*[20]

Its uniqueness has been acknowledged as well by a Jewish
scholar on the New Testament, David Flusser:

> It is clear that Jesus' moral approach to God and
> man . . . is unique and incomparable. According to
> the teachings of Jesus you have to love the sinners,
> while according to Judaism you have not to hate the
> wicked. It is important to note that the positive love
> even toward the enemies is Jesus' personal message.
> We do not find this doctrine in the New Testament
> outside the words of Jesus himself . . . . In Judaism
> hatred is practically forbidden. But love to the enemy
> is not prescribed.[21]

Another example of his insistence on the centrality of
personal worth appears in the account of his invasion of the
temple at Jerusalem. As was stated above, Jesus generally
shared the Pharisaic reserve regarding confrontation with
the Roman political authorities. But he was willing to forego
that reserve on this occasion for the sake of dramatizing
anew how much he considered the exploitation of people,
poorer people in particular, as a block to the emergence of
God's final reign. Scholars have begun to emphasize of late
that this gospel episode must be read as far more than mere
protest against empty ritual. His basic concern was the abuse
of worshipers by some of the temple priests who helped the
so-called money changers fix prices for ritual animals at in-
flated rates which the poor could ill afford.[22] Jesus was apparently so taken aback by the extent of this systematic exploitation of the poor that he abandoned his more customary
reserve on politically sensitive matters inherited from his
Pharisaic background to invade the temple precincts with
some of his disciples. Because the temple served as the local
center for political administration as it related to the Jewish
community of Palestine, his action clearly challenged the entrenched power elite of the day, and, indirectly, Roman impe-
rial authority. But protecting poor worshipers from these continuing abuses was so paramount a value for Jesus, a value
rooted in his general commitment to human dignity, that he
was willing to throw caution to the wind and engage in dramatic protest.

A third indication of Jesus' pervasive dedication to individual human worth emerges from his general willingness to include the "outsider," even the social outcast (e.g., tax collectors, prostitutes, and lepers) in his company. Many feminist theologians also see in Jesus' ministry a decided pattern of the inclusion of women to a degree previously unknown in Judaism, even in progressive Pharisaic circles, although some Jewish women authors have warned against exaggeration in this regard[23] (cf. the chapter "Feminism and Jewish-Christian Dialogue"). This feature of Jesus' activities assumes even greater prominence if we accept the theory that he espoused the cause of *am ha aretz* ("people of the land") —who are generally considered to be on the edge of the society of his day for various reasons, poverty being one of them —and that this identification with their cause put him at fundamental odds with Pharisaism. Jesus unquestionably exhibited great concern for these "people of the land." On this point there is little, if any, scholarly dispute. The disagreement among contemporary scholars revolves primarily around the question on whether this posture set Jesus against the Pharisees in a decisive way. The research undertaken by Ellis Rivkin and Michael Cook leads them to conclude, in Cook's words, that "the presumed antipathy between the Pharisees and the *am ha aretz* is . . . not easily demonstrable."[24] The work of Jacob Neusner, though it does not address this point directly, would seem to lay some basis for a fundamental contrast between the Pharisees and Jesus over the "people of the land." For Neusner has argued that in Jesus' time, unlike earlier periods, the Pharisees had evolved into exclusivistic table fellowship groups. If this is the case, then surely the "people of the land" were kept out by the Pharisees in contrast to Jesus' embrace of them.[25]

This is an area that requires further exploration. Presently, all that can be said is that there appears to be *some* difference between Jesus and the Pharisees with regard to the "people of the land." Whether the difference constituted a point of serious division between Jesus and the Pharisees remains an open question. Jesus did, however, in line with his deep commitment to the sacred dignity of every human being, appear to be more prepared to welcome the "people of the land" into the company of his disciples and perhaps even into his table fellowship meals.

These special features of Jesus' ministry began over time

to convince his disciples that indeed something decisive was happening through him. People began to sense a special presence of God in and through his person and his ministry emphasizing the special dignity of the individual person. But this process is gradual, as Robin Scroggs has reminded us:

> The movement begun by Jesus and continued after his death in Palestine can best be described as a reform movement within Judaism. . . . There is no evidence during this period that it attempted to break with its matrix. . . . There is, . . . prior to the aftermath of the war against the Romans (64–70 C.E.), no such thing as Christianity. . . . Believers in Jesus did not have a self-understanding of themselves as a religion over against Judaism.[26]

VI. The Emergence of the Church's Christology

Gradually an awareness set in that the church needed to express the distinctiveness of divine presence it had come to experience in more formal titles. At first, titles common to their shared Jewish tradition were used ("Son of Man," "Son of God," or "Son of David"), though their belief would be translated into more abstract Greek philosophical terminology by church councils. The point that needs to be underscored, as Raymond Brown clearly does, is that what the church calls christology is not dependent first and foremost on the meaning of a particular title assigned by the early Christian community to Jesus, but, instead, on the profound impact he had made on them as a person.

Brown puts it in these words: "If Jesus presented Himself as one in whose life God was active, He did so not primarily by the use of titles, or by clear statements about what He was, but rather by the impact of His person and His life on those who followed Him."[27] But even in the later parts of the New Testament, particularly the Johannine writings, where Jesus is viewed far more explicitly as God made human, a definite link remains between this divine dimension of Jesus' person and the deep commitment to individual human dignity that was a hallmark of his public ministry. Pope John Paul II reminded us of the depth of this connection in his first encyclical letter *Redemptor Hominis*.[28] Commenting on this letter, theologian Gregory Baum emphasizes that, according to John Paul's perspective, the church's concern for human rights abuses around the globe is not secondary to its primary mission but is an integral part of that mission because it is a direct consequence of christological doctrine.[29]

The more we examine Christianity's emergence from Judaism as a distinctive entity by the end of the first century, in the light of the new scholarship on the Judaism of the time, the more we come to recognize that Christianity's distinctiveness lies primarily in the proclamation of Jesus as God made human rather than in his clear fulfillment of central Jewish messianic prophecies. Professor Clemens Thoma makes this point quite strongly: "It is not correct to say that the decisive or even the sole difference between Judaism and Christianity consists in the Christian affirmation of Jesus as the messiah and its denial by Jews. There are certain assymetries and considerations on both sides that render unacceptable such an absolute statement on the messianic question."[30]

The critical issue for both Jews and Christians, Thoma hastens to add, is not ultimately the messiah, but rather the kingdom of God. And by the end of the first century it had become apparent that a decisive turn toward the realization of the kingdom of God occurred in the coming of Jesus. Yet it was impossible for the church to proclaim the full and final realization of this divine reign envisioned in Jewish tradition. Hence, both Judaism and Christianity stood in a condition of incompleteness awaiting the same final hope despite their differing understandings of how it would come about.

If the Christian churches continue to retain the term "messiah" in reference to Jesus, as they no doubt will, it is incumbent upon their members today to recognize the redefinition of the term that took place in the course of the first century and thereafter when "messiah" became one central way of expressing belief that, in Jesus, God became human. Such an understanding will go a long way in removing the traditional charge against Jews that in not accepting Jesus as the Christ they are being blind to their own messianic prophecies.

VII. The Church and the Jewish People Split

Reflecting upon the split between Christianity and the Jewish community that had come into place by the end of the first century, it is important for people in the churches to recognize its inevitability. Given the now central belief in God made human on the part of the church and the equally tenacious belief in the absolute gulf between humanity and divinity within Judaism, conflict was unavoidable. But, at the same time, there is equal need to join Cardinal Carlo Martini in acknowledging that, as a result of the separation which Martini calls the first and most decisive schism (split) in the history of the church, Christianity suffered a certain spiritual impoverishment.[31] Its health and vitality, its basic equilibrium, were affected in a negative way by the split. And only in recent decades is the church making a concerted effort to overcome the centuries-long effects of that impoverishment which also generated at times a fierce hatred of the Jewish people.

VIII.   Approaches to Covenant Theology

The contemporary church will also need to bear in mind, far more than it has, the strong insistence by Pope John Paul II, in numerous addresses,[32] that despite the separation between Christians and Jews generated by the early church's gradual awareness of God's special presence in and through the person of Jesus, strong bonds remain intact. In fact, the pope has spoken of these continuing bonds as involved with the very essence of Christian identity. In 1982, for example, John Paul II insisted that ". . . our two religious communities are connected and closely related at the very level of their religious identities."[33] Hence it becomes abundantly clear that Christians can never proclaim the uniqueness of their faith in a way that does not at the very same time emphasize the continuing bonds with the Jewish people, past and present.

Over the years various theologians and church leaders have grappled with the best way to categorize the complexity of the ongoing Jewish-Christian relationship, marked as it is both by separation and linkage. No clear consensus has yet emerged and none appears on the immediate horizon. Generally speaking, two approaches have achieved more or less equal prominence even though within each many colorations of the basic theme can be found.

The first approach is usually called the "single covenant" theory. It holds that Jews and Christians fundamentally belong to one covenantal tradition that began at Sinai. In this perspective the Christ event represented the decisive movement when the Gentile nations were able to enter fully into the special relationship with God which Jews already enjoyed and in which they continued. Some holding this viewpoint maintain that the decisive features of the Christ event had universal application (including Jews). Vatican and papal statements tend in this direction. Others, on the other hand, are more inclined to say that the Christian appropriation and reinterpretation of the original covenantal tradition, in and through Jesus, applied primarily to non-Jews. Paul van Buren and Monika Hellwig are two theologians who lean in this direction.

The double covenantal theory generally begins at the same point as its single covenantal counterpart, with a strong affirmation of the continuing bonds between Christians and Jews. But it prefers to highlight the distinctiveness of the two traditions and communities, particularly in terms of their experiences after the separation of the first century. Christians associated with this perspective insist on maintaining the view that through the ministry, teachings, and person of Jesus a vision of God emerged that was distinctively new in some of its central features. Even though there may well have been important groundwork laid for this emergence in the Pharisaic transformation of the Jewish people's understanding of the divine-human relationship, what came to be seen through Jesus as the Christ nonetheless must be described as a quantum leap.

This new revelation in no way obliterated the continued validity of the Jewish people's original covenantal relationship, nor did it dispense the new Christian believers from incorporating into their faith expression the fundamental insights of the covenantal tradition. The decision at the so-called council of Jerusalem described in the book of Acts (chapter 15) to free Gentile converts from observance of most of the Jewish ritual legislation may have been pastorally necessary. Unfortunately, it was often interpreted as freeing the church from all ties to the original Sinai covenant. Only since the Second Vatican Council has the church begun to restore its sense of basic bondedness to the Jewish people caused by this misinterpretation.

Monika Hellwig is a theologian who opts for the single covenantal outlook, while acknowledging that the other perspective has merit. Within a single covenantal framework Hellwig views Christianity's traditional proclamation that "Jesus is Lord" much more as a prophetic assertion which commits the Christian community to work toward the realization of human salvation rather than a claim about messianic fulfillment in the Christ event. Christians must rejoin Jews in basically seeing the messianic event as "lengthy, complex, unfinished and mysterious," however decisive they may regard the coming of Jesus to the process.[34]

Joining Hellwig in the single covenantal group of theologians is Episcopalian Paul van Buren who is in the process of completing a four volume analysis of the theology of the Jewish-Christian relationship.[35] In volume three where he focuses directly on christological questions van Buren argues intensely that all statements about Jesus as the Christ ultimately involve a statement about God the Father who must remain primary in Christian theology. Every proper christological statement must include an acknowledgement of the continuing covenant between God and Israel. Christology refers in the first instance to the church's critical reflection on the importance of Jesus as person. It has nothing to do with the Jewish concept of the coming of the messiah. So Judaism after Jesus' resurrection remains a religion of legitimate messianic hope rather than spiritual blindness.

According to van Buren "Israel" consists of two connected but distinct branches. Both are essential to its full definition. The Christian church represents the community of Gentile believers drawn by the God of the Jewish people to worship God and to make God's love known among the people of the world.

The shared messianic vision of Judaism and Christianity leads van Buren to advocate the notion of the "co-formation" of the two faith communities. By this he means that both of the branches of Israel must grow and develop alongside of each other rather than in isolation. While each will continue to retain a measure of distinctiveness, both will experience a growing mutuality characterized by understanding and love. This growing together in love will increase each partner's freedom to be its distinctive self while maintaining an awareness of the necessity for mutual cooperation.

An important proponent of the double covenantal approach is the German Catholic theologian Franz Mussner.[36] Mussner rejects any interpretation of the Christ event over against Judaism in terms of Jesus' fulfillment of the biblical messianic prophecies. Rather, the uniqueness of Jesus is to be found in the *depth* of his imitation of God, but even this dimension of Jesus as the Christ ultimately has important roots in the Jesus tradition. Mussner acknowledges that initially the early church tended to rely on biblical prophecies— what he terms "prophet christology." But without ever abandoning totally these early christological formulations, it gradually moved by the time of the Johannine writings to a much greater emphasis on "Son christology" in which the notion of the incarnation predominates.

IX. Conclusion

As we bring to a close our reflections on christology, in light of enhanced understanding of Jesus' profoundly positive ties to the Judaism of his time, we can certainly recognize that the process has only begun. The task must be undertaken with great sensitivity because we are touching upon the very nerve center of Christian theology. On the other hand, we also have a serious moral imperative to continue serious reflection, given what we know of the sufferings and extermination of Jews over the centuries as a result of christological outlooks that obliterated the basis of post-Easter Jewish existence. As we pursue this important work, we must do so with the conviction that, despite our continuing belief in the distinctiveness of the faith Christians have received through Jesus, this faith remains incomplete without incorporation of the central themes of human goodness, creation, and community, themes that continue to distinguish the Jewish people.[37]

NOTES

[1]Cf. Helga Croner, ed., *More Stepping Stones to Jewish-Christian Relations: An Unabridged Collection of Christian Documents 1975–1983* (Mahwah: Paulist Press, 1985), p. 226.

[2]Ibid. 227.

[3]Cf. Ellis Rivkin, "The Internal City," *Journal for the Scientific Study of Religion* 5 (1966): 230–31.

[4]Stuart Rosenberg, "Contemporary Renewal and the Jewish Experience." Paper presented at the 1968 International Conference of Christians and Jews, York University, Toronto, Canada, September 1968, 4.

[5]Ibid. 3.

[6]Albert Reville, as quoted in Jules Isaac, *Jesus and Israel* (New York: Holt, Rinehart & Winston, 1971), p. 44.

[7]Cf. Jacob Neusner, *From Politics to Piety: The Emergence of Pharisaic Judaism* (Englewood Cliffs: Prentice-Hall, 1973).

[8]Ibid. p. 83.

[9]Ellis Rivkin, *A Hidden Revolution: The Pharisees' Search for the Kingdom Within* (Nashville: Abingdon Press, 1978), p. 310.

[10]Cf. James A. Sanders, "Rejoicing in the Gifts" *Explorations* 3 (1989): 1.

[11]James Parkes, *The Foundations of Judaism and Christianity* (London: Vallentine-Mitchell, 1960), p. 177.

[12]Anthony J. Saldarini, *Pharisees, Scribes and Sadducees in Palestinian Society: A Sociological Approach* (Wilmington: Michael Glazier, Inc., 1988), p. 173.

[13]Michael Cook, "Jesus and the Pharisees—The Problem as It Stands Today" *Journal of Ecumenical Studies* 15 (1978): 457.

[14]James Sanders, "Rejoicing in the Gifts," p. 1.

[15]Cardinal Carlo Maria Martini, "Christianity and Judaism: A Historical and Theological Overview," in *Jews and Christians: Exploring the Past, Present, and Future*, edited by James H. Charlesworth (New York: Crossroad, 1990), p. 19.

[16]Cf. Joel Carmichael, *The Death of Jesus* (New York: Harper & Row), 1966 and S.G.F. Brandon, *Jesus and the Zealots* (New York: Charles Scribner's), 1967.

[17]Jesus himself is called "rabbi" in the New Testament, though some scholars feel this term may not yet have been in use in Jesus' own day and was therefore applied to him only by later New Testament writers. The scholarly dispute is to some extent immaterial since there is no question that the Pharisaic role of teacher paved the way for the subsequently more formalized rabbinical office.

[18]Clemens Thoma, *A Christian Theology of Judaism,* trans. Helga Croner (New York: Paulist Press, 1980), p. 115.

[19]Dieter Zeller, "God as Father in the Proclamation and in the Prayer of Jesus," in *Standing Before God: Studies on Prayer in Scriptures and in Tradition with Essays in Honor of John M. Oesterreicher,* edited by Asher Finkel and Lawrence Frizzell (New York: KTAV, 1981), p. 125.

[20]Donald Senior, "Jesus' Most Scandalous Teaching," in *Biblical and Theological Reflections on the Challenge of Peace,* edited by John T. Pawlikowski and Donald Senior, Theology and Life Series 10 (Wilmington: Michael Glazier, Inc., 1984), pp. 55–69.

[21]David Flusser, "A New Sensitivity in Judaism and the Christian Message," *Harvard Theological Review* 61 (1968): 126.

[22]Albert Nolan, *Jesus Before Christianity: The Gospel of Liberation* (Capetown: David Philip, 1977), p. 102.

[23]Cf. Deborah McCauley and Annette Daum, "Jewish-Christian Feminist Dialogue: A Wholistic Vision," *Union Seminary Quarterly Review* 33 (1983): 147–90 and Susannah Heschel, "Anti-Judaism in Christian Feminist Theology," *Tikkun* 5 (1990): 25–28.

[24]Michael Cook, "Jesus and the Pharisees," p. 449.

[25]Jacob Neusner, *The Rabbinic Traditions about the Pharisees Before 70.* 3 vols. (Leiden: Brill, 1971); *From Politics to Piety: The Emergence of Pharisaic Judaism* (Englewood Cliffs: Prentice-Hall, 1973); "The Use of the Later Rabbinic Evidence for the Study of First Century Pharisiaim," in *Approaches to Ancient Judaism: Theory and Practice,* edited by William Scott Green (Missoula: Scholar's Press, 1978), pp. 215–28.

[26]Robin Scroggs, "The Judaizing of the New Testament," *The Chicago Theological Seminary Register* 76 (1986): 42–43.

[27]Raymond E. Brown, "Does the New Testament Call Jesus God?" *Theological Studies* 26 (1965): 546.

[28]Pope John Paul II, "Redemptor Hominis," *Origins* 8:40 (March 2, 1979), pp. 625, 627–44.

[29]Gregory Baum, "The First Papal Encyclical," *The Ecumenist* 17 (1979): 55.

[30]Clemens Thoma, *A Christian Theology of Judaism,* p. 134.

[31]Cardinal Carlo Maria Martini, "The Relation of the Church to the Jewish People," *From the Martin Buber House* 6 (1984): 9.

[32]Cf. John Paul II, *On Jews and Judaism, 1979–1986*, edited by Eugene J. Fisher and Leon Klenicki (Washington: NCCB Committee for Ecumenical and Interreligious Affairs and the Anti-Defamation League of B'nai B'rith, 1987).

[33]Ibid. 37.

[34]Monika Hellwig, "Christian Theology and the Covenant of Israel," *Journal of Ecumenical Studies* 7 (1970): 37–51; "Why We Still Can't Talk," *Jewish-Christian Relations*, ed. by Robert Heyer (New York: Paulist Press, 1974), pp. 26–31; "Bible Interpretation: Has Anything Changed?," in *Biblical Studies: Meeting Ground of Jews and Christians*, ed. by Lawrence Boadt, Helga Croner and Leon Klenicki (New York: Paulist Press, 1980), pp. 172–79; "From the Jesus of Story to the Christ of Dogma," in *Anti-Semitism and the Foundations of Christianity*, ed. by Alan T. Davies (New York: Paulist Press, (1979), pp. 118–36.

[35]Paul M. van Buren, *Discerning the Way* (New York: Seabury, 1980), *A Christian Theology of the Jewish People* (Seabury, 1983), *A Theology of the Jewish-Christian Reality, Part III: Christ in Context* (San Francisco: Harper & Row, 1988), "The Context of Jesus Christ: Israel," *Religion and Intellectual Life* 3 (1986): 31–50. A fourth volume on Christ, Christian-Jewish dialogue and the wider dialogue of world religions is now in process.

[36]Franz Mussner, *Tractate on the Jews: The Significance of Judaism for Christian Faith*, trans. Leonard Swidler (Philadelphia: Fortress Press, 1984); "From Jesus the 'Prophet' to Jesus 'the Son,' " *Three Ways to the One God: The Faith Experience in Judaism, Christianity and Islam*, ed. by Aboldjavad Falaturi, Jacob J. Petuchowski and Walter Strolz (New York: Crossroad, 1987), pp. 76–85.

[37]For a fuller treatment of this topic, cf. John T. Pawlikowski, "The Jewish Covenant: Its Continuing Challenge For Christian Faith," in *The Life of Covenant: The Challenge of Contemporary Judaism. Essays in Honor of Herman E. Schaalmann*, ed. by Joseph A. Edelheit (Chicago: Spertus College of Judaic Press, 1986), pp. 113–24; *Jesus and the Theology of Israel* (Wilmington: Michael Glazier, Inc., 1989), pp. 88–99.

Discussion Questions

1. Was Jesus a Pharisee? Were his followers Pharisees? Explain.

2. As a result of reading this chapter, how do you understand the title "Christ" as applied to Jesus?

3. What are the five distinguishing characteristics of the Pharisees presented in this chapter? State and explain each.

4. How has your attitude toward the Pharisees changed as a result of reading this chapter?

5. What did the Pharisees mean by the resurrection of each individual person from the dead?

For Further Study

Cook, Michael. "Jesus and the Pharisees—The Problem as It Stands Today." *Journal of Ecumenical Studies* 15 (1978).

Culbertson, Philip. "Changing Christian Images of the Pharisees." *Anglican Theological Review* 64 (1982): 539–61.

———. "Re-thinking the Christ in Jewish-Christian Dialogue." *Ecumenical Trends* 13 (1984): 1–5.

Fisher, Eugene J. *The Jewish Roots of Christian Liturgy.* Mahwah: Paulist Press, 1990.

Lee, Bernard L. *The Galilean Jewishness of Jesus.* New York: Paulist, 1988.

Pawlikowski, John T. *Christ in the Light of Christian-Jewish Dialogue.* New York: Paulist Press, 1982.

———. *Jesus and the Theology Of Israel.* Wilmington: Michael Glazier, Inc., 1989.

Sanders, E. P. *Jesus and Judaism.* Philadelphia: Fortress, 1985.

Swidler, Leonard. *Yeshua: A Model for Moderns.* Kansas City: Sheed and Ward, 1988.

Vermes, Geza. *Jesus and the World of Judaism.* Philadelphia: Fortress, 1983.

VIII.

SANFORD SELTZER

Interdating and Intermarriage: Jews and Christians

I. Introduction

Jews and Christians[1] are marrying in ever-increasing numbers. The frequency of these marriages is such that unlike prior generations when intermarriage was a comparative rarity, its incidence today is considered normative and unremarkable. Individuals who intermarry come from all walks of life and diverse socio-economic strata. They include professing Christians as well as individuals whose origins were Christian but who in adulthood deny any formal religious orientation. Jews also exhibit a diversity of involvement and allegiances ranging from being religiously observant or active in the Jewish community to an absence of any formal Jewish institutional linkage, be it religious or cultural. While some studies would appear to show that the more intensive one's religious education and degree of practice during childhood, the less likely their intermarriage, no guarantees preventing intermarriage exist.[2]

Whatever the obstacles, couples in interfaith relationships are prone to believe that they are more than capable of surmounting religious differences. Faith is seen primarily as a personal matter rather than something to be shared in a marriage, the latter a luxury to be enjoyed when possible but hardly essential to a couple's happiness. Respect for a partner's convictions is deemed a far greater virtue than expectations that one individual will embrace the faith of the other, although significant numbers of non-Jewish men and women have converted and continue to convert to Judaism.

Over the years, some Jews have also left Judaism for other faiths.

The temptation to minimize the stresses inherent in an intermarriage is understandable when two people are in love, believing that feelings for one another will overcome any and all conflicts centering on religion, which after all, they often reason, is really not *that* important. That optimism is reinforced by a determination not to rock the boat and to avoid problems that can only jeopardize a relationship. Dating is often a laborious exercise. The necessity to start all over again once an attractive potential lover has been discovered provides little consolation.

The high rate of intermarriage is a dramatic example of the radical changes in the structure of the American family near the end of the twentieth century. It is an outgrowth of the influence of sociological trends which have been building in this country since the end of World War II. The mass mobilization and industrialization of the United States brought with it a concurrent reduction in traditional prejudices and negative stereotypes regarding the various faith communities and ethnic groups in American society. Although racial hatred and antisemitism are far from extinct and in fact today show some signs of resurgence, such attitudes are no longer acceptable among substantial segments of the population. Supreme Court decisions and legislation enacted by both the federal and state governments prohibiting discrimination in the marketplace on the basis of race, creed, or color have also been instrumental in reshaping the American scene.

The mass media, most notably television, have been particularly effective in bringing about these changes. Situation comedies as well as dramatic series and documentaries dealing with interracial and ethnic themes have dispelled widely held biases regarding minorities. New educational opportunities, particularly on a university level, have enabled Jews and Christians, blacks and Hispanics, to sit in the same classrooms and live in the same dormitories. The information explosion has been a boon for improved racial and religious understanding. College fraternities and sororities have largely abandoned traditional restrictive practices governing membership of non-whites, Jews, and other minorities. Few such organizations or private clubs retain their historic exclusivity based upon class, race, or religion.

The inevitable result of this transformation has been the phenomenon of numerous romantic involvements between individuals who a generation ago would have had little or no occasion to meet, let alone socialize. For many college students interdating is old hat, having already been in effect during their high school years. What transpires on the campus represents a logical extension of a well-established precedent. One's high school behavior was limited by the strictures of parental control and school regulations. Furthermore, dating, whatever the degree of intensity of a particular relationship, was seldom intended as a prelude to marriage. There were teenage pregnancies that resulted in marriage, but generally high school romances were just that—brief, temporary liaisons separate and distinct from the serious business of marriage.

To be sure, a great many college relationships are not permanent either. Dating on campus may be as varied and frequent as it was during high school. There are significant distinctions, however, between the high school and college dating experience. For one thing, many college students are legally "of age" and enjoy a far greater measure of independence and mobility than when they lived at home as teenagers. While their career and professional goals as undergraduates are often unclear, the academic atmosphere is one geared to the recognition that a university education is a prelude to the assumption of adult responsibilities.

Marriage too is no longer a remote possibility. The quality of romantic attachments is more likely to be molded by these new realities. Consequently, the implications of a relationship, especially a lengthy one, need to be weighed accordingly. Many couples in intermarriages met and dated during their undergraduate years. It is hoped that the information provided here regarding intermarriage will prove helpful for couples wrestling with what intermarriage holds for them and their families.

II. Some Insights Regarding Intermarriage

An ample body of literature on the subject of intermarriage is now available, drawn from both scientific research and the accounts of men and women who either are or have been in such marriages. (See the bibliography at the end of the chapter.) These findings have confirmed that despite many shared ideals and a common history, Judaism and Christianity remain distinct religions with diverse, sometimes conflicting theological positions. However successful the American experiment as a cultural melting pot, those who come from differing backgrounds do not easily relinquish deep-seated beliefs whatever their level of sophistication and worldliness. The frequency of intermarriage and its emergence as a familiar component of the contemporary religious scene have done little to reduce its troublesome aspects. These continue to generate tensions and pressure not present in marriages involving couples from similar backgrounds.

Among the more surprising discoveries made by couples who are interdating is that the prospect of an intermarriage causes discomfort even when neither partner has displayed any outward manifestations of religious observance. Customs and rituals connected with their faith are neglected. Synagogue or church attendance is sporadic at best. Still the discomfort persists and even grows as the relationship becomes more serious. It becomes evident that there are powerful forces at work, long buried but now awakened and very intrusive. Among them is the power of family ties and apprehensions regarding how parents will react when informed of the relationship. These preoccupations may sometimes act as a means of avoiding one's personal ambivalence, but they are legitimate and real nonetheless.

For Jewish parents the prospect that a son or daughter will marry a Christian will often evoke anger, resentment, pain, and a sense of betrayal. The latter is frequently connected with an accompanying self-criticism at having failed as a parent. Such sentiments will have little or nothing to do with their actual son- or daughter-in-law-to-be, who they will readily admit is very nice. They derive instead from a profound awareness that they have a responsibility for ensuring Jewish survival. This is true even when parents did not maintain a Jewish home, socialized with non-Jews, and did not interfere with their children's dating habits during high school. Anyone, they had stressed, was welcome in their home provided that he or she was a person of good character.

In a prior generation parental displeasure over an off-spring's choice of a mate would have meant the end of the matter. But at the onset of the twenty-first century, parents no longer control the destinies of their families. Well aware of their relative impotence in this matter, they will instead request or pressure, depending upon the nature of the family's style of communication, that the Christian partner convert to Judaism, or, if this is not possible, that the couple be married by a rabbi in a Jewish ceremony.

This conditional acceptance of the forthcoming marriage may have been already expressed by the Jewish partner, who has also broached the subject to his or her prospective spouse either as a non-negotiable demand or as a consideration that would be very much appreciated. If the non-Jewish partner is a woman, she will be asked to agree that any children born of the marriage be raised as Jews.

For many years the percentage of Jewish men marrying non-Jewish women far surpassed that of Jewish women marrying non-Jewish men.[3] The statistics had far less to do with the intensity of Jewish commitment predicated upon gender than they did upon the restrictive environment in which Jewish women lived, often thwarting their impulses and desires. New social forces, most notably the rise of feminism, have reduced the gender gap appreciably, so that the disparity between Jewish men and women in choosing a partner from another faith is far smaller than it once was. What has remained constant is the higher rate of conversion to Judaism by non-Jewish women in contrast to non-Jewish men.[4]

Although no analysis of the reason behind this imbalance has been done, one plausible explanation is male awareness that according to Jewish law the child of a Jewish mother is considered to be Jewish regardless of the faith of the father, while the child of a Jewish father and a non-Jewish mother is not, unless and until the child is formally converted to Judaism. Jewish women, it can be assumed, would be less prone to insist upon a husband's conversion under these circumstances, secure in the knowledge that their children would be Jewish by definition.

Over the years in counseling Jewish parents and partners contemplating an intermarriage, I have been struck by what resembles a mutual conspiracy of silence lasting as long as it is possible to avoid the issue. For example, the announcement by a son or daughter that he or she is marrying someone who is Christian rarely comes as a total surprise to parents. More often than not, they have been aware of the relationship for some time. The individual in question may have been invited to dinner on one or more occasions and, based upon the general tenor of the evening, polite but cool, parental feelings are quite evident. The implicit message "She's a nice girl, but . . ." has been transmitted in clear, albeit subtle terms.

Subsequent expressions of shock by parents or anger by an offspring when parental unhappiness is finally verbalized are somewhat suspect, and may be indicative of the wishes of all concerned that the problem go away by itself. It is only after those involved acknowledge that desire to be what it truly is, a fantasy, that a process of confronting the hard facts begin. Guilt, love of parents, the wish to placate and maintain sound family ties are genuine, sometimes irreconcilable emotions in the Jewish partner's abiding sense of personal Jewish identity notwithstanding his or her love for someone from another religious background. Christian partners and their families are subject to similar behavior patterns.

Short of dissolving the relationship and determining to date only persons of the same faith, each of the remaining alternatives for resolving the problems of intermarriage creates its own challenges.

III. Choosing To Become Jewish

Although figures are imprecise, a substantial number of men and women have chosen to become converts to Judaism, or Jews-by-choice, which today is their preferred designation. Conversion to Judaism is a comparatively recent phenomenon. Efforts at either open proselytizing (attempting to convert others) or even passive acceptance of new Jews virtually ceased upon the advent of Christianity as the dominant western religion and the imposition of formal restrictions upon Jewish efforts to attract proselytes. The latter were not merely avoided, they were discouraged as well. The record of numerous conversions to Judaism in the biblical and Graeco-Roman periods of Jewish history was forgotten and was replaced by the false assumption that proselytes were not welcome.

The Jewish community has developed formal courses of study designed specifically for persons interested in becoming Jewish, as well as informal networks and social settings intended to facilitate the transition process. Becoming a Jew-by-choice is a decision not to be made lightly. Prospective candidates should take the step only after lengthy and careful deliberation, as well as consultations with a rabbi. Agreeing to do so solely in response to the pleadings of a Jewish partner is not advisable and can lead to anguish and bitterness in later years.

Historically, Jewish law stipulated that no conversion was to be performed for the sake of a marriage, as this was the least valid justification for changing one's religion. Today the overwhelming majority of Jews-by-choice experience their initial exposure to Judaism by virtue of a romantic involvement with a born Jew. The fact need in no way detract from the integrity of a decision to embrace Judaism. It is to caution against making impulsive and superficial commitments.

Jewish partners bear a special responsibility not to exert undue pressure nor to make light of the ambivalence and doubts of a mate. Born Jews also have a tendency to ignore their own roles in fashioning a Jewish home once their wishes have been realized and their significant other has become Jewish. I have heard too many Jews-by-choice, usually women, lament the failure of their husbands to provide ongoing support and encouragement of their Jewish activities after their conversions. These husbands are content instead with an official declaration that their wives are Jewish. The need to keep up appearances is not a convincing rationale for expecting people to transform their lives.

The complexities of conversion are further magnified by problems within the Jewish community. The three major branches of American Judaism, Orthodox, Conservative, and Reform, have separate criteria for conversion. It therefore becomes incumbent upon potential Jews-by-choice to familiarize themselves with the differences between the three branches and determine where they will feel most comfortable and accepted as Jews. Here again, discussions with rabbis and wherever possible the insight of the Jewish partner and the Jewish family can be invaluable.

Whatever the rate of conversion to Judaism, it is exceeded substantially by the number of couples who retain their individual religious identities and decide to intermarry. Intermarriage is an alternative which, while avoiding the pitfalls of an ill-conceived conversion, brings with it other difficulties.

IV. What Is a Jewish Wedding?

Foremost among them is the question of who will officiate at the wedding. Many Jews are under the impression that being a born Jew automatically entitles one to the prerogative of having a rabbi solemnize their marriage. They are shocked and chagrined to discover that Orthodox and Conservative rabbis cannot and the majority of Reform rabbis will not officiate at an intermarriage even when the Christian spouse is willing to have children raised as Jews. Because the issue is so highly charged and the position of the rabbi so misunderstood, it is important to consider what a Jewish marriage connotes and what accounts for the unwillingness of most rabbis to agree to a couple's wishes to solemnize an intermarriage.

Marriage according to Judaism is far more than a private act of two consenting adults who pledge their love and fidelity to one another. The broader ramifications of matrimony are best summarized by the Hebrew word for betrothal, *kiddushin,* meaning to make holy. A marriage represents a sacred commitment on the part of a Jewish couple to be faithful not only to one another but to the Jewish community, the Jewish people, and a set of beliefs and practices known as Judaism. The ceremony marks an acceptance of that value system including the obligation to transmit the Jewish heritage by word and by deed to children. Historically, marriages that were childless were actually frowned upon by the community, for the family was understood to be the key to Jewish continuity.

The symbols of the wedding ceremony underscore the religious and communal obligations of the bride and groom and emphasize the bond between marriage and the collective experience of the Jewish people, both happy and sad. A case in point is the custom of the breaking of a glass at the conclusion of the ceremony. The shattered fragments commemorate tragic events in Jewish history, specifically the destruction of the ancient temple, thus reminding the wedding guests that even at moments of joy we must not forget the suffering that has marked the tenacity with which Jews have refused to surrender their right to worship and express themselves.

The rabbi was vested with the responsibility of presiding at the wedding, this formal declaration of mutual Jewish commitment. He was known in Hebrew as *msader kiddushin*, literally, the coordinator of this act of sanctity.

Before the advent of civil authority, the rabbi served as both the secular and the religious guarantor of the legal validity of the marriage. In presiding over the marriage ceremony and signing the wedding documents, he confirmed that the principals were Jews and had entered into this contract in accordance with the norms of Judaism. Even today the rabbi and, for that matter, all clergypersons who officiate at weddings, regardless of the faith of the participants, are considered representatives of the state when performing a marriage and signing the wedding license.

The central ritual of the Jewish wedding ceremony, which has not changed for centuries and which is the same in all branches of Judaism, is the declaration by the bride and groom that they are marrying in accordance with the requisite criteria of Judaism. "Be consecrated unto me with this ring as my wife/husband according to the law of God and the faith of Israel."[5] The pledge is direct and unequivocal and assumes that the couple is prepared to live in keeping with its mandate. In previous generations it was inconceivable that a couple would expect to have a Jewish ceremony presided over by a rabbi unless both partners were Jewish, by birth or by choice.

The current controversy is a dramatic illustration of the struggle between advocates of religious voluntarism and private versions of spirituality and those traditions such as Judaism which stress group solidarity and impose restrictions upon the autonomous actions of their adherents in deference to the best interests of the greater community. That overriding priority is best exemplified by the continued practice in both Orthodox and Conservative Judaism not only to grant a Jewish wedding certificate along with a civil one, but in the event of a divorce to require a religious proceeding in addition to the prescribed legal procedure dictated by a secular court of probate for terminating a marriage.

There are Reform rabbis who will agree to officiate at an intermarriage despite the contrary position of the Central Conference of American Rabbis, the official rabbinical body of Reform Judaism. In 1973, the last time the matter was formally addressed, a resolution issued by the Central Conference stated in part:

> The Central Conference of American Rabbis recalling its stand adopted in 1909 that mixed marriage is contrary to the Jewish tradition and should be discouraged now declares its opposition to participation by its members in any ceremony which solemnizes a mixed marriage. The Central Conference of American Rabbis recognizes that historically its members have held and continue to hold divergent interpretations of Jewish tradition. . . .[6]

Rabbis who officiate are of the opinion that whatever the precedents of the past, a willingness to participate in an intermarriage is in the best interests of Judaism. A wedding witnessed by a rabbi, they argue, can be a very persuasive impetus in motivating couples to rear children as Jews and, in some instances, to encourage the born Christian partner to convert to Judaism. There is ample opportunity, they say, to modify or delete those aspects of the wedding ceremony which, if retained, would be dishonest or hypocritical. The overriding consideration, they contend, is to offer the couple some supportive Jewish dimension at a critical time in their lives. While some rabbis who officiate set no prerequisites for doing so, many others obligate the couple to a prescribed period of study about Judaism as well as requiring a promise that any children born of the marriage will be raised as Jews.

There are occasions when couples may wish to have both a rabbi and a Christian clergyperson co-officiate at their wedding. Such so-called "ecumenical ceremonies" are again a reflection of late twentieth century sociological and pastoral trends in the United States. They also mirror the evolving nature of Protestant-Catholic relationships. In some Christian circles, intermarriage has been lauded as a unique opportunity for achieving a universal non-sectarian Christianity.

The following is illustrative: "Mixed marriages contain the possibility of becoming a prophetic sign of the triumph of the love of God over the division of the Churches."[7] In theory, ecumenical ceremonies appear to be the ideal avenue for resolving many of the most troublesome aspects of an intermarriage. In reality they may create as many problems as they seemingly overcome.

The presence of Jewish and Christian clergy symbolizes the respective religious traditions of each partner and relieves the anxieties of each family that the wedding will be one-sided. The demand for equal time, even when unspoken, is a powerful factor in the desire for an ecumenical ceremony. This grand compromise is also a manifestation of the prevailing American view, now somewhat less dominant in light of the resurgence of Evangelical Christianity, that basically we all believe in the same ideals, worship one God, and celebrate a common heritage.

Very few rabbis will participate in an ecumenical wedding ceremony. A limited amount of research has been done in an effort to ascertain whether, as has been claimed, the willingness of a rabbi to officiate at an intermarriage contributes to subsequent decisions on the part of parents to raise their children as Jews. The existing data show little or no correlation between the two. In other words, rabbinic participation in an intermarriage has no effect upon how children are subsequently reared.[8]

The question of who witnesses a wedding is not unrelated to the influence of a long-standing American folk ethic. While emphasizing the civil status of matrimony, it encourages the participation of the clergyperson, less as a spokesperson for a particular faith than as the official representative of the American civil, religious establishment with its own theological doctrine, a doctrine best expressed in the words of the Pledge of Allegiance, "one nation under God indivisible . . ." There are both Christian clergy and rabbis who espouse this philosophy and are perfectly comfortable conducting nonsectarian ceremonials.

The power of this folk ethic is such that when it is suggested that the couple consider having a justice of the peace conduct their wedding, the proposal is generally rejected— this despite the fact that such ceremonies are not only beautiful and dignified, but also inoffensive to families with different religious traditions. A civil marriage can be the setting for an honest and authentic articulation of a couple's distinct religious orientation, conveying a genuine appreciation of the unique messages of Christianity and Judaism, messages that should never be trivialized, least of all on one's wedding day.

The various branches of Judaism, most notably Reform Judaism, have undertaken extensive programs of education, support, and outreach in behalf of couples in intermarriages. Non-Jewish partners are welcomed at services of worship and at congregational functions. In many congregations they are granted a form of synagogue membership consistent with their non-Jewish status. Their membership prerogatives are generally restricted to not holding elective office and conducting or participating in specific synagogue religious functions which would be inappropriate for Christians.

These overtures have helped to lessen the apprehensions of both partners that given their situation, synagogues might be inhospitable and rejecting. Jewish community centers and other secular agencies have been equally forthcoming in their efforts to provide a congenial environment for these families.

V. Dealing with Children

There are problems and dilemmas that intermarried couples need to anticipate. The most critical is the Jewish status of a child of such a marriage. In 1983 the Central Conference of American Rabbis declared that children of intermarriages were presumptively Jewish if either parent was a Jew.[9] The declaration evoked a storm of controversy, since it marked a radical departure from Jewish tradition, which held that although the child of a Jewish mother and a non-Jewish father was automatically Jewish, the child of a Jewish father and a non-Jewish mother was not, unless and until the child was formally converted to Judaism.

This decision of the Reform rabbinate accorded gender parity to men and women and acknowledged that both played equal roles and bore equal responsibility in determining the Jewish status of a child. It went on to state that the presumption of Jewishness was contingent upon the performance of "appropriate and timely public and formal acts of identification with the Jewish faith and people," including "entry into the Covenant, acquisition of a Hebrew name, *Torah* study, *Bar/Bat Mitzvah*, and Confirmation.''[10] *Bar* and *bat mitzvah*, meaning literally son and daughter of the commandment, are rituals in which boys and girls at age thirteen symbolically assume full religious responsibilities. Confirmation is a ceremony which is held on the festival of Shavuot, which commemorates the giving of the ten commandments. The confirmands are usually teenagers, fifteen to seventeen years of age, who, having completed a certain level of religious education, reaffirm their loyalties to Judaism on this occasion.

This resolution was a response both to the high incidence of intermarriage and the changing parenting roles of men and women in the United States. It sought to address what it interpreted as an obsolete definition of women's duties as well as emerging family models that were forerunners of what would be the norm in the year 2000. The other branches of Judaism have not accepted the Reform position. The prospects of their doing so in the foreseeable future are not very bright.

Children of Jewish fathers and non-Jewish mothers who are raised as Jews in keeping with the criteria of Reform Judaism will not be granted Jewish status in Orthodox and Conservative quarters. Their non-Jewish identification may preclude them from observing a *bar* or *bat mitzvah* in a traditional synagogue, or in adulthood, should they plan to marry someone who is Orthodox or Conservative, from having a rabbi from either branch of Judaism consent to officiate at their wedding. They will also be considered non-Jews should they wish to settle in Israel and would have to be naturalized in accordance with the duly prescribed immigration statutes of that country. As previously mentioned, it is impossible to predict when, if ever, the Jewish religious community will develop uniform ground rules governing marriage, conversion, and the status of children.

The problem of intrafaith harmony aside, the religious upbringing of children remains the most challenging facet of an intermarriage. Many couples have premarital verbal agreements which they hope will resolve the matter, if not to everyone's satisfaction, at least to the smallest measure of discomfort. However valuable open and candid discussions about child-rearing may be, it behooves couples to remember that these conversations have taken place in a hypothetical context. Any parent can attest that the best-laid plans have a way of changing in the aftermath of a baby's birth. What may have seemed logical, at the very least a reasonable compromise premaritally and prenatally, may now be open to doubt. Couples should anticipate the need for new negotiations and a revision of agreed-upon intentions after a baby is born.

What follows is a look at some of the alternatives couples select in choosing a religious lifestyle for their children. All have problems. None is foolproof. Each not only is subject to modification but offers no guarantee that children themselves at some point later in their lives will turn their backs on their parents' aspirations.

A familiar strategy is to decide to allow children to choose for themselves. The format is one which fits neatly into modern American notions of multiple religious options as well as a philosophy of so-called enlightened parenting, which strives to make children autonomous and independent as early as possible. In truth, letting children choose is an excellent means of sidestepping the issue of religion in the interests of family peace. It allows both parents the luxury of treading neutral ground rather than being compelled to take a stand.

It also runs counter to the developmental needs of young children. Children crave an underlying sense of identity. They look to parents as models to emulate and as unimpeachable resources in celebrating life's joys, coping with its sorrows, and understanding the meaning and purpose of human existence. A solid religious foundation is an important ingredient for healthy growth.

Parents who provide little or no religious guidance for their children convey the impression that they have nothing of substance to give. Children, in turn, may interpret that void as an invitation to look elsewhere for such values. They will often do so, discovering alternatives which may be unhealthy or unwise.

Letting children choose is also a direct contradiction of how most parents relate to children during their formative years. Parents will establish clear and strict guidelines regarding bedtime, diet, cleanliness, friendships, and a host of other value-laden items. It is only in the realm of spiritual values that another standard is applied.

A second solution is to expose children to two religions in

a balanced and equitable fashion. Colorful, glowing accounts of dual-religion families are often featured in popular magazines and newspapers. Such superficial treatment of serious questions conveys the misimpression that there are simplistic answers to this problem. Some couples decide to have a baby baptized and also, if the child is a boy, ritually circumcised, or, if a girl, named in the synagogue. Ritual circumcision or *brit milah,* the covenant of circumcision, as it is known in Hebrew, is based upon the biblical injunction found in Genesis 17:12 which reads, "At the age of eight days every male among you throughout the generations shall be circumcised . . . thus shall my covenant be marked in your flesh as an everlasting pact." Since baby girls are not circumcised, naming them in the synagogue was introduced as an alternate ceremonial.

In their quest for religious parity, the couple underscore their own unresolved conflicts and demean the rite of baptism for Christians and the ceremony of *brit milah,* ritual circumcision for Jews. What are profound sacred acts are transformed into meaningless gestures in the name of a genial pluralism lacking any real depth.

A third option is a decision on the part of the couple to raise a child solely in one religion. It remains the most preferable choice albeit one fraught with complexities of its own. For example, if a couple resolve that children will be Jewish, the success of that endeavor may hinge upon how the decision was reached. If it is mutual and the Christian partner becomes an active participant in the religious life of the family, the message conveyed and internalized by the children will be affirmative. But if, as is sometimes the case, the non-Jewish parent is passive or hostile, acquiescent only because of tremendous pressure exerted by the Jewish parent, the prognosis is limited for a healthy religious environment.

Children quickly perceive the mood of a family. Parental ambivalence will take its toll and children will soon find themselves feeling guilty and anxious over issues of loyalty and betrayal when observing the tenets of one faith rather than another. In making a decision of such importance, parents should be mindful of a number of criteria.

An agreement under duress is empty and counterproductive. In the long run it will achieve nothing and run the risk of backfiring. When parents decide to affiliate with a synagogue and enroll their children in the religious school, they should arrange a meeting in advance with the rabbi and the school principal. Here the philosophy behind the curriculum should be described in detail in order that the couple can determine whether these enunciated goals are compatible with their own purposes and how active both parents will be in furthering them.

In the absence of a clear consensus, intermarried couples who enroll a child in a synagogue religious school not only are unfair to the child and dishonest with one another, but are insensitive to the needs of the other children in the classroom as well. A child who is the recipient of mixed messages can be a disruptive element, creating anxiety for children from homes where there is no equivocation about Judaism and the purpose of a religious education. This is not what these parents had anticipated when they joined a congregation. On the other hand, if an intermarried couple have determined in good conscience to live Jewishly, children will respond positively to a stable, consistent environment.

VI. Divorce and Blended Families

Just as dating and marriage patterns have been impacted by a host of societal changes, divorce, blended families, and both single parent and divorced parent households have all become culturally prevalent today. Figures show that nearly one-half of all marriages in the United States currently end in divorce, with the divorce rate among the intermarried somewhat higher.[11] These statistics, along with newly emerging family trends, lead one to assume that in the twenty-first century, religious differences will not only be a formidable cause of marital breakdown, but will play a decisive part in post-divorce interaction between parents and their children. Some discussion of the implications of divorce for the intermarried is therefore very much in order.

Reference has already been made to Jews who make conversion a pre-condition of marriage or who demand that the Christian partner promise to raise children as Jews. There are a growing number of divorces currently in litigation throughout the country in which the custodial parent, usually the mother, has repudiated her Jewish conversion and reverted back to her former faith, refusing as well to continue raising the children as Jews. In the case of an inter-marriage she has simply broken the promise to provide children with a Jewish upbringing. There are other situations in which Jewish ex-husbands have gone to court objecting to the practice of mothers who celebrate Christian holidays in the presence of their children, even though the children are being educated as Jews. These actions, the fathers maintain, undermine the intent of a Jewish upbringing and are evasions of the pre-marital commitment to which both parties agreed.

Given the nature of the legal system and the unpredictability of judicial decisions, there are no definitive rulings that can be demonstrated in these cases. Divorce laws vary from state to state. In the past, courts were reluctant to interfere in questions of religion and were predisposed to leave the matter of a child's religious upbringing to the custodial parent unless it could be shown conclusively that it was not in the best interest of the child to do so.

But even if court-ordered guidelines were consistent, their implementation would be quite another matter. What a court holds to be legal and binding in the area of finances is far more enforceable than when one is dealing with the teaching of a religious ideology. Furthermore, Jewish fathers, who in general are the plaintiffs in these cases, forget that the termination of a marriage implies the failure to live up to all manner of promises made by both partners before and during the marriage, of which religion was but one. Demands that an ex-spouse behave in a certain way religiously can be a violation of that individual's civil rights as well.

The matter is further compounded by the liberalization of laws governing the custody of children in a great many states. Formerly, when a divorce took place, mothers were nearly always granted sole custody of children unless it could be proved that the mother was unfit, a very difficult and generally unsuccessful endeavor. Today over thirty states provide some form of what is known as a presumption of shared legal custody. What this means is that while children may physically reside more frequently in the home of one parent as opposed to the other, both parents share equal responsibility in dealing with legal, medical, educational, and religious issues affecting their children unless one parent voluntarily waives that prerogative or is adjudged to be unfit.

The implications of shared legal custody for the religious training of children from divorced, intermarried households are enormous. Answers are not to be found in the courts but in the willingness and ability of couples who, whatever their other differences, are able to hold the welfare of their children as a mutual priority.

The rate of intermarriage among Jews in second marriages is high. The reasons accounting for this trend include a declining pool of available mates, particularly for women as they grow older. If the first marriage has been especially unhappy, there is a tendency to seek a partner from a religious or cultural background unlike that of the former spouse. The end result of this process is the blended family consisting of Jewish and Christian children living together regularly or intermittently, plus a new family configuration referred to as the bi-nuclear family, which is comprised of interlocking networks involving former spouses, their new partners, and the families of origin of all concerned.

Preserving religious integrity in blended and bi-nuclear families is not easy under the best of circumstances. When former spouses are locked in a bitter struggle over their children or when these new family arrangements evoke fears and insecurities within either parent, the task is even more difficult.

For example, the non-custodial parent may dread the spiritual loss of children. Whatever religious or ethnic prejudices have been harbored over the years may now be galvanized and openly expressed. Attempts may be made to undermine the stepparent and openly mock his or her religion. Ideally, and in light of shared legal custody, parents should and will almost always have to communicate with one another for many years after their divorce.

The impending marriage of one partner to someone of another faith should be disclosed early enough to afford time to discuss its meaning for children. Assurances need to be given that a child's religious upbringing will not be affected adversely by the new marriage, at least insofar as the parent with primary physical custody can control the situation.

The non-custodial parent, who in the past, when the couple was married, may have left the responsibility for the religious education of the child to the other parent, may now insist upon playing a greater role in that process and by law, in states awarding shared legal custody, is entitled to do so. Working out the details of his or her new duties will be an added responsibility assumed by the parents.

It bears repeating in light of the divorce rate among couples who stem from similar backgrounds, and the easing of the legal criteria for divorce, that simplistic maxims about happy marriages are naive and unfair. Nor is it appropriate to assert that intermarriages are bound to fail or destined to bring unhappiness to those who are in them.

VII. Anticipating Danger Signals

The facts of the matter do suggest that since intermarriage has the potential of creating additional tensions in relationships, couples should begin the difficult process of talking about themselves and their expectations of marriage long before the emotional intensity of being together gets out of hand and they are no longer able to exercise dispassionate judgment. Many persons are painfully aware of how the disclaimer, "It's only a date," proved to be illusory. The same individuals are often at a loss to account for the sudden surge of powerful Jewish associations immediately prior to an intermarriage. "I never thought I would feel this way" is a familiar refrain.

Couples in intermarriage pride themselves on having risen above biases and stereotypes. Their marriage, they say, demonstrates how liberal they are and how uncluttered their lives with the prejudices of older generations. Experience may prove otherwise. The scenarios that follow are drawn from interviews with many couples and should not go unheeded.

The possibility of name-calling and the use of other well-known negative references to a partner's ancestry in the heat of an argument is an all too common occurrence. Other manifestations of animosity rooted in the sorry history of Jewish-Christian relationships may also surface unexpectedly. Jews may refuse to attend church services or participate in the celebration of Christian holidays, even though their Christian partner is perfectly willing to go to the synagogue. Part of the reason may be traced to the fact that the New Testament contains many passages read in the course of a service of worship which Jews hear as overtly antisemitic. While

Christian ministers try to explain them as ancient references having nothing to do with present-day events, Jews experience them as direct, personal attacks.

Memories of the holocaust continue to affect Jews. What they evoke is not easy to convey to Christians who are far removed from the horrors of the Nazi death camps. As decent men and women, they may recoil with revulsion over the fact that six million Jews met their deaths, but their horror is impersonal. For them what happened is true. For Jews it is real. Many Christians, especially women, do voice open ambivalence about bringing Jewish children into the world who may be vulnerable to persecution at some future date by virtue of who they are. Both partners should anticipate that what the Jewish spouse may interpret as an antisemitic remark overheard at a cocktail party may seem perfectly innocuous to his or her mate. In turn, the latter's attempt to make light of the comment may only aggravate the situation.

For Christians matters affecting the state of Israel may be remote and inconsequential. The reactions of their Jewish partners may be a source of constant bewilderment. Some intermarried couples may find it less taxing to confine their social relationships to other couples in similar circumstances. Friendships with Christian or Jewish couples have often led to uncomfortable discussions about religion which they do not care to repeat.

Spouses may feel uneasy during visits with their respective in-laws. Stilted conversations, awkward attempts to talk about the weather or sporting events with people bending over backward to be on their best behavior, make such gatherings intolerable.

The problem is aggravated when there are grandchildren with each set of grandparents vying for their affection and sometimes for their religious loyalties. In some families, partners decide to avoid these visits, preferring to have spouses spend time alone with their parents rather than enduring stressful get-togethers. All of the aforementioned situations can build invisible walls and cause deep-seated resentment.

The following reminders may be helpful for couples planning to intermarry:

1. Intermarriages demand even more maturity, candor, and the capacity for compromise than same-faith marriages.

Anyone expecting to magically surmount long-held beliefs simply by uttering the words "I do" will be sadly disappointed. Love never conquers all. All marriages, to be successful, require continuous work.

2.   Normal marital misunderstandings may stimulate reactions wholly out of proportion to their surface causes. The compromises necessitated by the conditions of an intermarriage may stir angry feelings which will not always be expressed directly. Instead they may show up in incidents having nothing whatsoever to do with religion. They therefore become even more dangerous to marital stability since they cannot be localized or their origins identified.

3.   Religious and cultural experiences which should enrich a marriage may be difficult to achieve. Too often, intimacy is equated only with sexual fulfillment or the sharing of private thoughts with one's partner. While these are certainly highly desirable, closeness is not limited to these two areas of marital interaction. Couples should be able to touch spiritually as well. The joint celebration of religious moments is a deeply rewarding opportunity which may not be attainable when one is intermarried. Appreciating a spouse's heritage intellectually or dutifully going through the motions of reading a text at a festival dinner is a poor substitute for genuinely being a part of the event. That gap may always exist no matter how diligently the couple work to overcome it.

4.   The lack of spiritual alternatives sufficiently compensatory for the absence of such moments may have unforeseen results. The inability to be religiously synchronized within a marriage may lead to efforts to find such gratification outside of it. While these separate excursions may be perfectly innocent, the distancing they produce can only fray the relationship and contribute to a state of affairs where couples lead basically independent lives.

5.   The religious upbringing of children poses endless dilemmas. The subject has been more than amply treated in these pages. It is enough to add that, given the increase in the life expectancy and the emergence of multigenerational families as normative in the next century, the influence of grandparents in the years ahead will become an ever more important aspect of a child's environment.

6.   A successful intermarriage may be one thing. The quality of its Jewish dimension may be quite another.

VIII. What of the Future?

For those Jews who have been thoroughly assimilated into the American mainstream and wedded to secularism, intermarriage may pose few or no problems. If anything, it may hasten their avowed desire to leave the Jewish scene without resorting to outright conversion to Christianity. Throughout Jewish history there have been individuals who have made that choice. What is contained in these pages may be totally irrelevant for them.

There are others, however, who are determined both to share their lives with a non-Jewish partner and also to maintain their own Jewish identity and that of their children. They are joined by another group who are ambivalent about their Jewish identity and who still are searching for answers to who they are. Hopefully these men and women will find helpful insights in the information provided here. Perhaps they will avail themselves of the numerous opportunities now offered by the Jewish community in either attaining their goals or resolving their uncertainties.

Finally, it bears noting that however permanent or irreversible societal trends may appear, change is always afoot even at the very moment when the status quo seems most firmly entrenched. While that has always been true, it is even more pronounced in our day. No period has been more cyclical and less stable than the years following World War II. The advent of the year 2000 will probably bring more upheaval in its wake.

What the next century portends in the way of Jewish marital patterns and evolving family constellations remains to be seen. The next decade will offer us a clearer picture of how children of late twentieth century intermarriages, the adults of tomorrow, have dealt with their upbringing and how their own marital and religious choices will have shaped the Judaism of the next generation. By the mid-twenty-first century, the various branches of Judaism may have developed a common approach to intermarriage and conversions, thereby unifying the Jewish community as it copes with these phenomena. Possibly the return to religious orthodoxy may have become so dominant as to make intermarriage a curiosity rather than a matter of immediate concern.

Whatever the rapidity and unpredictability of change, it

is undeniable that the desire for Jewish survival is abiding and the pride in Jewish achievement ongoing. Intermarriage is hardly a new problem for Jews. It is as old as the Jewish people and is amply documented in the Bible and in rabbinic literature.[12]

Predictions of the demise of the Jewish community because of intermarriage are unfounded. Simplistic formulas for preventing it are futile and more often than not complicate an already complex situation. Judaism has ever withstood these forces both external and from within which have threatened to overwhelm it. There is no reason to doubt that the challenge of intermarriage will be met with the same resilience that has characterized other struggles of the Jewish people for nearly six thousand years.

NOTES

[1]Readers should note that the words Christian and non-Jew have been used interchangeably throughout this chapter. In some cases non-Jew is a more accurate designation due to the individual's rejection of any formal religious identity as an adult.

[2]For more detailed analysis see Calvin Goldscheider and Alan S. Zuckerman, *The Transformation of the Jews* (Chicago and London: University of Chicago Press, 1986), pp. 176–81. Also Sanford Seltzer, Steven Schweger, and Mark Winer, *Leaders of Reform Judaism*, Research Task Force on the Future of Reform Judaism (New York: Union of American Hebrew Congregations, 1987), pp. 113–37.

[3]Susan Weidman Schneider, *Jewish and Female* (New York: Simon and Schuster, 1985), pp. 334–37.

[4]Sanford Seltzer, *Who Enrolls in the Introduction to Judaism Program?* A Report from Four American Cities, Horizon Reports (New York: Union of American Hebrew Congregations, October 1984).

[5]*Rabbi's Manual* (New York, Central Conference of American Rabbis, 1961), p. 27.

[6]*Central Conference of American Rabbis Yearbook*, Vol. LXXXIII, New York, 1973, p. 97.

[7]*Living the Faith You Share: Ten Ecumenical Guidelines for Couples in Roman Catholic-Protestant Marriages* (Needham: Whittemore Associates, n.d.).

[8]Egon Mayer and Amy Avgar, *Conversions Among the Intermarried* (New York: American Jewish Committee, 1987), p. 21.

[9]*Yearbook Central Conference of American Rabbis*, Vol. XCIII, New York, 1984, pp. 157–60.

[10]Ibid.

[11]Barry A. Kosmin, Nova Lerer, and Egon Mayer, *Intermarriage, Divorce and Remarriage Among American Jews, 1982–87* (New York: North American Jewish Data Bank, Family Research Series, No. 1, August 1989), pp. 12–15.

[12]Biblical personalities married to non-Jews include Joseph, Moses, Solomon, Ahab, and Bathsheba. Those interested in reading more on the subject should consult Joseph R. Rosenbloom, *Conversion to Judaism: From the Biblical Period to the Present* (Cincinnati: Hebrew Union College Press, 1978). See also Bernard Bamberger, *Proselytism in the Talmudic Period*, rev. ed. (New York, 1968).

Discussion Questions

1. Would you consider marrying a person from another faith tradition? Why or why not?

2. What do you see as either the advantages or the obstacles to an interfaith marriage?

3. What are some of the issues surrounding intermarriage concerning one's family of origin, the desire to have children, the desire of one spouse to have the other convert?

4. How do you react to the fact that very few rabbis will participate in an interfaith wedding ceremony?

5. How do divorce, remarriage, blended families and the binuclear family affect interfaith marriage?

For Further Study

Cowan, Paul and Rachel Cowan. *Mixed Blessings: Marriage between Jews and Christians.* New York: Doubleday, 1987.

Gruzen, Lee F. *Raising Your Jewish-Christian Child: Wise*

Choices for Interfaith Parents. New York: Dodd, Mead, 1987.

Luka, Ronald. *When a Christian and a Jew Marry*. New York: Paulist, 1973.

Mayer, Egon. *Children of Intermarriage: A Study in Patterns of Identification and Family Life*. New York: American Jewish Committee, 1983.

———. *Love and Tradition: Marriage Between Jews and Christians*. New York: Plenum, 1985.

Mayer, Egon. and Carl Scheingold. *Intermarriage and the Jewish Future: A National Study in Summary*. New York: American Jewish Committee, 1979.

Petsonk, Judy and Jim Remsen. *The Intermarriage Handbook: A Guide for Jews and Christians*. New York: William Morrow & Co., 1988.

Rosenberg, Roy A. *Happily Intermarried: Authoritative Advice for a Joyous Jewish-Christian Marriage*. New York: Collier, 1988.

Seltzer, Sanford. *Jews and Non-Jews: Falling in Love*. New York: Union of American Hebrew Congregations, 1976.

———. *Jews and Non-Jews: Getting Married*. New York: Union of American Hebrew Congregations, 1984.

IX.

SUSANNAH HESCHEL

Feminism and Jewish-Christian Dialogue

I. Introduction

If someone from the last century were to visit the churches and synagogues of America today, the biggest surprise they would have is the presence of women on the pulpit, leading the services as ordained ministers and rabbis. Feminism has been the most significant and visible force for change in religious communities since the early 1970s.

The feminist critique of religion parallels, in numerous respects, the issues addressed by Jewish-Christian dialogue. Both feminism and interreligious dialogue are concerned with how Judaism and Christianity define and represent the "other"—in one case, women, in the other case, different faiths. Feminism exposes sexism, while interreligious dialogue criticizes anti-Judaism. In both cases the critique leads to the question of whether traditional beliefs and language should and can be changed or reinterpreted. Feminists argue, for example, that language referring to God and the religious community solely as male excludes women's experiences. The language of the liturgy and theology should acknowledge the presence of women in the community and the recognition of femaleness in the divinity. In Jewish-Christian dialogue the most frequently discussed issue has been removing anti-Judaism from the Bible, liturgy, and teachings of Christianity. In both cases, the assumption is made that negative teachings concerning women and Jews cannot be upheld within the heart of a religious tradition.

Proposals for change are not, however, implemented easily. The discovery of sexism and anti-Judaism in biblical texts leads Jews and Christians to question whether the Bible can be held responsible for women's suffering under patriarchy and for the persecution of Jews by anti-Semites. At the same time, some theologians and religious leaders are reluctant to sanction the removal or alteration of problematic texts because they consider the Bible to be divinely revealed or inspired and not subject to change.

While the challenges posed by feminists in exposing the sexism within Judaism and Christianity are similar to the challenges posed by Jews and Christians concerned about Christianity's anti-Judaism, the two groups have generally not been in dialogue with each other, but have proceeded independently.[1] Nevertheless, their proposed solutions to the problems they delineate ought to be considered in tandem. Feminists, for example, have been radical and innovative in proposing new theologies of Judaism and Christianity based on women's spirituality and morality. Similarly, some Christian theologians have developed new Christian theologies of Judaism that make a sharp departure from classical postures of supersession (the idea that Christianity has displaced Judaism).[2] By operating independently of each other, however, manifestations of sexism often remain in the writings of those concerned about eliminating Christian anti-Judaism, while some Christian feminist theology has retained classical doctrines of Christian anti-Judaism.[3] Christian feminist theology would best be served by combining awareness of sexism with elimination of anti-Judaism.

II. The Development of Feminist Theology

Feminism is not new to the twentieth century, although its impact on religion is relatively recent. During the nineteenth century in the United States, a feminist movement developed calling for woman suffrage, as well as increased involvement of women in social projects.[4] During the Second Great Awakening, for example, Christian women became prominent as leaders of religious communities, and women's voices were taken seriously as sources of religious insight and authority.[5] Although the feminist movement reached a peak at the turn of the twentieth century, it declined after women were granted voting rights in 1920.

The second wave of feminism arose in the United States during the 1960s, stimulated by the publication of Betty Friedan's classic, *The Feminine Mystique,* which became a best seller.[6] Friedan described American women who had achieved the professed post-war American dream of marriage, children, and a house in the suburbs. Yet with all their material comfort, Friedan described the dissatisfaction of these middle-class women, who suffered from the "problem which has no name." The homemaker's life was not satisfying, according to Friedan, because these women were defined relative to their husbands and lacked a sense of their own identity.

During the second wave of feminism, religion increasingly became a major concern. Feminists in the nineteenth century had been critical of religious teachings, particularly of biblical and post-biblical images of women as temptresses, whores, and sinners. In the twentieth century, however, feminists mounted a broader critique of religion that encompassed all aspects of theology and practice, and that also set forth an alternative, feminist theology.

An important starting point for feminist theology was the post-World War II feminist classic, *The Second Sex,* by Simone de Beauvoir, which set forth a critique of patriarchy within western civilization.[7] De Beauvoir argued that women and men are not born, but created. Whatever biological differences exist, their roles are social constructs devised by cultures and sanctioned by religions. The roles that are devised place men in positions of power, while women are kept subordinate. She writes,

> Humanity is male and man defines woman not in herself but as relative to him; she is not regarded as an autonomous being. . . . She is defined and differentiated with reference to man and not he with reference to her; she is the incidental, the inessential as opposed to the essential. He is the Subject, he is the Absolute—she is the Other.[8]

Drawing on the work of de Beauvoir and others, feminists began, during the 1960s and 1970s, to examine religion critically, uncovering the position of man as subject, woman as other.[9] The earliest feminist theological studies examined the teachings and laws of Judaism and Christianity. For example, Catholic feminists saw a pattern in the prohibitions against birth control and ordination of women as priests which they traced to teachings concerning Eve's responsibility for original sin. Blaming Eve for the fall, argued Mary Daly in her first book, *The Church and the Second Sex*, led to a negation of women and a view of sexuality as potentially dangerous and sinful.[10]

Jewish feminists found similar patterns of projecting guilt onto women.[11] For example, that women must sit behind a curtain during synagogue services in Orthodox congregations is traditionally explained as protecting men from distracting sexual thoughts during their prayers. As in Christianity, women are identified as seductive, and sexuality is defined in opposition to spirituality. Most disturbing to feminists is the assumption that only men's needs during prayer are taken into consideration. The separation of religion and sexuality has led both Jews and Christians to an identification of men with spirituality, women with physicality, providing a justification for retaining male control over religious institutions.

By the mid-1970s, however, the feminist critique of religion began to shift from discussions of religious teachings to analysis of religious symbols. The earlier feminist criticisms were hopeful, convinced that alterations in laws and customs could be made to include women fully in the activities of their religions. Indeed, feminism seemed successful during the 1970s, as ordination of women to the ministry and rabbinate became increasingly common. Yet precisely during this period the feminist argument shifted and took on a new, pessimistic tone.

The new feminist argument was inaugurated by Mary Daly's book, *Beyond God the Father*.[12] Daly argued that because the church worships a male God and a male savior, women will always be outsiders, regardless of how the church might change its teachings. By identifying its central images of holiness with maleness, Christianity, she claimed, inevitably excluded and denigrated women.

The symbol of the Father God, spawned in the human imagination and sustained as plausible by patriarchy, has in turn rendered services to this type of society by making its mechanisms for the oppression of women appear right and fitting. If God in "his" heaven is a Father ruling "his" people, then it is in the "nature" of things and according to divine plans and the order of the universe that society be male dominated.[13]

For Daly, it is symbols, rather than teachings, that are the central problem. However much women may be included in religious rituals—ordained priests or ministers or rabbis —sexism will not be eliminated within religion or society as long as God is male. Yet eliminating a male Father God from centuries-old theologies, liturgies, and sacred texts was clearly not an easy task, and feminists began questioning whether a transformation of Christianity or Judaism was even possible. Increasing numbers of feminists began to explore women's spiritual traditions outside the context of Judaism and Christianity, turning to Wiccan traditions or to ancient Graeco-Roman pagan traditions.[14]

For those feminists choosing to remain within the contexts of Judaism and Christianity, Daly's work sparked explorations of various alternatives to the male Father God. Christian ethicist Beverly Harrison, among others, has argued in her book, *Making the Connections: Essays in Feminist Social Ethics*, that not only God's maleness, but God's transcendence, omnipotence, and immutability are problematic.[15] Traditional theology's elevation of God above human beings, unaffected by human actions, teaches that it is precisely a lack of relatedness that is God's strength; that lack of relatedness fosters a society that promotes individualism rather than community, self-reliance rather than caring for others. Harrison suggests that not only should God's exclusive maleness be ended, but that God's attributes, too, must be altered. Daly herself had argued that a hierarchical understanding of God as a supreme king who stands in power over human beings undermines our potential for moral action.

Increasingly, feminist theologians have insisted that feminism is not only a question of gender ethics, but also a problem of social ethics. Overcoming oppression of women and others within society requires a different understanding of God. Harrison proposes a view of divinity as immanent rather than transcendent, and seen as sister or brother rather than as parent. God should be seen not as utterly self-reliant and disinterested, she argues, but in relation to us, responsive to humanity and in need of human deeds. A God who stands in relation to humans, rather than imperially inaccessible to us, forces us to take responsibility for social and ecological problems, argues Sallie McFague in her book, *Models for God: Theology for an Ecological, Nuclear Age.*[16] When God is in his heaven, ruling his earth, in the traditional theological imagination, societies turn over responsibility for the planet to him, and then may feel free to develop weapons of destruction, according to McFague. In other words, if God's got the whole world in his hands, why should we humans worry about the future of our planet?

Feminist theology—or, more properly, theologies—now span a wide range of positions. Some, like Carol Christ, who has argued persuasively why "Women Need the Goddess," have left Christianity behind in favor of reviving ancient pagan traditions of women's spirituality.[17] Others, such as Beverly Harrison, are concerned with a new understanding of divinity and its relation to social ethics. Still others are concerned to remain within the Jewish and Christian traditions, despite their sexism, and look for reconciliations between feminism and Judaism or Christianity. Black feminists, who call their approach womanist theology, are particularly critical of feminism, arguing that many of its assumptions concerning sexism are drawn from white, middle-class experiences.[18]

III. The Problem of Anti-Judaism in Christian Feminist Theology

Of major concern in the context of Jewish-Christian relations is the negative image of Judaism that often appears in Christian feminist writings. Frequently, in their effort to "rescue" the possibility of remaining Christian, despite Christianity's sexism, feminists blame Judaism for introducing and perpetuating patriarchy. There are, in fact, two major motifs of anti-Judaism present in Christian feminist theology. First, there is a tendency to blame Judaism for the origins of patriarchy, charging that the ancient Israelites, together with the Father God of the Hebrew Bible, murdered the ancient goddess and destroyed the peace-loving society that worship of her had promoted. Second is a motif that highlights the alleged positive treatment of women in early Christianity by negating first century Judaism's negative treatment of women. These motifs are certainly familiar—long before feminism, anti-Jewish motifs played an important role in traditional male Christian theology. They are troubling because they display a lack of awareness of the history of Christian anti-Judaism.

The first motif, blaming the Jews for killing the goddess and introducing patriarchy to the world, echoes the old Christian charge that the Jews killed Jesus.[19] The argument entered feminist writings beginning in the early 1970s, and is repeated in Elizabeth Gould Davis' *The First Sex*,[20] Sheila Collins' *A Different Heaven and Earth*,[21] Merlin Stone's *When God Was a Woman*,[22] and Gerda Lerner's *The Creation of Patriarchy*.[23]

In what became one of the most popular feminist books in West Germany several years ago, Gerda Weiler repeated the argument, in *Ich Verwerfe im Lande die Kriege* ("I Denounce the Violence of the Land"): "Patriarchal monotheism developed through the elimination of the cosmic Goddess; there is no father in heaven without the murder of the mother."[24] The dominance of patriarchy has left us, these feminists continue, with a society which is dualistic and disunified, in which body stands apart from soul, mind from nature, men from women. Worship of a male deity is claimed to set forth a pattern of social control of men over women. Moreover, the male religion described in the Hebrew Bible is said to legitimate violence and destruction.

On one level, the argument that an ancient goddess worshiping society once existed is important to feminism because it asserts the historically accidental nature of patriarchy, in opposition to those who claim that patriarchy is inevitable because it is biologically rooted. In addition, the argument tries to legitimate feminist goals by showing that they were once realized in an ancient woman-centered society. If patriarchy is an historical phenomenon, it can also be overcome by historical progress.

These assertions, however, are problematic. That a male Father God sanctifies patriarchy is clear; but the corollary is not necessarily true: that the simple presence of female deities will guarantee a feminist social order. Patriarchy has existed, and continues to exist, even among peoples who worship female deities. That the Hebrew Bible makes a strong case against worship of the goddess is uncontested, but the relation between her suppression and the actual role of women in biblical society has not been clarified. Women's real power in the agricultural society of ancient Israel was, according to Carol Meyers' recent study, *Discovering Eve,* much greater than we can realize from biblical narratives.[25] Finally, just as feminists have tried to reconstruct ancient female spirituality based on relics of goddess figurines, the biblical texts have also been interpreted by feminists to show that Israelite women may have had their own spiritual traditions. Reading between the lines of the Hebrew Bible, feminists suggest that prophetic condemnations of goddess worship are evidence for the persistence of goddess worship by Israelite women. Future research might indicate the persistence of unique women's religious traditions throughout the course of Jewish history.

What troubles me more, however, is when the argument extends beyond an affirmation of feminism to an historically unverifiable assertion that Jews introduced patriarchy and violence into the world. In describing the contrast between ancient goddess religion and what characterizes the religion of the Hebrew Bible, Gerda Lerner writes, "No matter how degraded and commodified the reproductive and sexual power of women was in real life, their essential equality could not be banished from thought and feeling as long as the goddesses lived and were believed to rule human life."[26] With the advent of Israelite religion, she continues, a dramatic change takes place: "This new order under the all-powerful God proclaimed to Hebrews and to all those who took the Bible as their moral and religious guide that women cannot speak to God."[27]

How do we respond to such arguments? Even a cursory survey of the mythology of other cultures yields evidence for the early introduction of patriarchy in other parts of the world. Curiously, this comparison has been ignored. In addition, the ancient goddesses were not always associated with peace and non-violence; on the contrary, ancient Near Eastern goddesses were often presented as bloody warriors, as in the Ras Shamra texts concerning Anat.[28] Moreover, it is obvious that women do "speak to God" in the Hebrew Bible, and we can point to women leaders, such as Deborah, and prophets, such as Hulda. On the other hand, such arguments are not a real answer. Biblical religion is in the hands of men, beginning with the patriarchal accounts, and continuing through the classical prophets, the priests, and the scribes. Yet the real issue at stake here is not the actual lives of Israelite women, but whether the Hebrew Bible (the Jews) can be held responsible for inventing patriarchy.

According to Elizabeth Gould Davis, when God accepted Abel's offering of meat (Gen 4:4) "the new male God was announcing his law: that thenceforth harmony among men and beasts was out, and killing and violence were in."[29] Emphasizing the violence described in the Hebrew Bible has often been used throughout history to denigrate Judaism. At times, that violence is contrasted with the supposedly peaceful actions of Jesus reported in the Christian scriptures. But the biblical reading is often distorted. The rape, murder, and other violence described in the Hebrew Bible is not intended prescriptively, but descriptively, as a picture of a social reality that scripture as a whole discovers, seeks to understand, and condemns. And the Jesus of the gospels is hardly a peaceful fellow; what he does not like he throws over (literally, when he enters the temple, Mt 21:12–17) or curses (the fig tree, Mt 21:18–22).

From a Jewish perspective, the God of the Hebrew Bible is a God of passion who expresses love and anger out of a sense of caring for human beings. The Jewish God is not remote and impassable, but passionate and affected by human action. The view that the Hebrew Bible introduced violence into the world is as absurd as the accompanying claims by Christian theologians that Jesus introduced love. Ancient Near Eastern documents pre-dating biblical materials make it clear that war, violence, and patriarchy pre-dated the Bible and coexisted with a pantheon of goddesses as well as gods.

For all their claims to be post-Christian, these feminists are setting forth a schema that seems to follow the traditional Christian model of the fall: first there was an idyllic state in the garden of Eden (worship of the goddess), then a fall through human sin (rejection of the goddess), and now a state of evil in which we await a future redemption (return to the goddess). In the feminist schema it is not women who brought about the fall, as in traditional Christian theology; it is the Jews. How ironic that the old antisemitic association of Judaism and deicide should resurface here in feminist writings. What is operating in these arguments is not historical evidence-because the garden of Eden is a myth, not an historic reality—but a new theodicy (explanation for evil) that blames the Jews for the suffering of women and the existence of violence.

The second motif of anti-Judaism is unquestionably the most prevalent, not only among feminists, but also among Christians eager to defend Christianity against the very need for feminism. This motif affirms Christianity through a negation of Judaism. It is a technique common to Christianity ever since Paul, and it is particularly dangerous because it assures Judaism a central role in Christian theology, but only when that role is negative.

The "negation" motif first became influential among feminists with the publication in 1971 of "Jesus Was a Feminist" by Leonard Swidler.[30] While Jesus is not reported in the gospels to have claimed to be a feminist, his rather unremarkable interactions with women can be made to seem remarkable if they are brought into comparison with a picture of a highly patriarchal, misogynist Jewish society in which he lived and preached. By painting a negative picture of first century Palestinian Judaism, Swidler, as well as the others who followed his lead, could make a claim for Jesus' message of feminist liberation.

Swidler's argument has been brought to bear either in denigrating or in supporting the contemporary feminist movement. Sometimes it is used to prove that Christianity has no need for feminism, because Jesus already liberated women. In other contexts the argument is used to legitimate the contemporary feminist movement, since Jesus himself was a feminist. In both cases, it is Judaism that ends up taking the blame.

The South American liberation theologian Leonardo Boff writes in *The Maternal Face of God:*

> It is against this antifeminist backdrop that we must view Jesus' message of liberation. Women in Jesus' time suffered discrimination at the hands of both society and religion. . . . In an ideological context like this, Jesus must be considered a feminist.[31]

In feminist accounts, the argument proceeds differently: Jesus (or Paul) was a feminist, compared to the misogynist

Jews of their era, or Jesus (or Paul) would have been a feminist, had it not been for their Jewish upbringing. A classic example comes in the writings of Elisabeth Moltmann-Wendel, a German Protestant feminist whose books, in English translation, have also become popular in the United States because they represent a "moderate" feminism. Moltmann-Wendel is able to rescue Jesus and Christianity from the more serious feminist criticisms by contrasting Jesus with early Judaism. She writes, in *Freedom, Equality and Sisterhood:*

> Jesus and his message are to be seen against the background of this world. Palestine, where Jesus appeared, was not a world with progressive views, emancipated women and insightful men who tolerated independent women. Palestine . . . was a small, conservative enclave. Jewish tradition and interpretations of the law still determined the people's consciousness and the customs of the country, despite some attempts at reform. The pious Jew still thanked God every morning that he was not an unbeliever, a slave, or a woman. . . . Women sat on the balcony of the synagogue and so never entered the inner sanctum of the house of God. The integrity of a worship service according to orthodox Jewish practice did not depend on whether or not women were present. Women were not permitted to say confession or thanksgiving prayers; only saying grace after meals was allowed them. The Jewish patriarchy was severe, although some of its traits were favorable to women. Naturally, there was no question of any emancipation of women.[32]

She then concludes, "This background makes Jesus' appearance and message even more impressive."

Moltmann-Wendel's account of Jewish women's position in the first century is inaccurate or even false, and is not supported by historical evidence. For example, recent studies have established that archeological remains do not show the existence of a women's gallery in first century Palestinian synagogues. That Jewish women of the first century—or any century—were only permitted to say the prayers of grace after meals is unsupported by historical sources.

At issue, however, is not only the reality of Jewish women's lives in the first century, but also the structure of Moltmann-Wendel's argument. She is deliberately painting a negative picture of the situation of Jewish women not to sympathize with Jewish feminists, but to highlight the alleged superiority of Christianity. Jesus is made to seem "even more impressive" by contrasting him with the allegedly wretchedly discriminatory treatment of women by other first-century Jewish males. It is difficult to respond to this charge from a Jewish feminist perspective because we are placed in a position of defending what we have grown used to criticizing: the position of women in Judaism during the second temple and rabbinic periods. Moreover, we are accustomed to Jewish apologetics which try to defend the classical treatment of women by comparing it to an allegedly worse situation for women in the ancient, non-Jewish world—an argument that is structurally the same as Moltmann-Wendel's.

Both Jewish and Christian feminists are trying to look between the lines of our evidence to recapture a positive picture of Jewish women's lives. For example, Christian feminists have read Pauline injunctions against women speaking out in church as evidence that women were taking active leadership roles in early Christian communities. Similarly, Mishnaic statements that women danced in the forests of Jerusalem on the 15th day of Av (a month in the Jewish lunar calendar) and on Yom Kippur (the Day of Atonement, a Jewish High Holy Day) can be read as indicating that at least some independent religious activities were undertaken by Jewish women in the period of early Judaism. Each constituency is trying to reconstruct a positive, redemptive picture of women's reality underlying whatever repressive, patriarchal measures emerged in rabbinic Judaism and in the church.

It is also striking that Moltmann-Wendel uses the word "Jew" to refer to Jewish men. Often in feminist writings there are subtle indications of an attitude that all Jews are male, and all feminists are Christian.

The negative depiction of second temple and Mishnaic Judaism (the period from about 500 B.C.E. to 250 C.E.) is also used in arguments by some West German feminists regarding the nature of Nazism. They argue that Nazism is a patriarchal phenomenon and therefore not a movement for which women bear responsibility. Perhaps the most outrageous statement is found in the work of Christa Mulack. She asserts, in *Jesus, the Savior of Women:* "We can say that the relations of Jesus with the law corresponded to typically female ideas, while those of the Pharisees and Scribes were at home in a typically male mental world." Mulack further argues that under patriarchal ethics, men absolve themselves of responsibility for their actions. In the following paragraph she draws a parallel between the Pharisees and the Nazis:

> Under patriarchy no one has responsibility for his deeds, because he behaves at the command of someone higher. They themselves wash their hands in innocence. These men would have done exactly as Pilate, if Jesus had let them, but also exactly like Rudolf Hess or Adolf Eichmann, who pleaded "not guilty," because in the last analysis they had only followed the command of a *führer*. And if this *führer* commanded murder, then his followers would have to murder. With all the differences, that are certainly present here, the inner methods of argumentation are still the same. It always shows the same obedience to authority that is so typical for the male gender.[33]

By contrast, Jesus, according to Mulack, never used a law or another authority, in order to secure his own deeds. Quite the contrary, his perspective was divine, regardless of what the law said about it. Jesus began neither with the law nor with God, but with the people themselves. What is the result? Mulack tells us: Women are liberated!

Mulack's argument is that ethical appeal to God or to a law—which, she says, characterizes Judaism—represents patriarchal thinking. Rejection of external authority is the female mode of ethics, a mode which Jesus also possessed, although he happened to be male. Judaism is male, patriarchal, and misogynist; Christianity is female, feminist, and liberating. The internal contradiction in Mulack's argument is clear: why does she require an external authority, in the figure of Jesus, to legitimate feminism?

But all of these considerations pale next to the consequence Mulack is drawing: that Hess and Eichmann are typical examples of this patriarchal (Jewish) morality which disclaims responsibility by appealing to a "higher authority." In an assertion almost too extraordinary to believe, Mulack blithely maintains that Jewish adherence to divine commandments is equivalent to Nazi obedience to the criminal orders of their superiors. What is Nazism, in Mulack's logic? The domination of Jewish morality over Christian morality. German Christians are thus in no way responsible for the holocaust; Jews are made by Mulack into victims of their own religion. And who is washing her hands here in innocence?

IV. Conclusion

That Christian theological anti-Judaism persists among Christian feminists should not be surprising, given the tenacity of anti-Judaism through the centuries. Certainly, it is easier to blame the external influences of Judaism for the existence of sexism than to accept the possibility that sexism is intrinsic to Christian theology. The danger that emerges, however, is that Judaism is once again labeled an inferior religion, and that Christian teachings are relieved of responsibility for radical change. What is required is a shift, from Christian feminists criticizing Judaism's sexism in order to elevate Christianity, to a recognition that feminism is a challenge shared by Jewish and Christian feminists.

Feminism should encourage both Jews and Christians to see their common agenda of eliminating sexism within their respective theological, textual, and liturgical traditions. Whatever hesitance may be encountered from religious leaders reluctant to make the needed radical changes in response to feminism might be encouraged by pointing out the similar mechanisms at work in anti-Judaism. Clearly, those who accept the argument that theological anti-Judaism is in some way connected to secular antisemitism and the persecution of Jews would have to accept the parallel argument that theological exclusiveness of the female is tied to society's patriarchy and misogyny.

The effort to draw a contrast between a Christian theology of relationship and a legalistic religion of Judaism and its Old Testament is hardly new. Feminists are taking an old Christian characterization of Judaism as a religion of law and labeling it male, in opposition to Christianity, a religion of love, which is labeled female. That this contrast, which reached a peak with Marcion's (a Christian heretic in the second century) differentiation between the God of the Old Testament and the God of the New Testament, was termed heretical and condemned by the early church did not result in its disappearance.

The law-love distinction is used by some Christian feminists to argue that Christianity and feminism are ultimately compatible, because the teachings of Jesus promoted precisely the kind of sensitivity and caring that characterize women's relationships. They build on the research of some feminist psychologists, including Nancy Chodorow and Carol Gilligan, who conclude that in responding to moral dilemmas males are concerned with establishing universal rules and principles, while females are concerned with fostering close relationships.[34] According to some Christian feminist theologians, Jesus, too, attempted to establish a new kind of relationship, shifting religion from matters of ritual to intimacy with God and other human beings. According to other feminists, regardless of Jesus' intentions, feminist spirituality must focus on reciprocal relation between human beings and divinity. Beverly Harrison writes:

> If our moral language is ever to interpret self/other duality in terms that affirm and embrace mutuality and support the whole spectrum of human fulfillment, autonomy, and as yet unrealized possibility, all of us must learn to envision all action as genuine interaction. Theological images that portray God as Lord or King, even those that describe God as Mother/Father, teach us that holy power is not reciprocal power. By contrast, metaphors and images that locate and identify holiness in sister/brother relations teach us to long for a "Holy One" who is a companion, one not diminished by our growth, power and fulfillment, one who does not need to rule by dictum. Such images and metaphors teach us social relations of mutuality. God/ess does not replace us through substitution or render us subordinate but is flowing, alive with us, in the world.[35]

Harrison's description is strikingly similar to the theological approaches developed during the twentieth century by several European Jewish theologians, including Martin Buber, Franz Rosenzweig, and Abraham Heschel. These theologians were clearly unaware of feminist issues, yet they, too, taught that God must be understood as standing in relation to humanity, rather than in transcendent superiority. Heschel, for example, developed a "theology of pathos," in which he argued that traditional rabbinic thought, as well as medieval *kabbalah* (Jewish mysticism), presents God not as the Unmoved Mover of Aristotle, but as the "most Moved Mover" of the Bible.[36] God is not aloof to human suffering, but is deeply affected by human deeds, in Heschel's theology. Central to the teachings of the prophets of the Bible, as well as rabbinic Judaism and later, medieval *kabbalah*, is the idea that God is immanent, gaining or losing strength as a result of human deeds.

The consequence of God's pathos, according to Heschel, is a new attention to social concerns. Piety, he argued, cannot be divorced from concern with others, as exemplified by prophets' continual preaching about widows and orphans. Whatever I do to another person, Heschel wrote, I do to God; when I hurt someone else, I injure God.[37] The intimacy between human beings and God is profound and is central to Judaism, according to Heschel's interpretation. Viewed in this light, some feminist theology could be seen as a Christian parallel to Jewish teachings, and not as teachings that are unique or superseding Judaism. Finding parallels, both in the critique of sexism and in the constructive proposals for alternatives, should lead to mutuality, rather than suspicion and denigration.

Both feminism and the Jewish-Christian dialogue are movements filled with the potential for overcoming deeply-rooted prejudices. Together their goals can make a profound impact as religion enters the twenty-first century.

NOTES

[1]One important exception is A. Roy Eckardt, "Salient Christian-Jewish Issues Today: A Christian Exploration," in *Jews and Christians: Exploring the Past, Present, and Fu-*

ture, ed. by James Charlesworth (New York: Crossroad, 1990), pp. 151–77.

[2]Paul M. van Buren, *A Theology of Christian-Jewish Reality.* 3 vols. (New York: Seabury, 1980–1988).

[3]A. Roy Eckardt, *Black Woman Jew: Three Wars for Human Liberation* (Bloomington: Indiana University Press, 1989).

[4]An introduction to the history of the women's movement in the United States is found in Jo Freeman, *Women: A Feminist Perspective* (Palo Alto: Mayfield Publishing Co., 1984) and, by the same author, *The Politics of Women's Liberation* (New York: Longman, 1975).

[5]See Ann Douglas, *The Feminization of American Religion* (New York: Knopf, 1977) and Carroll Smith-Rosenberg, *Disorderly Conduct: Visions of Gender in Victorian America* (New York: Oxford University Press, 1985); Rosemary Ruether and Rosemary Skinner Keller, eds., *Women and Religion in America.* 3 vols. (San Francisco: Harper and Row, 1981–86).

[6]Betty Friedan, *The Feminine Mystique* (New York, 1963).

[7]Simone de Beauvoir, *The Second Sex,* trans. and ed. by H.M. Parshley (New York: Knopf, 1953); first published in 1949 as *Le Deuxième Sexe.*

[8]Ibid. 16.

[9]For an historical review of various manifestations of sexism within Christianity, see the collection *Religion and Sexism,* ed. by Rosemary Radford Ruether (New York: Simon & Schuster, 1974).

[10]Mary Daly, *The Church and the Second Sex* (Boston: Beacon Press, 1968; reprinted with a post-Christian afterword by the author, 1985).

[11]For critical analyses of Judaism, see Susannah Heschel, ed., *On Being a Jewish Feminist: A Reader* (New York: Schocken Books, 1983).

[12]Mary Daly, *Beyond God the Father* (Boston: Beacon Press, 1973).

[13]Ibid. 13.

[14]See Starhawk, *The Spiral Dance* (Boston: Beacon Press, 1978) and *Dreaming the Dark: Magic, Sex and Politics* (Boston: Beacon Press, 1982), and the collection in Charlene Spretnak, ed., *The Politics of Women's Spirituality* (Garden City: Anchor Press, 1982).

[15]Beverly Harrison, *Making the Connections: Essays in Feminist Social Ethics,* ed. by Carol S. Robb (Boston: Beacon Press, 1985).

[16]Sallie McFague, *Models of God: Theology for an Ecological, Nuclear Age* (Philadelphia: Fortress Press, 1987).

[17]Carol Christ, *The Laughter of Aphrodite* (San Francisco: Harper and Row, 1987).

[18]See Jacqueline Grant, *White Woman's Christ and Black Woman's Jesus: Feminist Christology and Womanist Response* (Atlanta: Scholars Press, 1989); Katie Geneva Cannon, *Black Womanist Ethics* (Atlanta: Scholars Press, 1988); Susan Thistlethwaite, *Sex, Race and God* (New York: Crossroad, 1989).

[19]Some of the material following in this section of the chapter appeared earlier in a slightly different form in my article, "Anti-Judaism in Christian Feminist Theology," *Tikkun* 5 (1990), 25–28, 95–97.

[20]Elizabeth Gould Davis, *The First Sex* (Baltimore: Penguin, 1971).

[21]Sheila Collins, *A Different Heaven and Earth* (Valley Forge: Judson Press, 1974).

[22]Merlin Stone, *When God Was a Woman* (New York: Harcourt, Brace Jovanovich, 1976).

[23]Gerda Lerner, *The Creation of Patriarchy* (New York: Oxford University Press, 1986).

[24]Gerda Weiler, *Ich Verwerfe im Lande die Kriege* (München: Frauenoffensive, 1984); my translation.

[25]Carol Meyers, *Discovering Eve: Ancient Israelite Women in Context* (New York: Oxford University Press, 1988).

[26]Lerner, p. 160.

[27]Ibid. 179.

[28]See J. Aistleitner, *Die mythologischen und kultischen Texte aus Ras Schamra* (Budapest, 1959), pp. 39f.

[29]Davis, p. 136.

[30]Leonard Swidler, "Jesus Was a Feminist," *The Catholic World* (1971), 177–83.

[31]Leonardo Boff, *The Maternal Face of God,* trans. by Robert R. Barr and John W. Dierksmeier (San Francisco: Harper and Row, 1987).

[32]Elisabeth Moltmann-Wendel, *Freiheit, Gleichheit, Schwesterlichkeit* (München, 1977), 12. Translated as *Freedom, Equality and Sisterhood.*

[33]Christa Mulack, *Jesus—der Gesalbte der Freuen. Weiblichkeit als Grundlage christlicher Ethik* (Stuttgart, 1987), pp. 155–56; my translation.

[34]Nancy Chodorow, *The Reproduction of Mothering* (Berkeley: University of California Press, 1978) and Carol Gilligan, *In a Different Voice: Psychological Theory and Women's Development* (Cambridge: Harvard University Press, 1982).

[35]Harrison, p. 39.

[36]Abraham J. Heschel, *The Prophets* (New York: Harper and Row, 1962); see also *God In Search of Man* (New York: Farrar, Straus, and Cudahy, 1952).

[37]Ibid.

Discussion Questions

1. How does the feminist critique of religion parallel, in numerous respects, the issues addressed by Jewish-Christian dialogue?

2. Why would Christian feminist theology best be served by combining awareness of sexism with elimination of anti-Judaism?

3. How has the identification of God as male in Christianity contributed to the denigration of women?

4. What are some examples of the negative images of Judaism that often appear in Christian feminist writings?

5. Why is it historically unverifiable to state that Jews introduced patriarchy and violence into the world?

For Further Study

Christ, Carol P. and Judith Plaskow, eds. *Womanspirit Rising: A Feminist Reader in Religion.* New York: Harper & Row, 1979.

Eckhart, A. Roy. *Black, Woman, Jew: Three Wars for Human Liberation.* Bloomington: Indiana University Press, 1989.

Grant, Jacqueline. *White Woman's Christ and Black*

Woman's Jesus: Feminist Christology and Womanist Response. Atlanta: Scholars Press, 1989.

Heschel, Susannah. "Anti-Judaism in Christian Feminist Theology." *Tikkum* (1990): 25–28, 95–97.

———. *On Being a Jewish Feminist: A Reader.* New York: Schocken Books, 1983.

McCauley, Deborah and Annette Daum. "Jewish-Christian Feminist Dialogue: A Wholistic Vision." *Union Seminary Quarterly Review* 33 (1983): 147–90.

Plaskow, Judith. "Christian Feminism and Anti-Judaism." *Cross Currents* 28:3 (1978): 306–09.

Reuther, Rosemary Radford. *Religion and Sexism: Images of Women in the Jewish and Christian Traditions.* New York: Simon and Schuster, 1974.

Thistlethwaite, Susan. *Sex, Race and God.* New York: Crossroad, 1989.

Umansky, Ellen M. "Beyond Androcentrism: Feminist Challenges to Judaism." *Journal of Reformed Judaism* Winter (1990): 25–35.

X.

S. SAMUEL SHERMIS

Educational Dimensions of the Jewish-Christian Dialogue

I. Introduction

This is a chapter on learning how to participate in a Jewish-Christian dialogue. While all other chapters in this text are concerned with different aspects of the dialogue, this one deals with what happens when you want to communicate with others. The focus is on what you need in order to learn concepts that are as important as they are difficult to grasp. If the experiences of those who have participated in the Jewish-Christian dialogue are any guide, you will be participating in an insightful and intellectually stimulating experience.

In the last few decades, fueled by research in the United States and Europe, a serious exchange has been taking place between Jews and Christians.[1] The dialogue groups are small, usually a dozen or two, assembling in churches, synagogues, classrooms, universities, community meeting places, and homes. The topics range from rite and ritual to complex issues of theology. Much of the time the discussion begins with "safe" topics like holidays and traditions and then extends to the sensitive and controversial: Why don't Jews accept Jesus as their savior? or, Why did Christians sit by and allow millions of Jews to be slaughtered in the holocaust?

While there has been no radical alteration in the religious life of either the United States or Europe, in responses to the exchange between Christians and Jews many do report a gradually improving climate. Those who have participated—often in two or more dialogues—say that they have a much better understanding of the history, beliefs, and feelings of those in different faith communities. Many still have unanswered questions, but most report that they feel closer to others in the discussion group or that they have, for the first time, a good idea of why others feel as they do. Not revolutionary, to be sure, but sufficiently encouraging that the dialogue is spreading.

II.　The United States and the World in Context

The rationale for the dialogue in the context of the United States should be seen in terms of the concept known as pluralism.[2] Despite the pluralism that has characterized America since its colonial beginnings, there has not been a corresponding tolerance of differences, alternatives, and cultural options that have existed since colonial days. *In theory,* America has always been hospitable to all nationalities, races, and religions. But, *in actuality,* the Anglo-Saxon tradition and the Protestant religion have always enjoyed a kind of unofficial dominance. Other points of view, and other nationalities, religions, and ideologies, may be tolerated, depending upon the amount of social stress and anxiety at any given time.

The value of the Jewish-Christian dialogue can reasonably be interpreted as a coming of age, a maturity on the part of this American society. We are, in effect, beginning to behave the way we should, *according to the long verbalized tradition of tolerance and respect for differences.* Instead of saying "My religion is legitimate; what is wrong with yours?" many have begun to acknowledge that other religious convictions possess equal legitimacy. The Jewish-Christian dialogue, then, is the authentication of other points of view and modes of existence. It is understanding others *on their own terms* as if they truly had a perfect right to exist.

In a sense, what has been observed as characterizing American society is, to a lesser extent, true of much of the rest of the world. Events in the last few years have not simply shown the inability of communist forms of government to function, they have also revealed that the entire world is pluralistic: ethnically, religiously, and ideologically.[3] At present we are witnessing a good deal of serious and at times lethal conflict between different nationalities, religions, and ethnic groups throughout the world. Hence, joining traditional armed conflicts (Irish, Catholic-English, and Protestant in Belfast; Jewish and Islamic in Israel; Hindu and Islamic in Pakistan) are rivalries that have festered quietly for seventy years and have only recently surfaced, i.e. the Christian-Islamic and Armenian Orthodox-Roman Catholic animosity in Soviet affairs.

It would be a foolish over-simplification to suggest that the sort of Jewish-Christian dialogue that has begun in the United States will provide a speedy solution to global conflicts. But it does seem reasonable to suggest that the dialogue in the United States may offer a *model*. There are certain assumptions and attitudes that one finds in Jewish-Christian dialogues in American society that should prove useful in allaying the admittedly complex conflicts that have pervaded the world.

Assumptions are crucial to the dialogue: the supposition that the other person operates from different assumptions than you do; the assumption that *differences* in the other person's outlook are simply different and not a sinister error; that it is a good thing to exchange views peaceably; that beneath the many differences in philosophy, ideology, rite, and practice that separate us, the other person is as human as you; that if your experiences and starting points were the same as those of the other person, you might very well have reached the same conclusions.

III. Dialogue in the Classroom

The rest of this chapter will be devoted to the classroom context of the Jewish-Christian dialogue. There are certain characteristics of the dialogue as it takes place in classrooms which distinguish it from dialogue in informal settings. First, there is the requirement, always present in formal education, that students will eventually be called upon to demonstrate what they have learned. Second, precisely because it is a formal learning situation, it is possible for the instructor to do what is ordinarily not allowed in informal discussions: demand formal proof of any assertion. There are, in short, ground rules for classroom dialogues: everyone—including the instructor—can be made to provide evidence and support, to clarify, and to explain. While this may appear to dampen the enthusiasm that usually accompanies an informal "rap session," it can also be argued that the need for demonstration, for support, renders the classroom dialogue intellectually rigorous. And there is much that can be said in favor of intellectual rigor.

A. Goals of the Dialogue

A reasonable question is: What are the goals of the Jewish-Christian dialogue? This straightforward question yields several goals and objectives. Experience has shown that participants will approach the dialogue with different purposes. They may be motivated by intellectual curiosity. Christians often indicate that they wish to learn more about their own historical roots. Christian and Jewish young persons may find themselves romantically interested in someone who does not belong to their faith community. Some may wish to "test" their own faith—in the sense of finding out what they believe, why, and to what end. Certainly one of the most important goals is simply improving the relationships between members of two religions that have historically been at odds with one another.

Hence, there are many reasons to hold a Jewish-Christian dialogue, one of which is to strengthen this society by gradually creating a less tense, a less suspicious, and a less conflictual social environment for all of us. It is a way of improving a pluralistic society in which—to reiterate—there is not supposed to be an official ideology or religion and therefore a person has the option of choosing among alternative beliefs. In one sense, then, the Jewish-Christian dialogue is a means to an end, with the end defined as a better quality of *shalom* (peace). There is, however, another important goal, and that is to advance the Jewish-Christian dialogue. The dialogue is its own goal. Though this may sound circular, and although many would not accept this position, it means simply that *holding a dialogue is not a means to anything but an end in itself.* People participate in a dialogue because, in both the Jewish and the Christian traditions, such communication is inherently good and desirable. We talk and listen to each other so that we can learn more and grow in insight, compassion, understanding, and knowledge.

B. How Does The Dialogue Proceed?

The Jewish-Christian dialogue requires certain practical policies or guidelines. We assert that there are ground rules that all participants must accept. Among the more important ground rules are the following:

1. The dialogue must not be based upon a covert desire to convert, proselytize, or prove others' positions and beliefs false. This is simply another way of saying that dialogue participants must be sincere and candid but must not engage in the discussion with a hidden agenda. We also must recognize that such a ground rule is not self-evidently legitimate, for a great deal of Christianity is and always has been a proselytizing religion (to convert from one belief or faith to another) and many Christians are persuaded that their role, their obligation, is to spread the word of God.[4] Since Roman times, Judaism has not been a missionary religion.[5] If the intention to convert is not specifically avoided, then what happens is not a dialogue but something else.

2. Other participants in the dialogue have something to say that you should be hearing and understanding. At times some conversation is simply a monologue where one speaker is silent just long enough to think of a response to the other's misunderstandings. When this happens, there is no real listening. We argue that dialogue participants must be persuaded that what the other person says and thinks is significant.

3. Learning more about the other's faith, community, and beliefs cannot be done passively. This point is emphasized in contrast to the passivity that characterizes most formal education. For much of the time in many schools, it is sufficient simply to memorize enough information to pass a test. If you can hang on to "H_2SO_4," the definition of "peninsula," and the provisions of the Treaty of Versailles long enough, that is usually sufficient. We call this "passive" because it does not require much beyond simply receiving information and recalling it at a later time. However, to learn about the beliefs, faith, history, traditions, theology, philosophical assumptions, and world views of people from another religion requires *active* learning. You will need to adopt what is called different "learning strategies." Although more will be said on this topic later in the chapter, here it is suffi-

cient to say that active learning requires an empathetic feeling for the viewpoints of others and a genuine desire to want to know. It also requires the asking of many questions—some designed to gain a broad outline and others devised to identify specific details.

4. Your understanding of the other person's belief is not complete and is likely to be inadequate. You may *believe* that you understand, but it is likely that you do not. You may think that since you have used the "same" language, you are communicating. But this is likely to be deceptive. The reason for this is that *even though Christianity and Judaism may use the same terms the meanings are not identical.*

While terms such as "sin," "salvation," "God," "faith," and "charity" are used by both Jews and Christians, they have similar but not identical meanings. Second, there are terms that have rough equivalents. These include "social justice," "loving kindness," "compassion," and "concern." Third, there are also terms used by members of one religion that simply have no equivalent in the other. The Jewish concepts *am* or "people" and *mitzvah* or "commandment" are such words. The Christian concepts "the mystical body of Christ" and "the resurrection of the body" have no Jewish equivalent. Finally, some of the central concerns of one religion simply are not shared by the other, e.g. "eternal salvation" is literally the central purpose of some Christian faith communities. Jews have nearly nothing to say about this matter.

5. Emotions are part of the dialogue. You will need to deal with a wider and more intense range of feelings and emotions than is usually the case in an academic setting. To be sure, some aspects of the dialogue refer to historical events about which historians are in agreement. Some refer to specific behavior, i.e. the tendency of urban Jews to vote alike. These are not inherently upsetting concepts. However, there are concepts that are distressing, including, but not limited to, "the charge of deicide," "destruction of the entire eastern European Jewish community during the holocaust," "lack of Christian support for modern Israel in the conflict with its Arab neighbors," "Jewish anti-black racism," "Christian antisemitism" and "Fundamentalist Protestant anti-intellectualism."

At this point there are two implications to be considered.

First, while expressing feelings is often considered unacceptable in American society, it is probably better to express them than it is to smile on the outside and repress anger on the inside. This is not an invitation to a name-calling session but rather a recognition that being candid and honest about your feelings does not necessarily have to lead to insults and hurt feelings. Second, it follows that deliberate avoidance of the attitudes, emotions, feelings, and value conflicts inherent in the dialogue is simply another way of not taking the dialogue seriously. Religious differences *are not confined to distinctions in theology, rite, and historical interpretations.* Religious differences *necessarily include conflicts* and disharmonies concerning how people feel about themselves, their faiths, and their perception of what is called cosmology, i.e. their place in the universe. You will then need to accept the likelihood that you may feel strongly and that your emotions may rise to the surface. It is better to acknowledge your feelings and deal with them than to pretend that they do not exist.

C. Language and Concepts

An important word must be said about the nature of language and concepts in the dialogue. Concepts in the sciences and social sciences tend to relate to tangible, specific *things.* When meteorologists talk about a "cyclonic wind of ninety miles an hour," they refer to something that can be identified as an air mass. When a sociologist talks about "stratification" they assume that they are referring to specific behavior within a social group. These are "hard" empirical facts. There is an important difference between this approach to language and behavior and what takes place in the Jewish-Christian dialogue. Concepts in many areas of religion may not point to specific behavior. They may instead point to other concepts.

Hence, when some Jews talk about a messianic age, they cannot point to existing characteristic behavior. "Messianic age" refers to a time, somewhere in the unknown future, where there will be no more superstition, injustice, and exploitation of the poor. When Christians talk about "redemption," they are essentially using a shorthand term that stands for a large related cluster of ideas, like the salvation

254 S. Samuel Shermis

from sin through Christ's sacrifice. Other concepts that refer not to things but to other concepts include "sacraments which celebrate the mystical body of Christ" and the Jewish notion of "celebration of the covenant."[6] Because you cannot easily identify something clear and "solid," you may well experience difficulties getting the meaning of what the other person is saying. You will need to think in a more complex and sensitive fashion about what you hear, read, and say. It might be useful for you to read a more expanded discussion of language and concepts in, e.g., Jonas F. Soltis' *An Introduction to the Analysis of Education Concepts*[7] or George F. Kneller's *Logic and Language of Education.*[8]

D. Translating the Guidelines into Strategies

All of the observations above are preliminary. Now, assuming that all readers accept these guidelines as criteria for a fruitful dialogue, we will suggest certain procedures which come out of studies of learning and teaching and are intended to facilitate your understanding. Let us deal with some of the low-level strategies first.

The usual approaches that can be found in any "How To Study" text are certainly useful. Do not read each chapter three times in exactly the same way. Rather, use a combination of skimming and scanning to identify the main ideas, discover the structure of the chapter, and pinpoint differences and similarities with your own beliefs. Then read the chapter carefully. Underline, make marginal notes, identify concepts that you do not understand, and look up unfamiliar words—or, what is more tricky, familiar words used in an unfamiliar way. Discuss what you have read with others. Create a list of questions that might usefully be asked in class. However, there are more intellectually complex learning and thinking skills that you need to identify and develop.

1. Write your own summaries of major points in a separate notebook. Write a summary of the entire chapter in a paragraph. It is well worth the effort it will cost to rephrase ideas in your own words. You will avoid low-level memorization and will discover more meaning when you rephrase the ideas in your own fashion.

2. Go beyond summarizing. Ask yourself such questions as: Can I give an example of this position? Can I state the

relevant principle? Can I state the opposite principle? Can I find an example that contradicts the principle? Can I discover the implications or consequences of an idea? Can I provide a statement of this position that is completely acceptable to a proponent? This is a way of checking your own understanding. You may think you understand, but test your understanding. Can I compare or contrast this new idea with concepts in my own faith community?

The reason for this has to do with the nature of a concept. To know what a concept means requires one to know what *it does not include.* To understand the Jewish concept "human beings are co-partners with God in creating the world" requires you to distinguish this formulation from the idea that God completed creation in six days. Only by comparing and contrasting—seeing what is the same and what is different—can you build understanding. To continue a theme discussed above, how you *feel* about what you are learning is not only as important as *what* you are learning; the emotion about and the content of what you are learning are really inseparable. The ancient dualism between "knowing" and "feeling" will interfere with learning. You do not "know" on one side of your head and "feel" on the other. They occur simultaneously.

Most textbooks come equipped with a profusion of references that are usually ignored. References listed in texts, however, can function as learning aids. *Categories* of references usually found in textbooks include:

other text or text chapters on the same subject;

articles published in academic journals;

articles in specialized reference works—dictionaries and encyclopedias of religion, philosophy, history, and social sciences;[9]

articles in liberal intellectual journals—specifically designed for those who, while not necessarily specialists in religion, have keen intellectual interests in a wide range of subjects.

A different textbook may have a chapter on the same topic that is useful, for it may provide another explanation of the same phenomenon. The alternative explanation, with different language, dissimilar emphasis, and other examples and illustrations, often helps in gaining more insight. Ordinarily articles in academic journals because of their high level of abstraction and saturation with jargon and specialized vocabulary are beyond the grasp of all but experts in the field. There are exceptions to this generalization—but not many. Specialized encyclopedias and dictionaries have the same limitations: they assume a broad background in the subject. A possible strategy is to copy the page in the reference, underline unfamiliar terms, and discuss them with the instructor. Liberal intellectual journals such as *Commentary, Commonweal,* and *Christian Century* are extremely useful. These are more difficult to read than popular magazines and newspapers, but their style of writing is often clearer than academic journals and tends to emphasize the social context of religion.

The point of this section is to emphasize the meaning of the term "active learning," that there are sources of information beyond the text and the instructor, and that students who develop the motivation to read beyond the text will learn more and the learning will be more meaningful.

E. Asking Questions: The Interior Dialogue

At times learning can be compared with a dialogue that you are carrying on with yourself. This is especially true of the reading, listening, and hearing that you will be asked to do for the Jewish-Christian dialogue. Imagine that the interior dialogue consists of a series of questions that you will be asking of your dialogue partners, of the instructor, and of the material in this text and other sources. Here are some of the questions that you should be asking yourself:

Why do you say this? "Because I learned it" or "Because this is what I was taught" is not an answer. The question does not ask, "How did you acquire this idea?" It asks, "What support or rationale do you have for accepting this idea?" It asks, "What is there about this idea that recommends acceptance?"

What do you mean? This is not quite the same as saying: What does this term or this idea mean? The meaning that you need to be concerned with is not the meaning that "inheres" or "belongs to" a term. *The meaning of an idea lies as much in what you bring to it as what is in it.* The difficulty that this idea raises is that people bring different things to ideas. You may discover that what you bring to unfamiliar ideas is a truckload of rigid, resistant, unshakable beliefs. You may find out that what you bring to unfamiliar ideas stands in the way of understanding them. You may discover that you just do not bring very much because your reading, your background knowledge, and your experiences are insufficient. You may decide that you need to subject your stock of ideas to a thoroughgoing review.

Can you explain that further? An explanation is not repetition! There is little point in repeating the same phrases or words. If you do not understand or if someone does not understand you, then attempt to discover why. Here are some of the reasons why human beings do not understand one another:

1. They are listening too selectively. People often do not hear all of what is said. They sometimes select out of the whole only a few ideas and fixate on them. Try to pick up the entire position and not bits and pieces.

2. A term or a concept can prevent communication. Often it is a new or unfamiliar term, or, as we have already said, a familiar term used in an unfamiliar way. Try to discover if one word, phrase, or term is causing trouble.

3. The units of meaning are too large. You will have difficulty understanding the book of Job in one reading. You are not likely to make sense of John Calvin's or St. Augustine's concept of the elect[10] in one reading. If you feel that you are struggling with too many large ideas, break them down into smaller units of meaning. This suggestion applies not just to readers but to speakers and listeners as well.

4. A prior stock of concepts is interfering. This point was made above in the discussion of bringing meaning to an idea. If you do not understand the idea, you may need to stop for a moment and ask: Why am I confused? Am I confused because, based upon what I already know, this concept doesn't "fit"? What is there about my stock of ideas that is getting in the way?

5. The ideas are presented at a high level of abstraction. "The cross as a symbol" is an abstraction, as is "the natural world," and "supernatural existence." The second two concepts, however, are far higher on the "ladder of abstrac-

tions." This means that they include more and are more difficult to visualize than "the cross as a symbol." If you have the
sense that you are being confused by the highly abstract nature of some ideas, ask the participants or the instructor to
"break down the idea into some of its component parts."

6. "The ideas are simply new and perhaps threatening.
Consider the Hassidic idea that words get in the way of communication between human beings and God; and therefore it
is best to praise God with a particular kind of song called
Niggun which has no words." Words are replaced with di di di
and la la la. Upon first hearing, this may strike you as prepos-
terous. But think about it for a few minutes. From a Hassidic
perspective, there is a mystical realm, beyond the experience
of most, that cannot be understood in the usual manner.
Given this assumption, a wordless song is not quite as ludi-
crous as it sounds. Indeed, there are Christian conceptions of
mysticism, something like wordless communication, or
speaking in tongues, that will help you see what the Has-
sidim feel.

Can you illustrate that idea? Illustrations are often essential in making abstractions come alive. Ask for them! Discuss them, *but always within the context of how the examples relate to the principle.*

How does this idea differ from that one? As we have said,
ideas with the same name may actually differ. By the same
token, different-sounding ideas may have something in common. Learning will gradually improve as you become profi-
cient at analysis, i.e. creating differences and distinctions,
seeing similarities and likenesses.

Does everyone in your faith community take this position? Within any given faith community, as we have said,
there are bound to be differences in interpretation and understanding. The question Do all Catholics feel this way? or
Do all Jews accept this point? will probably reveal that the
position may not be universally held. And if this is the case, it
is worthwhile to bear down on the history, experiences, and
conditions that created divided interpretations within
the faith.

Let me see if I have the idea. With experience you can
become quite adept at reflecting and summarizing complex
ideas. A summary, however, is not a verbatim repetition. A
summary is like a synthesis: it attempts to capture the most

important concepts. Terms that describe summarizing are "getting to the heart of the matter" or "capturing the essence of the idea." Find as many opportunities as possible to develop the skills of summarizing, understanding, and distilling complex ideas.

IV. Conclusion

The analysis, suggestions, and prescriptions for learning how to carry on the Jewish-Christian dialogue cannot be considered definitive. There is much that you yourself will discover about learning as you discuss, read, and deliberate. Indeed, there is one point of view in the educational specialty known as "learning theory" which is that *what you learn about learning* is as important as *the content of learning.*[11] There is another point of view which maintains that the goal of education is more education, that your journey toward intellectual growth has as its end more intellectual growth.[12] We hope that as you participate in the Jewish-Christian dialogue, you will grow from strength to strength.

NOTES

[1]See the introduction to Michael Shermis, *Jewish-Christian Relations: An Annotated Bibliography and Resource Guide* (Bloomington: Indiana University Press, 1988), pp. xii–xv.

[2]The term "pluralism," while used frequently since the 1960s, is rarely defined and is admittedly ambiguous. However, any word which is defined as ". . . a historical phenomenon, a normative doctrine, and a mode of analysis" invites overbroad usage. See "Pluralism" in David L. Sills, ed., *International Encyclopedia of the Social Sciences* (New York: Macmillan), p. 164. Pluralism can refer to 1. the existence of a broadly based decision-making process, and 2. the presence of a wide variety of nationality or ethnic groupings, races, political theories, religions, ideologies, and economic positions. In this chapter we will argue that our society is and has been pluralistic in the second sense.

[3]See Graeme Gill, "Revolution in Eastern Europe," *Current Affairs Bulletin* 66 (1990): 4–12 and Peter King "Will the Soviet Union Survive Until 1994?" 13–14 in the

same issue. The authors provide an account—obviously dated by events since its publication—of the political, ideological, and nationalistic forces that surfaced almost immediately after it became clear that Gorbachev was serious about reversing the "Brezhnev Doctrine," which gave the Soviet Union the right to coerce its satellite countries into conformity.

[4]We need to recognize that at various times many religions have proselytized in response to an internal dynamic that requires divine commands or insights to be transmitted to all. See "Missions," in Mircea Eliade, *The Encyclopaedia of Religion,* vol. 9 (New York: Macmillan, 1987), pp. 563–69. Various wings within Protestantism and Catholicism in the United States have been committed to conversions and missionary efforts. For evangelicals in our society, then, it is no exaggeration to say that proselytizing is the *raison d'être,* the heart and soul of their belief structure.

[5]We would be less than candid to overlook the fact that in recent years the progressive, Reform wing of Judaism has been seriously considering the need for what is called "outreach," which is a euphemism for proselytize. The argument is that since 1950, Jews in the United States have reached zero population growth. Their numbers have stayed the same, and as a percentage of the total population, this amounts to a decrease. This decrease has worried Reform leaders about the continuing survival of Judaism.

[6]See Section I. "Christian Perspectives of Judaism and Jewish Perspectives of Christianity," in Michael Shermis, *Jewish-Christian Relations,* pp. 69–73.

[7]Reading: Addison-Wesley, 1968.

[8]New York: John Wiley, 1966.

[9]A "generalized" reference work includes, for example, *Webster's Dictionary* or *The Encyclopaedia Britannica.* For most purposes general references are perfectly adequate. For a more detailed source of information, however, there are "specialized" references. These include *Oxford English Dictionary,* an extremely large, scholarly work which traces the historical and etymological background of each word, and the *International Encyclopedia of Social Sciences, The Encyclopedia of Judaica,* and *The Encyclopedia of Religion.*

[10]This example was chosen because while Calvin's ideas

on the elect, predestination, and salvation by faith alone are a common staple in many texts and articles in history, sociology of religion, and other disciplines, most discussions are necessarily simplistic. Calvin's discussion of these concepts is scattered throughout his massive two volume *Institutes of the Christian Faith* (for which an old but still useful translation is by Henry Beveridge—(Edinburgh: T. and T. Clark, 1987); the central treatment in these two volumes is found in Chapter XI. A different problem exists in most discussion of the doctrine of the elect in Augustine; he wrote over an extended period of time and changed his mind frequently. See Robert E. Meagher, *An Introduction to Augustine* (New York: New York University Press, 1978). If the reader wishers a comprehensive overview of this topic, see the useful article entitled "Election" in Mircea Eliade, *The Encyclopaedia of Religion*, vol. 1 (New York: Macmillan, 1978), pp. 75–81.

[11]This idea is explored at length in "How Does Bruner's Cognitive Psychology Treat Learning and Teaching?" in Morris Bigge, *Learning Theories for Teachers*, 4th ed. (New York: Harper and Row, 1981).

[12]The philosophical position that the aim or end of learning is more learning and that the aim of education is growth is developed by John Dewey. A good introduction to Dewey is *Democracy and Education* (New York: The Macmillan Company, 1916).

Discussion Questions

1. How do our own personal presuppositions influence dialogue?

2. What are some of the misconceptions/misunderstandings you feel Christians have about Jews, or Jews have about Christians? Explain.

3. Why are "assumptions" crucial to the dialogue? What role does "language" play in dialogue?

4. What do you see as the various objectives and goals of the dialogue between Jews and Christians?

5. Why is it not possible for serious dialogue to be based upon any covert desire to proselytize or convert?

262   S. Samuel Shermis

For Further Study

A Jewish-Christian Resource Packet: Exploring a Theological Relationship Between Christianity and Judaism. Distributed by the Indiana Council of Churches, 1100 West 42nd Street, Room 224, Indianapolis, IN 46208.

Culbertson, Philip. "Doing Our Homework: Fifteen Steps Toward Christian-Jewish Dialogue in Local Congregations." *Journal of Ecumenical Studies* 20 (1983): 118–23.

Fisher, Eugene J. *Homework for Christians: Preparing for Christian-Jewish Dialogue,* rev. ed. New York: National Conference of Christians and Jews, 1985.

Fisher, Eugene J. and Leon Klenicki. *In Our Time: The Flowering of Jewish-Christian Dialogue.* Mahwah: Paulist Press, 1990.

Guidelines on Dialogue with People of Living Faiths and Ideologies. Available through the World Council of Churches, 150 Route de Ferney, 1211 Geneva 20, Switzerland.

Herschopf, Judith and Morris Fine. *A Guide to Interreligious Dialogue.* Available through the American Jewish Committee, Institute of Human Relations 165 East 56th Street, New York, NY 10022.

Interreligious Interaction: A Program Guide. Available through the Department of Interreligious Affairs, Union of American Hebrew Congregations, 838 Fifth Avenue, New York, NY 10021.

Klenicki, Leon and Geoffrey Wigoder, eds. *A Dictionary of the Jewish-Christian Dialogue.* New York: Paulist, 1984.

Pawlikowski, John T. *What Are They Saying About Jewish-Christian Dialogue?* New York: Paulist, 1980.

Shermis, S. and Michael Shermis. "Educational Aspects of Jewish-Christian Dialogue," in *Jewish-Christian Relations: An Annotated Bibliography and Resource Guide.* Bloomington: Indiana University Press, 1988. Pp. 1–16.

Contributors

Sister Mary Christine Athans, B.V.M. holds a Ph.D. from the Graduate Theological Union, Berkeley, and is an associate professor of Church History at The Saint Paul Seminary School of Divinity of the University of St. Thomas, in St. Paul, Minnesota. She writes in the area of Catholicism and Jewish-Christian relations and is currently working on a book on Jewish-Christian relations in the United States to be published by Paulist Press.

Rabbi Michael J. Cook pursued his doctoral work, which focused on the second temple period, at Hebrew Union College—Jewish Institute of Religion in Cincinnati, Ohio, where he is a professor of Intertestamental and Early Christian Literature. He has published *Mark's Treatment of the Jewish Leaders* (Leiden: Brill, 1978) and numerous articles, and is currently at work on a book on patristics, another on masculine spirituality, and still another entitled *New Testament Dilemmas and Jewish Responses.*

The Reverend Dr. Philip Culbertson is an Episcopalian priest who acquired his Ph.D. in Religious Education and Jewish Studies from New York University, and is professor of Pastoral Theology at St. Luke's School of Theology at the University of the South in Sewanee, Tennessee. He has published several articles on ecumenical and interfaith relations, a book on patristics and a book on masculine spirituality, and is currently at work on a book on the parables of Jesus in rabbinic context. He is also on the staff of the Shalom Hartman Institute, Jerusalem.

The Reverend Robert A. Everett is an ordained minister in the United Church of Christ and received his Ph.D. from the joint program in Religion at Columbia University and Union Theological Seminary in New York, New York. He is pastor at Emmanuel United Church of Christ in Irvington, New Jersey, and chaplain at Fairleigh Dickinson University in Teaneck, New Jersey. He has published several articles on Jewish-Christian relations, and his book, *Christianity Without Antisemitism: James Parkes and the Jewish Christian Encounter*, is in press.

Susannah Heschel is an assistant professor in the Department of Religious Studies at Southern Methodist University. She received her Ph.D. in Religious Studies from the University of Pennsylvania where she concentrated on the field of Modern Jewish Thought. She is the author of numerous articles on feminist theology, has edited a collection of essays, *On Being a Jewish Feminist: A Reader* (New York: Schocken, 1983), and will soon be publishing a book entitled *The Quest for the Jewish Jesus*.

Reverend Michael McGarry, C.S.P. is a Paulist priest who received his ministerial and theological degrees at the University of St. Michael's College in Toronto. He is currently rector of St. Paul's College, the Paulist Fathers' seminary in Washington, D.C. He has published several reviews and articles and a book, *Christology After Auschwitz* (New York: Paulist, 1977).

Reverend John T. Pawlikowski, O.S.M. is a Servite priest and professor of Social Ethics at the Catholic Theological Union in Chicago, Illinois. He received his doctorate degree from the University of Chicago, has contributed to many journals, and has authored eight books, including *What Are They Saying About Jewish-Christian Relations?* and *Christ in the Light of the Christian-Jewish Dialogue*.

Rabbi Sanford Seltzer is the director of research of the Union of American Hebrew Congregations and the director of the Committee on the Jewish Family. He has contributed articles and reviews to many magazines and journals and is the author of *Jews and Non-Jews: Falling in Love* and *Jews and Non-Jews: Getting Married.*

Michael Shermis received his M.A. in Religious Studies from Indiana University in Bloomington, Indiana. He is currently editor of *Parents and Children Together,* assistant editor of the *American Journal of Theology and Philosophy,* and projects coordinator of the Family Literacy Center at Indiana University. He has authored *Jewish-Christian Relations: An Annotated Bibliography and Resource Guide.*

S. Samuel Shermis, professor of Educational Studies at Purdue University, W. Lafayette, Indiana, teaches history and philosophy of education. He is the author of numerous articles, books and papers in this field and is presently a co-author of the fifth edition of a text on learning theory. He is also currently program director of Purdue University's Jewish Studies program and has written on educational issues related to the Jewish-Christian dialogue.

Arthur E. Zannoni taught on the faculty of the School of Divinity of the University of St. Thomas from 1985–1991 and served as associate director of its Center for Jewish-Christian Learning. He has written numerous book reviews and articles and is in the process of publishing a bibliography on the Old Testament. He currently resides in St. Paul, Minnesota.

Biographical Index

Topical Index